# Shark City

James Murray's first novel *The Pale Sergeant* (1986) was long-listed for the Booker Prize. His second novel *OlympiAntics: A Factasy* was electronically published to coincide with the Sydney 2000 Olympics. His short stories have appeared in various publications.

He has supported his fiction habit with corporate histories including *Phoenix to the World: the History of Clyde Industries* (1992), *Calling the World: The First 100 Years of Alcatel Australia* (1995), *Beds, Boots and Backpacks: YHA in Australia* (co-written with John McCulloch 1997), *Lifework: Heroes of Australian Health* (1997), *The Woolworths Way* (1999).

Books he has copy-edited include *Killing the Messenger* by Dr William McBride, *The Hard Way* by Harry Gordon and *America's Cup – Sailing for Supremacy* by Gary Lester and Richard Sleeman.

He wrote and produced the videos *Gold, Silver and Bronze: Australians at the Olympics* (1984) and *Olympic Glory: The Golden Years* (1993).

Born in Govan on Glasgow's South Side, James Murray's working life has been equally divided between the United Kingdom and Australia (with working excursions to continental Europe, the United States and Asia). He currently contributes film and book reviews and media commentary to the monthly magazine *Annals* Australasia while continuing to write fiction.

# Shark City

JAMES MURRAY

ARCADIA

This Project has been assisted by the Australian Government through the Australia Council, its arts funding and advisory board.

The Press On series of novels was founded by Michael Wilding and Phillip Edmonds. Edmonds was the managing director of *Wet Ink*, the magazine of new writing, and Wilding is Press On's commissioning editor.

Press On – 14

This is a work of fiction. Names, characters, places and incidents are the products of the author's imagination or are used fictitiously. Any resemblance to actual events, locales, or persons, living or dead, is entirely coincidental.


First published 2013 by Arcadia
the general books' imprint of
Australian Scholarly Publishing Pty Ltd
7 Little Lothian Street Nth, North Melbourne Vic. 3051
TEL: 03 9329 6963 FAX: 03 9329 5452
EMAIL: aspic@ozemail.com.au WEB: scholarly.info

ISBN: 978-1-921875-35-9



A Catloguing-in-Publication entry is available
from the National Library of Australia.

*Cover design* Art Rowlands
*Design and typesetting* Art Rowlands
*Printing and binding* Tenderprint Pty Ltd

Set in Fairfield LH 45 Light 11pt

In Memory of My Son
FRANCIS PRITCHARD MURRAY
London 1964 – Sydney 1989

## Acknowledgments

In writing this novel, I was helped in various ways by a number of people. They include: Philip Barnett, J. W. Burgess, Christine Humphries (Sydney Aquarium), Paul Fregosi, John Hodgman, Barrie Leffler (Videopak), Gary Lester, Richard Mirabello, Bill and Sherryl Macartney (Grand Prix Sailing), Ted and Sisko Morrisby, Jeff Patterson (UP Video Sports), Denis Phelan (Videopak), Ron Pile (MV *Frejya*), Chris Purser (Water Taxis), Robert Purves, Barrie and Elizabeth Watts, my children: Clare, Sarah, Kate, Joseph, Norah and my wife Jenny (always). My thanks to them all.

My thanks also to my editor, Carl Harrison-Ford, who combines a fine eye for detail with rare generosity.

Books on which I drew include: *The Atlas of Australian Surfing* (Angus and Robertson) by Mark Warren, *Inside the Brotherhood* (Grafton Books) by Martin Short, and *Who Dares Wins* (Arms and Armour) by Tony Geraghty.

# 1

Durman had retained a childhood image of Christmas in Sydney: sun-sleek police horses crapping gold at the Market Street–Elizabeth Street crossing. Now there weren't any—not even a Shetland pony ridden by one of the new tiny cops he'd noticed on the way in from the airport.

Strange to leave a place because it reminded you of what you didn't want to remember and yet be irked that it had changed when you returned.

Next to him in the mob waiting for green on the traffic lights was a guy of his own vintage. A guy who'd been in front of him at Park Street and who'd been staring into an antique shop window when Durman re-emerged after ducking into an office block foyer.

'What's happened to the police horses?' Durman said. A heel-shit would've been confused. The guy stared Durman up and down and back up as if measuring him for a king-hit. 'Economy measure. The pollies prefer their own high-priced bullshit.'

The lights went to green. The guy jockeyed himself into the lead, heading for DJs.

It, too, had changed. Chilly after the melting heat of the streets. And gone was the ambience of dim good taste. It had the hectic look of a French brothel in old Beirut, run by a madame with unlimited supplies of petrodollars. Pinkish marble everywhere.

Marble? Well-chewed nougat, allowed to set. Every plate-glass edge gilt and glittering under bright chandeliers.

All it needed was a pianist. Geez, it had one—a guy with a screwed-up eye and a voice to match, sitting at a white grand piano in a dinner jacket, singing 'Lady Be Good'.

And were the ladies ever being good, darting and jostling with something ecstatic in their stare. Not shoppers.

Worshippers amid golden groves of trees and leaping golden reindeer, which were some arty-farty's fantasy of Christmas chic.

The escalator to the first floor creaked like the stays of the women of yesteryear. Gowns. A beer-bellied guy, rubbing a rasping chin, was saying to a tiny, black-clad shop-assistant: 'I'm looking for something for my … uh, wife. She's about my size.' Durman paused for the shop-assistant's reply: 'Maybe you should try maternity, sir.'

The beer-bellied guy belched a laugh. Durman took the firestairs down, pausing on the half-landing to listen. The door above did not open.

At the Regal Tower Hotel, he was expected. Yes, a suite had been booked in his name. No, a package had not arrived for him. 'If you will just sign here, sir, we'll let you know as soon as it does arrive.'

Another change? Were there more sirs in the air than he remembered? The reception desk guys certainly didn't look Aussie. Clones from a flunky-factory in Switzerland.

As he waited for a lift, Durman had a glimpse of the atrium entrance where guests sat on cane chairs having afternoon tea. Poshos. How could so many afford it? Same way he could. Someone else was paying.

In the suite, the porter put Durman's holdall on the bench at the foot of the bed and waited. Durman gave him a dollar coin. The porter looked at it. 'You do realise, sir, the dollar coin's the large one. The two-dollar coin's the small one.'

Durman took the coin back. 'Shit, mate. You're right,' he said. And jerked his head towards the door. The porter seemed to get the message. To make sure, Durman kicked the door against his backside.

Yeah, definitely more sirs. And more bloody cheek. Durman sat on the edge of the bed and waited for the knock on the door. And waited. The telephone twittered.

'You've done good, mate.' Sydney accent, unmistakably sun-dried Cockney. The accent that'd come with the First Fleet and eventually dominated the brogues of Scotland and Ireland, the lilt of Wales as well as English accents of more genteel pretensions. 'Yeah, real good. Now listen, mate.'

Durman did. There was something else besides sun-dried Cockney in the voice. Something he knew but couldn't quite place: German? Italian? Greek? And a hint of mockery as it issued instructions. Durman replaced the phone. Someone was playing games. Amateur? Pro?

On the bedside table was a basket of fruit: *Compliments of the Management*. Durman took an apple, changed his mind and selected a mango. Had to be a pro. Otherwise, he wouldn't've known of Durman's game.

In the bathroom there were more mirrors than allowed him to ignore his flab. Have to get it off. The heat would help. Twenty-four hours ago, he'd been shivering in the stockyard melee of Heathrow. Now here he was in Sydney, mango pulp warm and sweet in his mouth and mango juice sluicing down his chest with the water from the shower, hot first, then cold, colder, coldest.

Dried and towel-draped, he thought about calling the operator to ask for a wake-up call. Geez, he must be getting flab on the brain to want to advertise he was going to have a kip. He set his watch alarm.

He had a recurring dream: a series of massive, solid doors swung open before him, each blacker than the previous one until he confronted a final door. This door remained closed but despite its solidity it had a quality of engulfing menace. He awoke then in a cold sweat to the whine of the alarm and wondered at the mind kink that could create such a dream, when he remembered its inspiration all too vividly.

Pro games.

The kind he was playing again.

With the same offsider. He'd placed the accent.

Not German.

Dutch.

Circular Quay was a counter-dance of pleasure-seekers, moving this way and that to the pulsing drone of a didgeridoo competing for coin with the riotous beat of a one-man band.

Amid the dance, companies of Japanese moved purposefully, telescopic lenses fixed, guidons fluttering as they followed their leaders to the strains of, 'When the Saints Go Marchin' In'.

Cafes jam-packed with customers occupied the quay's landward side. High above on the Cahill Expressway, wild traffic growled while trains rumbled on the Harbour Bridge approaches. As many people again were chewing the cud from take-away shops on the seaward side. A couple of hand-line fishermen from a more frugal past were filleting their catch before going home for a feed. And an older man from an even more frugal present was tickling empty cans from the rubbish bins.

Ahead, the Opera House sails shone as with the promises of the millions of lottery tickets that had gone into its building.

Old guy in a blue T-shirt marked *AllDay*. Durman took the newspaper he offered and moved to pay. 'Where've you been,' the old guy said, 'Tim-bloody-buctoo? It's free.' He gazed up at Durman, catching his grimace as he took in the front-page headline:

BIG IG LOSES FINAL APPEAL

'Bastard,' the old guy said. 'Don't care who he is. Deserves it. Press the tit meself.'

The tit. Ex-digger, talking about firing a heavy machine-gun.

Durman moved on, re-reading the story squeezed onto the front page alongside a colour picture of a giant, fair kid with a big cheesy grin.

> BANGKOK: World Ironman Champion Ian Graeme today lost his final appeal in Thailand's highest court, the Dika, against his death sentence for possession and trafficking in heroin. Graeme, 25, known to thousands of fans as Ig, was found guilty earlier this year of being caught holding 5 kg of heroin with an estimated street value of $7.5 million. (Full story, Page 2)

Know the full story, Durman thought. Been briefed.

Ian Graeme. On QF1 returning to Australia from a promotional tour of America and Europe. Hailed everywhere as a younger, finer inheritor of the Anzac tradition. A national icon. Stopped over in Bangkok for three days and was back at the airport to catch a flight for Hong Kong when heroin was found in his possession. Claimed it was planted on him. Five keys. Double Uoglobe. Grade 4. Ninety per cent pure. Among the Golden Triangle's finest. Planted. Amazing, he didn't claim the porno magazine he was carrying was planted on him. *Stud's Eye*.

Man o' War steps. The MV *Norn*. Dark blue. Gilt trim. Twin hull. Less a gin palace than a floating boardroom.

As soon as Durman crossed the gangway, crewmen cast off and the *Norn* headed out into the scaly glitter of the harbour, twin diesels creating a double wake which merged to a single white roar.

The island known as Pinchgut came up on the starboard, its name a remembrance of the starvation rations once doled out to its prisoners.

'They say no person ever escaped from it, mate.' The telephone voice. The mockery in it stronger. 'But you weren't around then, eh?' Stronger too the accent. Dutch. For sure: Anton Van Diemen.

'Bastard,' Durman said. 'Why don't you wear your bloody clogs instead of creeping up on a man?'

'Still the old joke, mate. I hope you are in better nick than your jokes.'

Durman had been tensed, waiting. But Anton had yet again reached him unaware, had got close enough to pat his back to make sure he wasn't tooled up or wired under his bush jacket. Only when he had his irritation under control did Durman turn.

'Shit,' Anton said. 'You've been leading with your nose. And the beard, mate. The beard is too much.'

Anton was obviously in very good nick. Only five-seven and 140 but with the cockiness of the fitter, smaller man who's proved to his own satisfaction the bigger they are the harder they fall. Not a skerrick of flab on him. Blond hair slicked back. Brown silk shirt opened halfway to the waist of his tan daks. Gleaming on his chest, a gold medal that hadn't been awarded for any campaign, except maybe service in bed. Over the shirt a whipcord wind-breaker with brown leather trim.

One garment too many. Probably to conceal a shoulder holster. And Anton being such a dandy, a shoulder holster matching the jacket's trim.

Anton slouched to the companionway, doing his harmless slob bit, but couldn't resist the command bark: 'Follow me.' Durman counted down from ten before obeying.

The main saloon was padded in brass-studded red leather. For'ard, a teak bar backed by a gaudy bare-breasted ship's figurehead surrounded by racked bottles and glasses.

Anton expressed surprise—spiked with more mockery—when Durman refused his offer of a drink. 'So we are off the grog …' He helped himself to a whisky … 'these days.'

Anton having a dig at the past. Durman sat down at the table in the centre of the saloon. Anton kept up the rubbishing. 'Always the poker face. Yet you must be surprised to see me.'

'You know everything.'

'Stop playing for time. You are not under interrogation.' Anton put the whisky bottle on the table along with a second glass and sat down opposite Durman.

'This is a deniable op. Totally deniable. Your contact was approached through a safe intermediary. My name was not mentioned.'

Deniable op. Durman had been intrigued as to the identity of his ultimate paymaster. Anton's use of the jargon suggested who it might be.

'How come you're back with the government?' Durman said.

'You mean after the way The Unit was disbanded following your …'

'Stuff-up,' Durman said. 'Cock-up. Fuck-up.'

'Or any lethal variation thereof,' Anton said.

The whisky was Talisker. Tempting drop. Durman reached across the table and hefted the bottle. 'How come?'

Anton held out his glass. 'You forget the way the government works, mate. You did a runner overseas. I stuck around. I knew once the remains of the shit dried on the fan, there'd be an opening.'

'And there was.'

'Had to be. You can do without an aircraft carrier or a chopper or a battle tank—not without covert action guns.'

'The Unit's been reactivated?'

'Not as such. Always scope for a specialist consultant on contract though.' Anton crooked his trigger finger. 'You know how it is.'

Durman did. And poured Anton a refill. Special consultant. It fitted. The smoothies had failed. Send in the roughies. He put this to Anton. 'Not quite. Diplomacy's still being tried. Highest level. But we don't quite have the in we had when our man played jazz piano to the king's sax.'

'And bribery's tricky up there.'

'Yeah, almost as tricky as it is down here. Or anywhere. One cop will take it on sly grog but not on illegal drugs. Another will do it on drugs but not on vice. One on female prostitutes but not male. Shit, there's cops who'll take free hamburgers from the Greek but not fried rice from the Chinese. The Thai contacted was notorious for being on the take from pimps. When our guy approached him with double the usual 100,000 bahts—no go. The Thai put the arm on him.'

'Our guy's in gaol, too?'

'Na, luckily another Thai was found who didn't have a thing against bribes about bribes. Still, the whole effort raised a quiet stink which doesn't help the diplomatic approaches. And just to keep things simple, our government's been bending over backwards—or maybe forwards—to prove its Asian credentials.'

'So?'

'So the Thais usually commute the death sentence on farangi. Now the point can be made that an Aussie drug trafficker should be treated the same as any other Asian.'

'But if they do commute the sentence, what about releasing him to serve his gaol term here?'

'No go.'

'Time frame?'

'Problematical. There's a queue. Ig may not be leading it—there again the Thais could line them all up in front of the machine-gun in short order. No worries.'

'Great way to go.'

'Yeah, they're a funny mob all right. They used to put their royals in a velvet bag and beat them to death with padded sticks. For commoners these days, it's a machine-gun. And—gentle touches—the prisoner is tied to a support with his back to the executioner and a screen between them. The executioner can salve his Buddhist conscience by thinking he's aiming at the screen not the prisoner. As for the prisoner, well, he doesn't know when he's going to cop it.'

'He hears the executioner cocking the gun.'

Both of them had heard the cocking of a machine-gun. They were silent as if listening to it. Into the saloon came the squeal of a gull. And the *Norn* heaved to a steeper sea.

'Crossing the Heads,' Anton said.

'How long's he got?'

'Two months. Absolute max.'

'Not much.'

'Certainly not enough for a tunnel.'

'I'm the judge of that.'

'Come on. Wham-bam's the go. And given the time constraints, I've already made preliminary contact with some auxiliaries.'

'I'd rather you'd laid on the plans of the Bangkok sewerage system.'

'Bangkok itself is the sewerage system.'

'It's no worse than Rio.' Durman got to his feet and crossed to a porthole. The *Norn* was putting about. Geez, Manly'd changed, too. High rises everywhere. No more seven miles from Sydney. A thousand miles from coronary. Or whatever.

'You got in there using scuba gear,' Anton said.

'Right. The main sewer went under the gaol. Carried a spare set of gear with me and brought the guy out the same way.'

'Neat. But not fast, right? Just tell me one thing—the time frame in Rio.'

'Six months.'

'See what I mean? It's got to be wham-bam. The guys are rearing to go.'

'SAS?'

'Ex. In fast. Out faster.'

'Oh, sure, with the Thai Rangers right behind. No thanks.'

'I've already made an up-front payment.'

'Tough. But better cash-in-hand than gaol. There's a fourteen-year stretch for Aussies engaging in mercenary activities.'

'Depends who they're engaging in them for—as who knows better than you.'

The remark convinced Durman his paymaster was the government. Anton continued: 'We're not talking blunt instruments. These guys are multi-skilled. All weapons. Unarmed combat. Chopper pilots. Parachutists. Boat handlers.'

'No war party. You said yourself it was a deniable op. It'll be easier to deny if there're no bang-bangs.'

To avoid further argument, Durman went back on deck. The *Norn* was on its return leg, moving along the north shore where houses clambered on top of each other to get the kind of harbour views enjoyed by the denizens of Taronga Zoo. Anton joined him. Durman said: 'Legacy ward, this Ig?'

'Only child. The Legacy people looked after him and his mum when his dad copped it. Vietnam. Then when his mum died, Legacy was there for him even more.'

Legacy. It was a name that conjured for Durman something of the Australia he'd once loved. Legacy, the organisation of servicemen who took it upon themselves to look after the widows and orphans of fallen comrades. 'So why does a kid like that with everything and everyone going for him get involved in drug trafficking?'

'Come on, mate. You know. He was loaded up by the Thais.'

Durman faced Anton. 'Loaded up? With five k's? You believe that? We know, everybody knows, he had the stuff stashed in his surfboard cover.'

'Indeed. Everybody does know—just as everybody did know he always carried his surfboard with him, booked a seat for it. The virtuoso with his instrument.' Anton's eyes held on Durman's. 'If he hadn't been loaded up, this op would not be on.'

'What I can't work out …' From the zoo, a lion roared, challenging the roar of the *Norn's* engines. 'The porn mag he was carrying. It doesn't seem to fit.'

'Mate, you always were a bit prim and you've been away too long. Porn's now a bigger Aussie export than bullshit.'

The *Norn* was passing the area, discreetly infamous as the location of the Australian Secret Intelligence Organisation's HQ. This, too, had changed. The area was being redeveloped.

At least the long, low stone jetty and walls of the Marine Barracks appeared to be immune to redevelopment. Behind them rose Admiralty House, and the sharp high gables of Kirribili House—residences, asylums of the Governor-General and the Prime Minister.

No way either of them would be in on the op. They'd be getting the top-grade mushroom treatment the same as their predecessors when The Unit carried out its exercise to secure Kirribili House as part of a coup d'etat scenario.

'You haven't forgotten, mate,' Anton said.

'Forgotten what?' Even as he responded Durman knew Anton had the true rubbisher's ability to tune into his victim's thoughts.

'No,' Anton said, 'I don't suppose you can.' He gripped Durman's arm in mock, strong sympathy. 'It was an accident, mate—an accident. It could've happened to anyone.'

Durman knew Anton meant the opposite. Their training had been designed to eliminate the accidental. What had happened could not've happened to anyone—only to a man who'd blurred his conditioned reflexes with one drink too many.

The *Norn* was curving back, heading for Man o' War steps, snaking its way among leisurely yachts, scudding hydrofoils, kayaks, beetling ferries and—for Durman—another novelty, a water-taxi, coming alongside a figment of someone's daftness: a fake Mississippi stern-wheeler from which came whiffs of smoke and Kentucky fried chicken.

Anton laughed. 'We could board her for a meal—except it's Thai for us.'

Thai deniable, thought Durman. And no one was more deniable than he. The government had already dismissed him with the Australian version of extreme ignominy—no superannuation.

'I'll need a ground plan of the gaol,' he said.

'If you'd come via Bangkok as instructed.'

'Just get it. I had my reasons for coming the other way.'

'Yeah, you couldn't resist having a squiz at Alcatraz.'

Durman was startled, Anton delighted at his startlement. 'Had you heel-shitted all the way. You hired a portable tape guide and saw it all—the shower room, the A-block gun gallery, D block for the intractables. Could you have broken someone out when it was in screaming order?'

Durman was silent, trying to work out who could have followed him. He had checked the whole jumbo load London–New York and New York–San Francisco. Then Los Angeles–Sydney. Checked them, waking and sleeping. One of the reasons he always travelled first—first could visit steerage but steerage couldn't visit first.

'Bull,' he said. 'Absolute bull. No one heel-shitted me.'

'Except maybe someone you didn't think could, mate.'

'No one.'

'If you want to believe that, mate—okay. But you haven't answered my question. Could you have broken someone out of Alcatraz?'

'I think so.'

'How?'

Durman wasn't saying. Alcatraz might have been decommissioned. Who was to say it wouldn't be recommissioned?

Submersible would be the go. Midget submersible. Like the one the East Germans built to sail across the Baltic. Only better. It never made it. Attacked by swans during a trial run.

A sub lying off the Thai coast might also be the go.

'How far's the government prepared to push this one?' Durman said.

'As far as it needs to.'

'Then the ground plan should be no problem. Get it.'

'Okay. Okay. Or should that be jawohl? Pity about the Wall coming tumbling down, eh? Bad for your business.'

The gap between Man o' War steps and the *Norn* was narrowing. Durman did not wait for the gangplank but leapt the gap, leapt from Anton's rubbishing, knowing that Anton was going to bring up the Kirribili House exercise.

As Durman passed the Customs House on Circular Quay, he sensed he was being heel-shitted. He kept walking until he reached a fountain of bronze, cast in the shape of a creek with trees and native animals. He moved round. Here a terrapin. There a shag and a lizard. And all the time, he was searching the crowd for a possible heel-shit. No one seemed to fit the hint given by Anton.

On a hunch, Durman broke into a run, heading into George Street. Once in the lee of the first building, he halted behind a bush. Jasmine? He wondered and waited.

What he expected to see, rounding the corner, was a guy in dark glasses and carrying a white walking stick—like the guy who'd been on the flight to San Francisco.

The guy who did round the corner was so surprising that for a moment Durman could not place him. Then he made him: the beer-bellied bloke in David Jones looking for a dress for his wife.

He must have been heel-shitting from in front then. Now Durman was behind him and he stepped up and punched him once, twice in the kidneys. The guy buckled. 'Tell Anton I said you need a refresher course,' Durman said.

'Wait,' the guy gasped. 'I've got to talk to you, mate.'

Durman kept going, ignoring him as the passers-by had ignored the incident.

## 2

In a golden haze, part sweat, part smoke, a girl lay in a foam-filled oyster shell, her breasts covered to the nipple with the foam that broke away in bubbles and floated ceilingwards, rainbow-glinting in the spotlights.

Wet dream as cabaret. Too much for one patron, a fast-food fat in a blue polo-shirt. He rose from his ringside table, shaking a bottle of beer and held it spurting between his legs as he moved towards the shell.

The rest of the audience roared like surf. The fat was at the edge of the stage when a bouncer reached him. Smaller—much smaller—than the fat, but he knew his stuff. He grabbed the bottle from the fat and placed it on a table. He then got one arm under the fat's crotch and lifted him clear of the floor.

It was done so smoothly, it could have been part of the act. The audience took it that way and roared again as the bouncer carried the fat from the room. The roar took on a baying note, counter-pointing a hidden drum, as the girl rose in the shell to reveal that she was naked but painted to resemble mother-of-pearl.

A vision unattainable, increasing the demand for the B-girls available and numbered.

No. 11 shimmied across the floor in a glisten of golden skin, smelling of Arpége. Or its locally bootlegged equivalent.

'She's for me,' Anton said. He tucked the required 150 bahts into her black-satin bikini top. She smiled and showed she was investing in gold-teeth futures.

Behind her, No. 33 waited for Durman to make a move. Anton said 'Be in it,' 'It's not porking, it's bargain basement R and R.'

No. 33 was still fresh in a hot pink bikini, her number pinned where the bikini dipped towards her crotch. No more than nineteen. She smiled but her eyes already showed how unmerry her life was. In a better world, her beauty would have won her the domestic happiness of which she dreamed. Here she was merely female, a brief distraction on some guy's path to the brief nirvana of loveless nookie.

Anton put an arm round No. 11 and said to Durman: 'You're not carrying a torch for some old boiler in Europe? Or …' His smile was all white venom. 'Your old comrade-in-arms. Not with chicks like these available.'

No. 33 waited. Durman was caught between his operational rule—no grog, no women—and his past, his pity. This woman more than likely was bonded. Needed money to pay a family debt.

'You want katoi?' she said.

'Ladyboy,' Anton explained. 'Transvestite.'

The woman nodded, smiling brilliantly. No contempt. Simply an alternative deal in which there would be a profit for her to share.

Durman handed her 150 baht. 'No, you want boy. Real boy.' He made himself stooped and doddery. 'Too old,' he said. 'I am too old.'

She smiled. And Anton laughed. 'Yeah, too old at thirty's the rule here.' He put an arm round No. 33 as well. 'Not to worry. Now you're paid for, I'll look after you.'

He moved with both women towards the inner darkness of the Bar Cooee.

Durman hailed a tuk-tuk, gave its driver his destination and asked how much. The driver named his price. Durman shook his head. The driver's face expressed ritual indignation. Durman offered half the quoted price. The driver split the difference and grinned when Durman said okay.

Leaning back in the tuk-tuk, Durman grinned, too. Away from Anton, he might be able to jig together a plan.

One of his main problems surrounded him: Bangkok's traffic—a roaring, hooting, jangling tide, wild in its accelerations and unpredictable in its stoppages. No way an escape vehicle could get through this traffic at a high-sustained speed. The only vehicle he'd seen moving swiftly was the royal Oldsmobile.

Was that a possibility—synchronising the escape with the movement of a royal personage? Tagging along in the slipstream? Yeah, yeah. And the sacred white elephants might fly.

On the back of the driver's seat was a notice. Durman leant forward to read it. 'It is better to be a beggar in the corner of heaven than a rich man in the middle of hell.'

Hell. For sure. A-flicker with neon, red and green, blue and gold. An occasional flare of older fuel. Carbide? Naphtha? Kero? Yeah, and the oldest fuels: sweat, sperm and eggs.

Sperm and eggs. With a side dish of fried rice. Cow pat gai?

Hell. With the floodlit, gilded cocks of wats pointing towards nirvana.

He'd seen farangi among the monks in their robes, making the early-morning, begging rounds. Was that a possibility? Lie-up in a monastery until the Code Red was over. Then work towards a border and goodbye Bangkok. East into Kampuchea? No way. North into Burma or Laos? Worse. You might get in but you'd never get out. South? Yeah, Malaysia might be the go. Travel by train—as backpackers?

The tuk-tuk came to a complete stop. Durman found himself looking at a little hand holding a little pistol.

'Two hundred.' The little hand cocked the little pistol and a little flame of butane was reflected in the dark eyes of the little girl holding the pistol. She had a child on her hip and another child standing near. Siblings? Or her own?

'No,' Durman said. And: 'Non.' And: 'Nein.' But the little girl cocked the pistol again and the child on her hip laughed.

The hand and the pistol. Durman felt the panic surge of a rising memory. He reached into his pocket and thrust a crumple of notes into the child's clutching hand.

The tuk-tuk moved on with the traffic flow. An arranged stop? Would the tuk-tuk driver get a cut later for stopping to allow the approach to the rich farang?

Rich in the middle of hell. Not rich enough. Not yet. But this op would do it. Then the one, safe, green place was his forever more.

Sooner he returned there, the better. So no lying-up in a monastery. No backpacking. No border-crossing.

From a compound adjacent to the road came a sound Durman knew well, the sound of a vehicle siren—a banshee keening.

Time: 23.05.

Police? he wondered. Paramilitaries? Fire brigade? The tuk-tuk halted again and inside the compound were rows of ambulances, painted jungle green. One emerged from the compound's entrance and into the traffic bedlam where it was blocked despite the increased volume of its keening, calling up death future—and death past. As Anton had—with his rubbishing: *comrade-in-arms*.

The tuk-tuk driver edged round the front of the ambulance while its driver and attendant screamed at him. He accelerated into a gap in the traffic ahead of a stalled silver-grey Mercedes and across a bridge spanning one of the city's klongs which out-stenched the tide of traffic.

Durman tried breathing through his mouth and acrid exhaust fumes caught in the back of his throat. Bastard Anton. Absolute bastard.

Absolutely right: Bangkok itself *was* the sewerage system. Tunnelling wasn't on. Wherever you worked, there would be water. And shite. And no chance of tapping into existing main sewers.

The tuk-tuk had stopped yet again. '*Vite*,' Durman said. The tuk-tuk driver, not to be outdone by any farang, said '*Voila*.'

Durman paid him off, ignoring his offers to wait. The Tiara had been quiet when Anton introduced Durman to it earlier in their recce. Now it was frothing at the mouth with reporters and photographers who had filed copy and pictures to deadlines half a world away, with TV crews who had bounced their images from satellites to the global village's idiot boxes.

As he moved towards the long mahogany bar, Durman caught a snippet of conversation. 'So he said to me I should learn to keep my nose clean. And I said to him: "You mean a lighter shade of brown than yours?"'

As the ensuing guffaw ended, Durman reached the bar and ordered a mineral water. He was served—from some time-warp, leftover cache or bootleg backroom—Apollinaris. There was a bowl of peanuts on the bar and a bigger bowl full of book matches advertising the pub. Durman took a handful of peanuts. Half-turning, he scanned the room. In its laughter, there was wariness. The drinkers were all watching each other.

No one, he noted, pissed alone. If one guy moved out of the bar to the lavatories, another was sure to follow him. Queer the lot of them. He took one of the books of matches and studied it. Queer for news.

Earlier Anton'd explained how the press build-up had begun when King Bhumibol's birthday had passed without a royal pardon for Ig.

A tubby guy, who looked like a jockey who'd decided the hell with wasting, raised a tweed cap to scratch his bald head. 'What I still can't understand is why Ig had himself booked on a Hong Kong flight. Ex-Honkers-Sydney security's tighter than an eel's bum. I mean 90 per cent of Oz heroin goes through Honkers and he had five keys.'

'A face. He's a face.' The respondent was slung with cameras and wore a sleeveless jacket pouched for film. 'He expected to breeze through all the way—not be busted.'

'Boofhead's what he is. The original bronzed boofhead. I hear he's been offered half a million for his story.'

'And the rest.'

'But he won't talk, the boofhead.'

'Evens he does before he's executed.'

'You were offering me odds two beers ago.'

'Okay. Three to one.'

'Bahts?'

'No way. Exes may be down but they're not that bad. Dollars.'

'Aussie?'

'Shit, no. US.'

'Okay.'

Durman knew he should not have let them catch his attention when the tubby guy turned to him. 'Forgotten your name.'

Durman gave him a name. The tubby guy said: 'Beirut, wasn't it?'

'Not me.'

'Ric Wyler-Star.' The tubby guy gave the name of his newspaper as if it were hyphenated to his surname.

Durman was mystified. Ric Wyler-Star irked, 'Come on. At the Inter. Every time the bloody parrot squawked 'Incoming', you yelled, 'Pieces of eight'.

'Not me,' Durman said.

'Where then?' Ric Wyler-Star said. 'Berlin?'

This was too close for comfort. Durman had operated in Berlin. But he hadn't been using journalist cover. Never did, though it was common enough practice. Real journalists had a way of turning journalist cover inside out by seemingly harmless anecdotes about mutual acquaintances. Or a bloody parrot.

'It *was* Berlin,' Ric Wyler-Star was saying. 'I knew it. Everyone was there when the Wall came tumbling down.'

'Listen. I'm not a journalist,' Durman took a book of matches from the bowl on the bar. 'I'm a tourist.'

'Not another bloody one,' Ric Wyler-Star said. 'Read about this place in your local rag, right?'

Durman did not need to answer. Ric Wyler-Star was off. 'Wreck every decent boozer in the world, they do. Bloody amateurs writing up their trips so they get freebies and then flogging their compositions for less than the rate. If I …'

The ringing of a telephone halted him. It was answered by a tall, broad-shouldered guy, the back of whose denim jacket carried the faded legend: 'Bao chai.' Even as he unhooked the telephone from its wall bracket, those nearest the door were already turning towards it. Then as suddenly as a flight of swallows wheeling in flight, and as inexplicably, they were all fighting to get outside.

Durman was carried with the rush out of the air-conditioned cool into the sweating heat of the night. Not swallows. Hounds quarrelling on a scent, faces contorted by the need to be first, some talking on mobile phones.

Other journalists were already at the Bang Kwang Central Prison in Nonthaburi, a satellite town out on the Chao Phraya River where it was still possible to sense that the concrete and glass sprawl of Bangkok and the roar of its feral traffic were having to contend with the primordial jungle and its quietude in a battle the jungle could win.

Not that the journalists were subdued. As the pack from the Tiara arrived to reinforce them, they were milling about, some yelling, some beating on the prison gates.

Drunk, the whole mob. But on something stronger than alcohol—overproof adrenaline.

Durman held back. He had reconnoitred the walls of Bang Kwang in daylight several times, travelling with Anton by river and road—the river, as Anton had pointed out, being the quicker and the obvious option as a line of retreat.

Now at night, the walls of the prison were less like stone than the crumbling, grey crust of some giant, sweating cheese. Behind the walls, cockroach hordes and rat tribes made common cause against 30,000 prisoners who shared its ten-man cells, its raw plank bunks, its 50-man hutments, its 200-man lavatories, its meagre rice, its richer heroin, its TB, its hepatitis and its AIDS.

A wicket gate opened and two uniformed guards appeared. They took up position on either side of the gate, fingers on the trigger guards of their slung sub-machine guns: Uzis.

Time: 01.30.

Behind them came a third uniformed guard, his shoulder-boards those of a colonel, his cap visor shining with more gold. On his chest, paratrooper's wings rose from a spectrum of military ribbons.

The baying excitement of the journalists increased. Still cameras buzzed and clicked on motor-drive. Hand-bashers attached to television cameras flared. Microphones and tape-recorders were thrust forward.

Was Anton right after all? Durman wondered. Was a war party the way? But a war party got up as a television crew, weapons concealed, ready to go in during such a scrum? Wham-bam. Steam straight in, snatch the prisoner and withdraw over the prison wall to the river—and a long-tail boat with engine running?

Only way to go here.

Or the too-obvious way?

'Come on, Colonel,' a voice yelled. 'If you want to be served piping hot, let's have the news.'

The baying increased. The colonel spoke a word in Thai. The guards cocked their weapons. The rattle and snap silenced the journalists. Durman began edging towards the wicket gate.

The colonel spoke rapidly in Thai, ignoring the mutters of the journalists.

'What's the little bastard saying?'

'Shut up, you Aussie berk, and we might hear.'

'Who're you calling berk, you Pommie drongo?'

'Pardon.'

'Fair enough.'

'I mean it's a pardon, you berk.'

'Don't call me berk.'

Durman halted. Through the gate was a guardroom, a guardroom enclosed in a glinting new cyclone wire cage. A floodlit cage, swarming with moths. And beyond the cage in the murk, Durman surmised, there would be a machine-gun, ready to turn the cage into a killing pen.

From the journalists came a babble of questions, addressed to the colonel and to each other: English in various versions, mixing with French and German and with Japanese from a TV crew who had forced their way to the forefront. Here and there the babble resolved itself into cross-talk acts. Durman picked up on the Berk and the Drongo again.

'Who? Who did he say?'

'The Nigerian.'

'But he was the world record swallower, eighty eggs—count them—eighty condoms reinforced with electrician's tape in his guts when arrested. Street value at least 500,000 smackeroos.'

The Nigerian had been ahead of Ig in the death queue. One out. Four to go before Ig: two Thais, a Frenchman and a Chinese. The babble increased in volume as the colonel, covered by his escort, about-turned. The Berk and the Drongo continued their cross-talk.

'… took him out in an ambulance, clever little bastards.'

'Shit a brick, I was here when it arrived. Military job.'

'Dozey git, I told you to look sharp. What time?'

'Time you said you'd be back from your massage.'

'Sorry about that, old boy. Bonking massage. Delightful. So what time? In *and* out.'

'In, ten past twelve. Out, say another ten minutes.'

A few of the journalists were running to their vehicles to try for interviews with the Nigerian at the airport. The Berk and the Drongo joined them. Durman watched them go. There would've been a stampede if Ig had been aboard the ambulance.

Beyond the jagged line of buildings opposite the prison, a blue neon sign blinked on and off against the night sky: Sapphire Hotel.

Durman strolled to where he had left his tuk-tuk and its driver. Beneath the street lamps hung replicas of the area's durian fruit.

Shrivelled rugby footballs with spikes added. 'The heaven and hell of fruit,' Anton'd called it. 'Heaven for taste. Hell for stench.'

A painted sign pointed towards the Museum of the Department of Corrections. Durman grinned. Juxtaposition was crucial for tourists. He and Anton had taken in the museum's collection of torture and execution memorabilia, including a giant wicker ball, spiked inside, where an offender could be placed before the ball was rolled among elephants for a lethal kickabout.

Time: 01.43. Less than five hours to reveille in Bang Kwang. Less than five hours until Big Ig rose to face the new day and a shorter queue ahead of him, waiting to be kicked to death by a heavy machine-gun.

Durman settled into the tuk-tuk. He had passed the ambulance depot at 23.05. The journo had said the ambulance had gone into the prison at 00.10. So it had taken 65 minutes for the ambulance to get from the depot to the prison. Say 55 to be safer.

The blue neon sign continued to blink on and off.

Sapphire Hotel.

Sapphire Hotel.

Anton had offered an alternative name.

Forward Command Post.

In Durman's suite at the Royal Lotus, the ground plan of Bang Kwang draped a coffee table like an over-starched linen tablecloth, figured in blue. On the floor, he was into his push-ups—on 45, heading for 50—when Anton came in. A surprise entrance on two counts. First, Durman had locked the door. Second, he had been congratulating himself that Anton would be too shagged-out to engage in any exercise.

Anton was in running gear, however, orange T-shirt sweated to his chest, blue shorts to his thighs and on his feet joggers that looked to have been built from multi-coloured bubblegum. 'I did my push-ups last night,' he said. 'with some help from the girls. Yours, mate, was a real little goer.'

Durman did not stop when he reached 50. Anton surveyed him when he stood up after 100 and Durman was conscious of the roll of flab above the waistband of his boxer shorts. 'You surprise me,' Anton said. 'From the look of you I thought you'd given exercising away. If I'd known, I would've invited you for a run. Only 10 k's.'

'In this place? People must've thought you were mad.'

'People paid no attention. Everything the farang does here is thought mad. Like paying for a girl, then not using her.'

'Or coming into someone's room uninvited.'

Anton held up a jingle of picklocks. 'My area of expertise.'

Durman had been waiting for his moment. 'You weren't so expert when you had the beer-belly follow me.'

Anton's eyes did not waver. Sea-blue. Sea-deceptive. 'Beer-belly? I do not understand.'

'You understand all right. After our meet, you stuck a big turd on my heels.' Anton shook his head. 'Come on,' Durman said. 'I gave him a message for you. And a couple of bruises.'

Anton continued to shake his head in a nice mixture of puzzlement and amusement. Durman began rolling up the ground plan of the gaol. 'This is out of date,' he said. 'The Thais have set up a new security box inside the main gate.'

'You've been inside?'

Durman explained how he had seen inside when the announcement of the pardon for the Nigerian was made.

Again Anton surprised Durman. This time by his lack of surprise—and the extent of his knowledge.

'Yeah. I heard about him from our contact. Apparently, the Nigerian authorities were working on the Thais to persuade them their national was a simple mule, a desperate victim of the globalisation of drug trafficking. People forget transport costs are as critical to profit margins in drug trafficking as …'

'Save the lecture.' Durman thrust the rolled-up ground plan into its carrying cylinder. 'The next on the queue are Thais. There's no way they're going to execute their own—or Ig—after sending the Nigerian on his merry way.'

'If you'd let me finish my lecture, I would've told you how merry,'

Anton said. 'The Nigerian had his executioner with him—full-blown AIDS. The Thais have their own sense of irony. They'll commute the death sentence and free a prisoner providing his death is guaranteed. As for not executing their own, they offed one of the Thais at dawn.'

'Shit.'

'Yeah, everywhere. Maybe they should strap them to a potty instead of a support.'

'So it's down to three ahead of Ig?'

'Correct. A Thai, a Frenchman and a Chinese.'

'The French'll get their guy off. That'll set a precedent for Ig.'

'No, it won't. The top guy at the Quai d'Orsay had a daughter and she OD'ed six months ago. He's let the Thais know he'll man the machine-gun himself with his wife as his number two.' Anton took the cylinder. 'I'll get this back where it came from.'

'The Embassy?' Durman said. 'Like your gen about the Frenchman.'

'Don't you worry about that.' Anton grinned at some joke Durman did not get. 'Our contact'll see to it and point out to his Thai opposite number who got the better deal.'

'He should ask for the bribe back.'

'No bribe. It was a barter deal. The Thais wanted the ground plan of the first Australian Federal Penitentiary. And that's still so secret it hasn't even been talked about in the Non-Members Bar dunny in Canberra.'

Durman crossed to the window. From up there, the Chao Phraya River had the look of a great snake, a python whose green and black markings were transformed to glistening gold by the sun.

Anton was playing a game. A double game. Otherwise he wouldn't've denied that the beer-belly was one of his people or been so cagey about his contact. Had to be someone in the Embassy.

A long-tailed boat, filled with tourists, sped up river and swung in towards Wat Arun—the Temple of Dawn. The lights on the tips of its five towers were still on. Forgetfulness? Or a memorial for the Thai who had died? Another long-tailed boat sped past, its long egg-beater drive shaft and propeller whipping up a plume of foam.

Tunnelling was out because of the water but water might still be the answer. Not for Anton. Not yet. Two could play at double games.

Durman turned from the window. 'I've been thinking.' He made a spiralling motion with his index finger.

Anton clapped his hands. 'Beauty. I can lay on the best. The Black Hawk.'

The Black Hawk *was* the best chopper around. For sure. Australian Army. Anton was definitely plugged into top contacts. 'Okay,' Durman said. 'Then it'll be a matter of arranging for Ig to be outside his cell.'

'Day extraction, of course.'

'Night.'

'Not on.'

'What about your other area of expertise—whiz-bangs?'

'Irish porridge—fertiliser, diesel, soupcon of Semtex?'

'Thermite, bring Ig out, light up the scene.'

'He's fettered, don't forget. Wrists. Ankles. And both linked.'

'Haven't forgotten. The way I see it, I'll be going down to pick him up.'

'That'll mean a winch and—there's no way he won't be guarded—you'll need bones. SMG. Stun grenades.'

'Okay on the grenades. Forget the SMG.'

Anton began a protest. Or a needle. Durman overrode him. 'The grenades? You'll get them here?'

'Too risky. There are other ways.'

Yeah, Durman thought, the diplomatic bag. And said: 'I'll leave it to you.'

'Do that, mate. Maybe I'd better lay on side-gunners with the chopper.'

Durman hesitated. 'As long as you realise every round they fire is more shit for your diplomatic contacts to clean up.'

'Who said anything about diplomatic contacts?'

'You didn't have to.'

Anton laughed, truly amused. 'No, mate, I didn't.'

Behind Anton's insouciance, Durman sensed another element. 'Ig,' he said. 'He must've lost some condition on gaol tucker.'

'Condemned men are like pigs,' Anton said. 'Their keepers like them to be fat for the slaughterhouse. Ig's been doing better—much better—than the standard bowl of rice and piece of chicken which may be rat.'

There was definitely another element. Durman waited. Anton held his stare for a stretched second. 'All right,' he said. 'You do need to know. The prison doc's on side. He's keeping his eye on Ig—diet, vitamin supplements, vaccination shots.'

'Money or another barter deal?'

'Barter. The doc's on the waiting list for immigration to Oz.'

Anton smiled frankly. And Durman wondered whether the sense he had of a hidden element wasn't merely a touch of the paranoids brought on by the nature of the game. The wilderness of mirrors, the unholy Jesus, James Angleton of the CIA had called it before succumbing to more than a touch of the paranoids himself. Durman returned Anton's smile. 'At least your doc seems to be keeping Ig's lip in good order.'

'His lip?'

'Been keeping it tightly buttoned, Ig—considering he's been offered half a million.'

'He's been told he's going to be extracted. And when …' Anton's smoothness broke in a swirl of uncertainty: a trout sensing the hook in a lure, going round for another look. 'If … you know?'

'No, I don't. What're you trying to tell me? He's not sick, is he? He's fit enough?'

'Not as fit as he was. But fit enough. This is a kid who used to win 42-k iron-man contests. And at world level—surf-ski paddling, board paddling, surf-swimming and running on sand. Oh, he's fit enough, mate. Yeah, fit enough to make a run for it—if he wasn't fettered.' Anton took a couple of jogging steps towards Durman. 'The question, mate, is, are you fit enough?'

With that he spun round and launched a kick at Durman's stomach. It was no more than half-serious. Yet it was enough to send Durman backwards over his bed and onto the floor on the other side. He would have let it pass—a souvenir of the days when putting on sudden turns was part of Unit training—except that as he got to his feet, he saw that Anton was into a fighting crouch, fists extended, swaying as if the eyes of a sensei were on him, and saying 'You're soft, mate. Out of training.'

Training, Durman had learned, was only a way of getting you to where you had to survive. And if he was going to survive this op, he had to show Anton who was in charge.

Bastard expects me to bow before we engage. Durman picked up a stainless steel Thermos jug from the bedside table and threw it at Anton's head. Anton swayed to one side and the jug shattered a mirror, and Durman's reflection, as he rampaged across the bed, trailing the bedcover and flicking it out to envelop Anton. 'You want to ponce around like Mr Suzuki. Durman punched Anton to the head as he struggled beneath the bedcover. 'Find a Mr Suzuki. Again he punched, this time connecting with Anton's jaw … 'who wants to ponce around with you.'

Anton went down. Durman swung his foot and stopped in mid-swing. His fist was sore enough.

There was a knock on the door and a room-service waiter pushed in a trolley loaded with Durman's breakfast.

He took in the broken mirror and groaning bed-cover. He giggled. 'Rock 'n' roll, man.'

Bangkok, Durman thought, city of angels, city of golden brilliance and beautiful people disappearing up its own fundamental orifice to become a gut tangle of strangulated roads and a slow peristalsis of stinking vehicles. A sour notion inspired by a sour circumstance.

Anton had insisted on hiring a Volvo for the trip to Don Muang airport, saying it was necessary for him to get used to the traffic if he was going to drive a get-away vehicle—a role Durman let him presume was his.

The possibility of the presumption becoming fact was diminishing with every futile attempt by Anton to make headway in the traffic jam hemming them in on the Phahon Yothin Road.

'I should have hired a bulldozer,' Anton said as he won an advance of 100 metres.

'Or a tank,' Durman said.

The people of this city like so many others were delusional about the motor car. Because it was designed for speed, they believed they were going fast—all evidence to the contrary.

'Victory Monument.' Anton took a left from the roundabout on which the monument stood, at its base a traffic cop, robotic in a gasmask, was trying to orchestrate the traffic, his white-gloved gestures precise, programmed, futile.

The going was easier all the way to a bridge over the Chao Phraya and beyond. Anton swung right, intent on finding a route roughly parallel to Phahon Yothin to get ahead of the traffic jam. The Volvo was now doing thirty. Anton managed to accelerate to forty when he glimpsed a train speeding along and the Volvo shot under a bridge as the train thundered overhead. 'Pharam Sixth Bridge,' he said.

Smug bastard. Durman slumped lower in his seat. He'd memorised the map. If he said, 'Time spent on reconnaissance is rarely wasted …'

Anton said it.

'Absolutely, General,' Durman said.

The road now ran parallel to the railway and as the Volvo crossed another loop of the Chao Phraya, the train pulled ahead.

In the distance, between the road and the railway line, rose a weird massif. 'The hell's that?' Durman said.

'Don't know,' Anton said. 'Not on the map.'

As the Volvo closed with the massif, Durman could see that it was made up of vehicles of every vintage and model. 'Forget Detroit,' Anton said. 'This is where they breed.'

At first sight, the vehicles did indeed look as if they were copulating—multi-coloured turtles in metallic orgasm. And Durman was reminded of the iridescent, discarded cicada carapaces—butchers, grocers, black knights—he had collected for Christmas as a boy in Sydney.

Boys were at work on the massif along with men and women and girls, cannibalising the vehicles. At the foot of the massif was a plain of refurbished vehicles: trucks, vans, semi-trailers.

Anton had the Volvo on sixty-five.

'Stop,' Durman said.

Anton accelerated. 'We've got a plane to catch.'

Durman reached across, turned off the ignition and, as the car slowed, got out. He jogged towards the massif of vehicles while Anton yelled: 'What the hell do you think you're doing?'

Durman did not know what he thought he was doing. The posse of salesmen who surrounded him thought they knew. Their command of English was concentrated in one word: 'Cheap.' Durman held up a 35 mm Pentax. As he strode among the rows of vehicles, he focused the camera this way and that. A more persistent salesman followed him and kept saying: 'Let me, boss. I will take good shot of you.'

People—privileged workers?—were living in some of the vehicle shells. Clean, bright washing fluttered on ropes strung clear of the rusting, metal rubbish between vehicles. The stench and black smoke of burning tyres was countered by the smell of a brave stew. Somewhere a child laughed, a tiny, shrill sound like a bird calling up spring in a desolation.

Finally, Durman spotted what he was hoping for. He stopped in front of a hearse, decorated with elaborate chromium-plated side lanterns.

Next to the hearse stood a couple of armoured personnel carriers on one of which a mechanic was working. He handed his camera to the salesman and, as Anton drove up in the Volvo, was in front of the hearse. 'I'll see you in one of these before you see me,' Durman shouted.

Anton's reply was lost in the roar of the APC's engine being revved by the mechanic. Durman hit its side. Full throttle. Unstoppable.

The salesman kept punctuating his spiel with shots. Predictably this involved giving, 'best price, very best price' on the hearse. Less predictably, it involved the offer of, 'optional extra at no extra cost'. This he insisted on demonstrating. It was inside the hearse on a raised platform: a massive coffin. Durman smiled but he was looking across the path at three ambulances, each painted jungle green, each marked with a red cross and each with its rear doors open to show that it was fully equipped with stretchers.

The salesman was impressed when Durman handed over what was left of his Thai currency as a tip. He reciprocated with 'Khawp khum'—thank you—and his business card.

After the sweating heat, the Volvo's air-conditioning was as chilly as Anton's silence on the drive along the parallel route before he swung right to come back on to Phahon Yothin Road. He was delighted to find himself just ahead of the reason for the traffic grid-lock: a pair of elephants swaying along, ghostly white and richly caparisoned—so delighted he broke his silence. 'No, mate,' he said, 'I am not stopping for you to get a photograph.'

'I think I've got what I need,' Durman said. He was conscious of the business card against his chest all the way back to Sydney.

The book of matches from the Tiara.

And the name, Ric Wyler-Star.

## 3

When the Town Hall clock began striking, its reverberations seemed to be made visible in the heat shimmer ahead of Durman. He waited for the tenth stroke before beginning his run. George, Pitt and Castlereagh Streets might have been newly named, so light was their Sunday morning traffic as he crossed them.

His sense of time warp was increased by a procession of vintage cars trundling along Elizabeth Street in the direction of Circular Quay. A merry procession, men drivers straw-boatered, blazered and moustachioed; women passengers in top-heavy feathered hats and frilled dresses. Among them sat a geisha in an elaborate kimono and a samurai in a winged helmet.

Durman crossed between a charabanc and a Stanley Steamer. He waved away a leaflet thrust at him by a dowager in pink.

'Bastard,' said the dowager. 'Can't you see I'm working?'

Durman reached back and she slapped the leaflet into his hand.

> PARRAMATTA … KEENEST PRICES SINCE GRANDPA WAS A KID … BARHOLM FORD TOYOTA …

Durham dropped the leaflet and glanced left, expecting to see the RC cathedral. Not a sign of the bloody place. To his right, the Anzac War Memorial was as he remembered it, squat implacable, a different kind of temple, awaiting a different kind of sacrifice.

He ran on. His memory was playing tricks. When he glanced left again, the RC cathedral was there. But no longer fronted by the bowling club where Dad used to play. Now a piazza on top of a swimming pool.

Durman was halfway up William Street, his running figure reflected in the glass cliffs of the buildings opposite, when he was confronted by a figure dressed in formidable pink. At first, he thought the dowager had somehow got ahead of him. Then he saw the pink was some kind of glitter stuff and the figure was a guy, morning beard thrusting black from beneath his make-up, eyelids batting flirtatiously despite their freight of false lashes. Shit, Durman thought, if I were as strong as his eyelids, I wouldn't be feeling this knackered. The guy might have caught his thought. 'Take a spell.' His eyelids batted again over pupils that were zonked-out black. 'With me.'

'Yeah, Georgie'll give you a real workout.' In an adjacent cul-de-sac was a cluster of pros, their night finery draggled in the morning light.

'Sorry, mate.' Durman kept going. 'I've got a date with your sister, Charlie.'

'Cheeky.' The voice fluted from masculine depths and a ripe swell of boobs netted in Lurex. Durman increased his pace. The guy kept up, his high heels clacking in unison with the squish of Durman's joggers. Durman thought about backhanding the guy. He thought again. All he needed was a stoush with a guy in a glitter frock who kept himself fit. And the cops taking their names.

Two laggard drunks were letting gravity and the occasional fart take them downhill from Kings Cross. Durman waited till they were almost level with him and shouldered the guy into their path.

On a whiff of rum, Durman heard: 'Where've you been, darl?'

And: 'Get your lousy paws off.'

The guy in the glitter frock obviously had his standards.

Durman was running clear except that the whiff of rum had set off a yearning for a drink. And a huge, red-and-gold Coca-Cola sign was glittering above him.

Time enough for a drink—and a good one—when he'd got Ig the Mule out.

Innocent mule or guilty mule?

Fitted-up mule? Or fated mule?

Not his problem. His problem was to get the big boof out, make sure the final payment was in and then get back to the one safe place.

Spring. He would be there by spring. After the gales of winter had blown themselves down to breezes shaking the bog-cotton.

Summer to come, and the trout rising to the midges on the evening lochs.

Near the bottom of the reverse slope from Kings Cross, he got his second wind and as he passed Rushcutters Bay the traffic roar eased so that he could hear the jingle of the running gear against the alloy masts of the moored yachts.

Anton had the chopper on stand-by. Was a transfer to a yacht the next stage? Or a sub?

He climbed away from the jingle of the running gear and at Edgecliff Station had an impulse to cheat: catch a train to Bondi Junction. Instead, he accelerated to beat the traffic lights for the downhill run into Double Bay. It, too, had changed. Glitzier. Triple not Double Bay if the multi-million dollar traffic smash was an indicator: a Rolls-Royce Silver Spirit, a Jaguar Sovereign and a Porsche with attendant mourners.

After the hill out of Double Bay he could take pleasure in the ample curve of Rose Bay, yachts, stinkboats and windsurfers signing its green-blue waters with vanishing white wakes.

A seaplane was lifting off in a glitter of foam. It banked to head north. Was that it? A seaplane transfer. A seaplane landing and taking off from the Chao Phraya, its arrival and departure masked from radar by the high-rise hotels along the river.

Ahead now Durman could see the S-bends leading up to and past Rose Bay Convent School, focus of so many of his boyhood fantasies.

At the end of the first S, Durman was glad he'd confined himself to using the haversack on his back only for a change of gear and not loaded it with extra weight.

Anton would have. He'd been rapt by all The Unit's training exercises. In the Blue Mountains. In the Simpson Desert. In the Snowies. Tough as the SAS course, mate. Tougher. Anton had been tougher. Able to go straight to the Killing House after a 20 k forced march, carrying 56 k, and score max kills. Any weapon. Never a fumble in the fire and reload drill which was why his rubbishing was so sharp.

Durman caught himself there. If he kept thinking along those lines they'd lead back to where Anton wanted the rubbishing to take him.

By the third S, Durman knew it was not enough to go off wine and women when he was operational. He knew he'd been wrong to let his fitness go, using the excuse that fitness could be a giveaway in certain situations. He'd seen an undercover soldier banjaxed in a Derry pub, his fitness making him a stand-out among a crowd of paunchy tearaways and hard cases.

As he reached the top of the S, a skinny lad on a red racing bicycle passed him as if he was standing still. And maybe he was. The lad turned his head as he passed, white teeth gleaming in a spotty face. 'Race you,' he said. And flicked into a gear change for the low-road swoop to Watsons Bay.

Durman had to turn for the high road: Military Road. He passed a cemetery and felt like lying down with the truly silent majority who knew what life was all about.

The salesman who'd sold him the joggers had said their unique aerobic structure guaranteed them against blistering. Yeah, guarantees *them*, Durman thought, as the pain of the blister on his heel intensified. He moved faster against the pain along the Dover Heights plateau and caught a glimpse of the sea.

Soon he was running downhill towards Bondi, its golden bow of sand, its white string of waves, shooting surfers beachwards. He worked his way down to the esplanade for the final stage, threading his way among the family groups and knots of teenagers. More Asians than he remembered. Mostly Vietnamese. Geez, and more tit, here, there and everywhere on the sand.

North Bondi clubhouse had grown a second storey. An aged Jewish couple were checking their watches by the clubhouse clock as if making sure they'd escaped from their terrible past.

Bondi clubhouse had also grown a second storey. As he passed it, a derisive yell went up. He kept going. He didn't want close encounters of the knuckle kind. Or any others.

The archways of the Pavilion had the look of a bazaar. Jewellery, leather and clothes stalls. Spruiking sellers. Thronging buyers. From the Pavilion itself rose the rhythms of a South American band. Chips

Rafferty, he thought. And wondered whether the full-length black-and-white photograph of him still decorated the stairs leading to the Pavilion theatre. There were others. Peter Finch. The aboriginal, Raymond—was it?—Tudawali.

Durman had on a towelling headband. Now it was sweat-soaked. Sweat drops, glittering, dripped from it before his eyes and refracted by the sweat drops he saw the figure of a surf lifesaver heading for the sea across his path. He pulled up to let the figure pass and realised it was a bronze statue, complete with beltman's harness, leaping perpetually towards the breakers as if to join the skull-capped lifesavers of the present, riding a rubber duckie on patrol, focus of a mob of Japanese tourists, paddling in the shallows. Like bloody Poms, he thought.

Out at sea, kids on surfboards were jockeying for the best waves. On shore, other kids on skateboards were performing even more fantastic manoeuvres on concrete waves.

Time: 11.10. Not bad for 14 k's. But not as good as his last when he'd come in ahead of a drongo got up as a nun.

He stripped to the bathers he was wearing beneath his running shorts. At the beach's southern end, he climbed down to the seaward rocks. He waited for a lifting swell and dived. The backwash carried him out as the stinging sea obliterated the heaving sweat of his run. He settled into his freestyle, trying not to think of the distance to the north point: 1000 metres.

He reckoned he was about a third across when someone said: 'Thought it was you when I saw you waddling along like a ruptured duck.'

Jerry Telfer, thought Durman, and said so.

'Yeah.' Jerry laughed. 'Didn't you hear me yelling?'

Durman had no breath to spare for a reply. Jerry had plenty. 'Still mad as a meataxe,' he said. 'The rip's carried you outside the line of the shark nets. Better angle back in.'

He did so himself and Durman followed. Jerry kept ahead of him, swimming with an easy, accustomed power. When they reached the seaweedy shallows of the north end, he stood up.

Beyond him, Durman saw another change: a rainbow snake of coloured tiles and broken mirror decorating the wall that ran alongside the children's swimming pool.

He turned for the swim back. 'You *are* mad,' Jerry said and followed him; followed him and couldn't resist passing him. Durman was content to go stroke for stroke, kick for kick. Not laugh for laugh when Jerry out there in the long, lifting swells guffawed at something.

As they angled towards the pool, Durman tried to catch a wave and beat Jerry in. But Jerry reached the poolside steps first. He guffawed again in handing Durman a condom. 'Welcome home, mate,' he said. 'As I remember, you were always too mean to buy your own.'

Still the old, overbearing, raw-tongued, raw-boned Jerry—except for his head. Where he'd been bald, there was a mat of hair. A wig? But how did it stay on in the surf? Anchored to the remnants of Jerry's dark, natural growth? Jerry caught him wondering and gave him a grin that was part defiant, part embarrassed, part appeal.

The appeal got to Durman and he refrained from asking whether Jerry'd had a transplant from his hairy chest or his hairy balls, which were barely covered by his royal-blue, red-striped Pierre Cardin bathers.

Instead he threw the condom at Jerry. 'Not my size,' he said. And thought, not Raymond Tudawali. Robert. Great footballer, too.

The condom had come from the sea. Jerry's royal-blue Mercedes 260E was fresh from the showroom, its brown leather upholstery shining.

Jerry sniffed it and exhaled. 'Two point six litre. Six cylinders. Electronic engine control.' He pushed a button. 'Electric windows. Automatic climate air-conditioning. More than one-twenty built-in safety features.'

'No thanks,' Durman said. 'The back wheels fell off the last one I had.'

'Rave on,' Jerry said.

Durman, caught between a past he did not want to remember and a present he needed to control, said: 'Good procession of your people this morning.'

Jerry Telfer was one of those drivers who manage to conduct conversations in the rear-vision mirror. 'Now what're you raving about?'

'Procession of cars,' Durman said. 'You're still selling them, aren't you?'

The horn on the Mercedes played the first notes of 'Colonel Bogey' and Jerry knew the first word. 'Bollocks,' he said. 'Where've you been? This isn't a sample. This is mine.'

'I thought …'

'Heard you,' Jerry said. 'You thought I'd stood still, polishing the bonnet of some clapped-out Holden. Anyway, what about yourself?

What're you doing for a crust these days?'

Durman had learned to play his cover story vague unless sharp detail was absolutely necessary. 'I'm looking at a few possibilities.'

'Like that, eh?' Jerry said. 'You ex-public servants're all the same—find it hard to adjust to the real world.'

'You may be right.'

'Of course I'm right. I mean there you were in your cosy public service job. Superannuated in. Next minute you're shooting through overseas. If you'd come to me, I might've been able to help you. Nothing as cosy as the job you had, of course. What a hoot.'

It was a hoot. A deliberate hoot. A hoot The Unit had put into circulation itself by way of the National Press Club leak-house in Canberra. A hoot based on The Unit's full name, the Policy Action Unit Special Executive: PAUSE—cover activity, chasing up the parliamentary draughtsmen to ensure speedy presentation of bills.

'Yeah, a real hoot,' Jerry said, adding the punchline: 'Establishing delay norms in the parliamentary process.'

'We were axed.'

'Yeah, I know. Been seeing a bit of your offsider, the Dutch guy.'

This was the kind of connection Durman had hoped to avoid. 'Anton?' he said, and stopped himself from adding, 'Haven't seen him in years.'

'He's doing better than looking at possibilities.'

'Is that right?'

'Yeah, much better. Where did you say you were staying?'

Durman hadn't said. He did so.

'Beats the Matt Talbot Hostel,' Jerry said. But he was impressed and tapped a number into his car phone. 'Missus there?' he said. And after a wait: 'Syl? Have I got a surprise for you.' He chuckled. 'No, not that. You know I'm always horny.'

Durman wondered about the chance of bailing out at the next traffic lights. Jerry was saying: 'I kid you not. Large as life, twice as dopey and wait till you cop the beard.' He spoke into the rear-vision mirror at Durman. 'Nothing much. Just the usual Sunday brunch. Few mates. Buck's fizz. Bit of tucker. No butter but. Syl's got me on cholesterol watch.'

'I'm watching my weight myself,' Durman said. 'Some other time.'

'You must be shortsighted. Anyway, you're expected. Syl, you know her. She'll be ropable if you disappoint her.'

*Again* may have been in Jerry's mind because he smiled in the rear-vision mirror. *Again* was definitely in Durman's mind. And Syl. Sylvia Taranton. Ropable.

## 4

The house was stepped back in three terraces on the contours of a rock face from which a ground-level garage had been hollowed and above which the terraces climbed to overlook the inner reaches of the harbour. Designed to astonish, the house. Yet it did not surprise Durman. It was Jerry and Syl in steel, glass and concrete. They said as much, explaining how they'd bought a weatherboard cottage and demolished it to free the site for rebuilding.

'Something that was more us,' Syl said.

'Bloody local basket-weavers tried to get a preservation order slapped on the place,' Jerry said.

'Fitted with aluminium window frames,' Syl said. 'Obscene.'

Some in the group agreed. Others ran to totally obscene. Durman remembered the pride with which his Dad had fitted aluminium window frames to their house.

'Greenies,' Jerry was saying. 'What do they know? If everyone planted an instant rainforest like ours, there would be no problem.'

Palms, tree ferns and gums shaded the terraces and the few mates. Not so few as Durman discovered drifting among them. A steady 30, entering and exiting from the first terrace with its swimming pool and games room, complete with bar and changing facilities. Nor were they mates. Clients, as Syl made clear. 'No, no—selling cars was never really Jerry's bag. But I didn't have to tell *him* twice.'

Under her burnished, coppery head of hair, her eyes had a slumberous quality as of a night-time creature caught by daylight. To what she'd said, her eyes added a gloss: 'Not like you, you dill. If you'd listened, you would've had all this. And me.'

A considerable reward. She stood as she always had, shoulders back, tits up, legs apart, arms akimbo, as if waiting for a starter's alert before bringing her feet together, and her hands, for the dive, the race and the winning touch.

A touch she retained. She put her hand on his arm. 'A drink, a real one,' she said. 'For old time's sake.'

He refused. She took a glass of Buck's Fizz from a white-coated manservant. There had been a maid on the front door. Filipina. Durman surveyed the upper terraces. Did the manservant and the maid live in? Maybe he should ask Syl to get her off the subject of Jerry. As if he could.

'What happened was the dealer Jer was working with hired a PR and Jer saw how much the PR pisspot was getting.'

'Yeah.' Jerry detached himself from the group he was talking to and joined them as Syl went on, 'And how easily he earned it.'

Jerry moved them nearer the pool where the noise of those who'd decided on a swim covered his remarks. 'The bastard had a troupe of tame journos who did the real work. Ex-journo himself, the bastard. Told me, better a ponce than a prostitute. So I though …'

'Yes, you did.' Syl drifted to another group. Jerry took a refill from the hovering manservant. 'All right, mate?' he said to him. And the manservant said: 'Wouldn't be dead for quids, Can.'

Can was Jerry's nickname. The manservant was an old mate, Ern Crimmond. Jerry introduced Durman as another mate. Then Jerry and Ern got into a discussion about football which might've gone on for the rest of the day had not Syl, making it clear Ern wasn't an old mate of hers, waved her empty glass at him.

'What was I saying?' Jerry said.

'Canterbury,' Durman said. 'Odds on for the premiership.'

'Bullshit. Bullshit two ways. They haven't got it in the forwards. As if you would know what you're talking about. League was never your game. What got you into poofter soccer, I don't know.'

Durman did: ethics. Soccer was their game—Olympic, Marconi, Croatia. Penetration was his.

Jerry was saying: 'No, what I thought was, that's for me, resigned, picked up me entitlements and set up as a PR.'

'Just like that?'

'Well, I did have to get some journos of me own lined up.' He spluttered into his glass. 'Or lunched up. Anyway I went to a rival dealer who'd once tried to hire me and offered him a concept—honest Injun.'

Durman looked at his glass of lime and soda, longing for an anaesthetising whisky, a stunning rum or a thud of vodka as Jerry went on: 'You don't get it, do you? Injun. Engine. No worries. The dealer—Lachie Thomson out at Blacktown—did. Real keen. Dressed up in fringed buckskins, war bonnet, the lot. My journos thought the whole concept was so piss-weak hilarious they had to run it. Pic of Lachie all dressed up, of course, and driving his price-breaker of the month—a red Mustang.'

Indicating the other guests, Duman said: 'They don't look like car dealers to me.'

Jerry winked. 'They're not. I got shut of the car dealers. I'm into doctors.' He lowered his voice. 'And are they ever into making money.' His eyes shifted to a group across the pool. 'The Macquarie Street Squatters,' he said. 'See the skinny dude?'

Durman could not miss the skinny dude. Battered Akubra hat, washed-out denim shirt, white moleskins and elastic-sided boots which had seen more cowshit than polish. 'Runs Simmental studs. One north, one south. Millionaire north, south, east *and* west from his medical centres. Patient through-put's his motto. Is it ever?—CAT-scans, X-rays, cardiographs, blood pressure, the lot. I've had one of my journos do a mammography piece. Quoting my doc, of course. If you quote them, you've got to locate them. So another nice plug for the Merimbula Medical Centres.'

'Clever.'

'Oh, I just give it a nudge. Doctors already have it made. Take the appendix. Now there's a nice little earner. What's more I don't have to promote it. One of my docs reckons he bought his Bentley with appendixes. If in doubt, whip it out's his motto. No shortage of doubt either, I can tell you.'

'Very clever,' Durman said. 'You must've your work cut out handling them all.'

A breeze from the harbour ruffled the trees and Jerry's wig. He grinned at Durman as he patted it down. And Durman realised that the appeal in the grin was not for sympathy; it was for complicity. 'Only some of them are my actual clients.'

'You're hoping to get the rest?'

'Wrong way round, buddy. They're hoping to get me. As I see it—and I don't care how multi-talented you are—you can't steer more than ten clients. Not properly.' His grin widened as he went on: 'What I do is keep renewing the ten. No shortage of prospects, right? So when I get an approach, I tell the prospect he'll have to better the terms of the lowest payer on my list.' He snapped his fingers. 'I don't have to tell you what it does for my fee structure, do I?'

'Not with this place to show me, you don't.' Durman returned Jerry's grin.

Sydney, the grin, Sydney with its congenital corruption. There was a local slang name for it. What was it?

'Excuse I,' Jerry said, hurrying to Dr Squatter who was leaving. Which left Durman a shag on a rock, gazing at the pool where Syl was backstroking elegantly, seal-silky in a black one-piece, her curves cupped in the azure curves of the water. She broke her rhythm to wave Durman to her.

From long ago, the wave, but not so far away: 20, 25 k's. The Basin camping area, fronting Pittwater and with the Lagoon behind. Syl had waved him out of the water then to where she lay under a Norfolk Island pine as the topmost gums on the far ridge of Kuringai Chase brushed the darkness down across the lagoon to them, and the tent he'd labelled Weekender in jokey backing of the alibi given her mad Mick olds—that she was at a Rose Bay Convent friend's weekender on Pittwater, a name connoting residential substance whereas the Basin was fly-by-night. Oh, they had flown.

He was trying to leave by way of the games room where he'd left his haversack when he was intercepted by 'Dr Binney—Jason' who had a penguin on his polo shirt.

Miniature portrait—except it lacked a miniature moustache.

'Noticed you having a yabber with Jerry,' he said. 'Old mates, eh? Wondered if you could have a word to him about me.'

'Doctor—cattle breeder?'

'Deer. Easier to manage and there's a good market for venison here. Not as strong as overseas but growing. Then there's the antlers. Fetch $500 a kilo in Honkers as aphrodisiac material. You might say, I get people coming and going.'

'You reckon?'

'Well, my speciality *is* venereology.'

Durman smiled—though he had the impression Jason expected a laugh—and said: 'You wouldn't know about the appendix?'

Jason ran his finger and thumb up and down on his miniature moustache as if estimating the number of hairs in it. 'No one really knows about it—except the little bugger's like Everest. It's there and potentially a killer.'

'That bad?'

'Gangrene's no fun. Nor septicaemia. But when and why's a mystery. And the stats aren't exactly glorious. Twenty per cent of patients operated on for appendicitis are found to have a perfectly healthy appendix. Fact is, you can present with classic symptoms.' He began prodding Durman's abdomen on the right. 'Pain there. Yet the appendix can be okay.' Durman drew back from the prodding. 'Shivers,' Jason said. 'You're not trying for a freebie, I hope. Not running a temperature?' He stood on tiptoe to feel Durman's brow. 'No, you seem to be all right.'

Durman agreed.

'So why the inquisition about the appendix?'

'I don't know,' Durman said.

And he didn't.

Then.

Jason said: 'The quid—I think I've earned the quid pro quo—the word with Jerry. The thing is I've branched out—you know?'

Durman didn't but he nodded.

'Occasional vasectomy,' Jason said. 'My kind of patients—they don't get what they get curling up with a good book. Or even a bad lavatory seat. Dick artists, every single one. So ...' He grinned. 'If I got on Jerry's list and he lined up a celebrity or three for the snip-trip. Nothing like a celebrity story to spread the word.'

'I'll see what I can do,' Durman said. Bugger all, he thought. And: The Giggle, that's what those in the know call corruption here.

The picture windows of the games room looked out on the inner harbour to Cockatoo Island. Another change: no sign of shipyard activity but he recalled seeing a humped, black submarine alongside one of the island's quays.

Sub, he thought. Best option.

Jason read his thought. 'Gone cultural, Cockatoo Island. Art shows. Rock-'n'-roll.'

Jerry's bit of tucker was on a long table shaded by an awning: smoked salmon, leg of ham, croissants, cheese and a line of silver chafing dishes.

Durman said: 'I might get myself a bite to eat.'

'Try the smoked salmon,' Jason said. 'It's Tasmanian. Definitely moreish.'

Durman felt sick. Cockatoo Island without a shipyard. Cockatoo Island where his dad had worked. Electrician. As he was to have been. Until he went up to Fort Street High and was shown the mock-Gothic towers of Sydney University.

Durman tried the smoked salmon. Jason was right. He tried some more. He was hovering over the cheeses when Syl came to the table.

She cut a slice of cheese and offered it to him on the point of the knife. 'I thought you were joining me in the pool.'

He took the cheese. 'Got trapped.'

She feinted at him with the knife. 'I'm surprised, elusive rat like you.'

She was wearing a red towel, tucked sarong-style over her bathers. Her hair was slicked back. Her eyes in the shade had lost something of their slumberous quality. He took the knife from her and cut himself another piece of cheese. She said: 'Aren't you going to say anything?'

The cheese was tremendous but that was not what she wanted to hear. 'If I was pissed,' he said. 'I would make a pass. Since I'm stone cold sober, I'd better go.'

'Not yet,' she said. 'There's a special guest I want you to meet.'

Jerry appeared, the old Jerry—disappointed and anxious. Yet different, too—irritated with himself for being either. 'He's not coming.'

Syl said: 'You told me he was a definite.'

Jerry held up a portable telephone. 'He's just rung to tell me.'

The frown on Syl's face went from murder to manslaughter. 'He rang himself?' She caught Jerry's assent and went on: 'He must be planning to use you again. Otherwise, he wouldn't've rung you personally, he'd've left it to that creep of a so-called personal assistant.'

'Easy on the so-called,' Jerry said. 'I suggested personal assistant. It's not an image-plus to have a bodyguard.'

'Creep.'

Jerry turned to Durman. 'Tell her that's no way to talk about your ex-offsider, Van what's-his-name?'

Durman was surprised—and nonplussed. Anton as a bodyguard? But for whom?

Others had less difficulty. There was a lowering of the level of anticipation which Syl counteracted by ordering Ern to lash out more champers. 'The Veuve. We've been patriotic long enough.'

She got a cheer for that. And a louder one for back-flipping into the pool.

Jerry drew Durman towards the games-room bar. 'Merv,' he said. 'Merv Vesmar. I'd give my left nut to have him on my list as a permanent.'

'Another doctor?' Durman said.

'Company doctor.' Jerry was so pleased with his reply he repeated it, adding: 'I've seen a few operators in the big end of town. He's got to be the greatest.'

The grin was back. Mervyn Vesmar, as Jerry described him, emerged as the latest in the long line of supernovas whose larcenous ploys ran back through Sydney's history to its convict origins.

Jerry harped on one ploy as if hoping that because it had happened once, it would happen again. And to him, not Merv Vesmar.

'On the bones of his arse, near as,' Jerry said. 'Office lease running out. Bank manager, a three-ulcer basket case. But Merv's always had more front than the Taj Mahal by moonlight. Got himself involved in a round-robin deal, you know—flick-passing a cheque through a number of bank accounts to disguise its origin.'

Durman knew. 'Only $25 million.' Jerry's chuckle failed to create the impression such a sum was his idea of petty cash. 'Each member of the round robin had to keep it in his account for a couple of months—the tax boys were awake to short-timers. Bastards had programmed their computer on a thirty-day alert and check.'

'He kept the money,' Durman said, hoping to cut Jerry off.

'Not this money. Not Merv—though it's been done, and if I told you who by and what he's doing you would laugh your socks off.'

'They're already off.'

Jerry checked and went on: 'No, what Merv did was use the twenty-five to buy a controlling interest in Ausgravure Holdings—an iffy-whiffy if ever there was one, then use its real estate to raise a loan of thirty-five. He duly flick-passed a cheque for twenty-five to the next player which left Merv ...'

'Ten million in debt.'

'You're joking.' But Jerry was serious, as shocked by Durman's mistake about money as a God-fearer might be about a blasphemy. Durman himself was embarrassed at his mistake, result of his eagerness to cut Jerry off. Sensing this, Jerry piled on the shock. 'Shit, how do you survive?'

Cash, Durman thought. Half up front, the rest on completion. 'Merv was into the bank for thirty-five, ya mug,' Jerry said. 'Not for long but. Not for long. He soon turned Ausgravure round.'

'Great.'

Jerry ignored Durman's tone. 'Yeah, he's an operator, Merv. No question. Among Ausgravure's assets was a string of magazines, mainly hobby but some general—*Lens*, *Leatherwork*, *Tantalus*, *Wool and Thread*, *Walton's Weekly*, *Woodturner* and—*boom! boom!*—*Stud's Eye* as well as—can you believe it?—*Country Property*, *Angora* and *Green Fingers*...'

Durman waved to Syl who was getting out of the pool. She turned to allow one of the clients to drape a towel over her shoulders while caressing her bum with his paunch.

'Dirty little sod,' Jerry said. 'Think he'd get enough as a gynaecologist. Now where was I?'

'About to rescue your wife from a dirty little gynaecologist.'

'Funny,' Jerry said. 'I can give you the number of a guy who does TV warm-ups. Aw, yeah, the magazines. Merv arranged for them to be printed offshore—Hong Kong—and contracted out the editorial packaging on a split-advertising revenue deal. Couldn't lose. Hong Kong cut the printing costs. And editorial contractors get writers for the smell of an oil rag or your-cheque-is-in-the-mail, whichever is the cheaper. Merv's retained distribution—not something I would've done myself—but I suppose he saves on Abe.'

'Handy guy.'

'Not a guy, you dill. A system—ABE—All Binds Enveloper, shrink-wraps and palletises magazines—or any other publications in quires.'

'Sounds like quires of money.'

'Sounds like you're bored rigid.' Jerry feinted a punch at Durman's midriff. 'You shouldn't be. You've been away, things change, people… Maybe you should listen.'

'I have been listening.' Durman was to realise he had not been really listening—or he would've got the two-and-two of Ig and the op.

'Then keep listening,' Jerry said. 'Merv's big one's *AllDay.* When he took over Ausgravure, it was an afternoon rag so bad the raw prawns refused to be wrapped in it.'

'You're promoting it.' Durman was delighted with this key to Jerry's yabber. 'And the magazines.'

'Wouldn't say no, but Merv's got an in-house team for that. I have acted for him personally. He felt his image needed … well, not exactly a polish, more a solid-citizen aspect.'

'Like you?'

'Mug!' This time Jerry's punch was no feint but Durman took it. 'The speech circuit—I put him on the speech circuit, schools included. Basic yet effective. They loved him—especially the Micks. Went goggle-eyed, the lot of them, as he talked about his business interests, his racehorses and his powerboats. Really into powerboats, he is. And you know Micks. You could hear their thick Mick minds going tick-tick as they worked out that if this richie-poo was talking to them about such things, he must think they were capable of having them, too. No more the old AMDG and the Public Service, eh?'

Durman had been allowing Jerry's yabber to drive him back towards the wide, cedar-and-brass railed spiral stair that led from the games room to ground level. He had to step aside when a new guest arrived—straight off his yacht: weathered, face under an old peaked cap, striped jersey, sawn-off jeans and leaky boatshoes.

He did not return Jerry's welcoming grin but thrust a glossy, coloured brochure at him. Jerry tried a joke. 'Sorry, no junk mail.'

His joke worked no better than his grin. 'Look at it,' the guy said.

The brochure was for The Pearl Haven Retirement Village. The guy said: 'Heart-stopping views.'

'That's right,' Jerry said. 'Absolutely fan… Oh, shit, I see what you mean—it being your project and you, you being a heart specialist.'

Durman, on his way down the stairs, did not catch the reply.

Outside, a couple were coming up the yellow brick driveway. He was basketballer-tall in a plaid shirt of cowboy cut, jeans and pointy black boots. She was even taller with footballer padded shoulders. 'You've got your notebook?' she said. He said: 'Yes. And a sharp pencil. And a clean hankie.'

The journo who'd written the brochure? Durman wondered.

Downhill, he could catch a ferry to the city. Uphill was the old house. He went uphill. At the sight of a vacant cab, he changed his mind. The old house might be demolished—not only did it have aluminium-framed windows, it was also timber-framed and fibro-clad.

And anyway, Mum and Dad were in a smaller place. The smallest.

## 5

Anton set the meet for 1200 hours at the Dingoes' Den, the cool mockery he was affecting on the phone not quite masking his urgency.

Trying for a little counter-rubbishing, Durman said: 'Take it easy. I'm not Mervyn Vesmar.'

'Say again.'

'The guy you mind. You sound as if he'd just shat himself and you were rushing to clean up the mess.'

'Who told you about Merv?'

'Come on, you know Sydney—everyone's a town crier here.'

'Listen. Whoever did should also have told you it was a one-off.

Mervyn had a spot of bother and—end of story—I dealt with it.'

Karate chop? Durman wondered. Or 9 mm parabellum?

Anton went on: 'This is Australia, mate. If you don't have a second string to your bow, you're up shit creek without the proverbial.'

In a leaky mixed metaphor, Durman thought.

And on: 'So, okay, I do the occasional one-off minding job.'

'All right.' Durman was pleased to have got Anton going. 'All right.' Too pleased. 'You don't have to panic.'

'No panic. But the frog's no longer in the queue.'

'Released?'

'Self-released. He OD-ed.'

'I didn't see anything about it.' The morning newspapers were scattered around Durman's breakfast trolley near one of the windows of his suite.

'It's not in,' Anton said, 'Yet.'

And hung up. Durman stayed by the window. From there, the Opera House's sails looked like the hoods of conspirators.

His own line of work.

And he had his method. Its elements had come together like one of those wooden spheres made up of seemingly random pieces. But Durman'd been taught that the longer the lead-time to the implementation of a method, the more likely, and more lethal, the leak.

The trick was to disassemble the sphere and present the pieces separately to Anton and other collaborators so that they did not know until the last possible moment what the complete shape was.

Before leaving the hotel, Durman checked at reception about the package he was expecting. 'Sorry, sir. Nothing.'

The Swiss-movement flunky must, he thought, rival the cuckoo clock as an export.

Outside the hotel, he was in the big end of town, among banks and business houses. The streets were thronged with office workers, many of them execs in elegant suits munching from brown-paper feed bags. This made it difficult for him to check whether Anton had laid on a replacement for the beer-bellied heel-shit.

On Macquarie Street, there were fewer pedestrians. He continued his check, stopping occasionally and turning and, in a rush, crossing the street on changing traffic lights, all the while puzzled as to why the old Anton should've put a heel-shit on him and then deny it.

Heel-shit training exercise? Trying to find his bolthole? No, it couldn't be that. Anton would know it was too early to choose a bolthole. An operator, Anton, but taking his chances doing one-off minding jobs while on government service.

Durman was half-right, half-wrong: his fate.

Outside State Parliament, a demo was in progress. Teachers. Some of them language specialists. Basic Anglo-Saxon. But not *Beowulf*.

Gotcha.

Durman slowed. Across the street, a young, fit-looking guy in a motorised wheelchair slowed, too, and began scrutinising the entrance to a building. Durman moved on. So did the guy. Durman was halfway across the street when the guy steered his chair into an office block. A genuine patient, bound for the consulting rooms of a Dr Squatter who had a stud bull to keep in the rampant style to which the guy was no longer accustomed.

In front of the Royal Sydney Hospital, a group of Yank tourists were photographing each other rubbing the shiny snout of the hospital's totem—a bronze boar piddling into a basin.

Wrong place, Dad'd always said. Should've been put outside State Parliament—oldest trough in Australia.

In the defile of Martin Place, the city's make-do public square, women wove their bright way in pairs, trios and quartets. Not as piss-elegant as the women of Paris, as machine-turned as the women of New York, as gaudily sexy as the women of Rio.

Sexy enough though. Elegant without affectation. Challenging.

By the post office, workmen were starting to dismantle a giant tree, plastic branch by plastic branch.

Christmas. How'd he survived it? He knew the answer: by falling off the wagon. Well, not falling. More a sentimental slip, trying for a toast in Dad's favourite Aussie whisky. Unavailable. Shit, unspeakable. The room service waiter'd said, 'Corio?' as if *he'd* said 'Curare'. And then segued into a ballad of blended Scotches: Dimple Haig, Highland Nectar, Cutty Sark, J and B, Crawford's Three Star, Teachers, Vat 69, Ballantine's, Johnny Walker Black Label, Chivas Regal. And from the ballad to an epic of single malts: Scapa, Glenallachie, Knockando, Laphroig, Glenmorangie, Talisker, Glenfiddich, Bowmore, Lagavulin, The Macallan, The Balvenie and one that was new to Durman.

New, twelve years old and irresistible.

Named after the harbour from which he'd sailed on a whim and found the one safe place.

Oban.

He wouldn't've slipped off the wagon into bed as well—except for a lingering fragment of naiveté: he did not know whether prostitutes worked on Christmas Day.

The Cenotaph was before him. At either end, a bronze soldier and a sailor stood eternally easy, holding a .303 short magazine Lee Enfield with fixed bayonet. On either side of the Cenotaph was engraved:

TO OUR GLORIOUS DEAD and LEST WE FORGET.

Time: 11.55.

Shouldn't be 'forget'. Who could forget?

Should be suppress.

'First the long perv on the living sheilas, eh? Then the short time remembering the dead comrade-in-arms.'

Anton Van Dieman, exhibiting once more his heel-shit skills. And his talent for rubbishing.

'How the hell …?' Durman said.

'That is for you to work out.' Anton ranged himself alongside Durman. 'But you make it easier, perving on the sheilas, getting misty over the …'

'The meet. The meet.' Durman halted. 'You said here. In here.'

They were at the entrance to the Dingoes' Den, the Commonwealth block where the Federal Government kept suites of offices for its various departments, ministers and, on occasions, their mistresses, prepared to be laid between the in-tray and the out-tray, liquor and prophylactics courtesy the taxpayer.

Anton had said Suite 721, seventh floor—The Unit's former offices. Now he said: 'There's a sticky in.' He drew Durman away from the entrance. 'RCSC.'

Durman understood sticky—stickybeak—Unit slang for a member of the Australian Security Intelligence Organisation. He did not understand RCSC. 'Random Cross-Security Check,' Anton said. 'Key element of the latest reform package. Each arm of the secret service can undertake checks on any other arm. The sticky who's in is from the old days. Knows me. Might recognise you. Can't risk it. Not on a deniable.'

Lying bastard, Durman thought—saying The Unit had not been reactivated, then saying it was under an ASIO cross-security check.

The Australian Imperial Forces Club was unchanged behind its nameplateless cedar door near Wynyard Square. No one-armed bandits had secured a bridgehead here. No jukebox disturbed the memory of military marches. On the cedar-panelled walls were cased medals, regimental crests, silver trophies and a mix of portraits of senior officers and battlescapes ranging from the Maori Wars to Afghanistan.

Anton led Durman to the bar, dominated by a huge replica of the sunburst badge of the Australian Imperial Forces.

'Pity your membership lapsed,' Anton said. 'Otherwise you could have made history by buying a drink.'

'Shit, that's rich, coming from the guy who invented the Dutch round.'

Anton laughed. He was already high, Durman decided. High on adrenaline, his face, his eyes exhilarated. He tried to persuade Durman to have what he was having: gin and tonic. 'Dutch gin.' Durman settled for the tonic.

At the far end of the bar, a group was playing the club game of spin-the-bayonet to decide who should buy the next round.

Anton raised his glass to Durman and then in the general direction of the group, his gold links glinting in the double white cuffs of his striped shirt, peeping demurely from his blue blazer sleeve.

One of the group responded, a stocky, dark-suited bloke—definitely a bloke—with the face of a grizzled pug-dog and a knowing eye which rested on Durman briefly and—to Durman—conclusively.

The once-over.

The bloke had to be The Unit's new Boss Cockie, unable to meet him formally on a deniable but needing to have sight of him.

'Like old times,' Anton said.

'Cut the crap.'

But it was like old times. He had been here with Anton when both were in the University Regiment before they resigned from it noisily and were recruited quietly into The Unit to prepare for local counter-insurgency when the Vietnam domino toppled and the Red hordes thrust south. He smiled.

Anton said: 'What's the joke?'

Durman shrugged. He had been smiling at the memory of the Red hordes in Germany, toppling the Berlin Wall and thrusting west in search of life, liberty and the pursuit of a supermarket trolley.

The group from the bar moved into the dining room and the club's long, centre table, reputed to have been rescued from Darwin after the first Japanese bombing raid. Durman expected Anton to join the group and to find himself under further scrutiny. Instead, Anton ushered him to a reserved table near a window.

The menu was still typewritten on a plain card, headed Orders of the Day. Oysters were the traditional starters here. Both Anton and Durman ordered a dozen.

Main courses included steak and kidney pie, liver and bacon, Chicken Marengo, Beef Wellington, Barramundi Blamey, mixed grill and steaks.

Anton made the ancient joke about the Barramundi being named after the Australian field marshal 'because he drank like a fish' and ordered the Chicken Marengo. While Durman was deciding, Anton went into an aria on the wine list which ended with his ordering half-a-bottle of Huntington Estate semillon from Mudgee.

'One of the great secrets, mate. Austeo.'

Austeo—Australian Eyes Only—an in-joke that irritated Durman. He ordered the mixed grill with chips and tea and asked for tomato sauce.

'Rosella?' There was a glimmer of humour on the face of the waitress, who like the rest was a serviceman's widow.

The window next to the table overlooked a wharf where a container ship was being loaded.

'Is that a possibility?' Anton said. Durman shook his head. Anton went on: 'It worked for your Rio client. Camp-bed, tuckerbox and a chemical closet, I heard. Not to mention a …' He broke off as the waitress laid the oysters before them.

'Nice touch that—the woman.'

Durman was concentrating on his oysters. The taste of summers past. Knocking oysters off the rocks of the Hawkesbury River. Opening them with Dad's clasp knife and slurping them down. Alive, alive-o.

'Container ship,' Anton said. 'Seaborne withdrawal linked to the chopper extraction?'

Durman was silent while the waitress served their main courses. She had decanted the Rosella into a silver sauceboat and left the table with the air of someone whose victories, though petty, were significant. Durman picked the lamb cutlet from his mixed grill and dipped it in the Rosella. 'Seaborne, yeah. But not a container ship. Bluebags. A cigar,' he said, using Unit slang for the Navy and a submarine.

'A cigar?' Anton took a sip of his semillon. 'I'm not sure about a cigar.'

'With your contacts?'

'It's not … It's not a matter of contacts, it's a matter of cigars—there are only six.' He didn't seem to be enjoying his Chicken Marengo. 'In my view, a container ship will make for easier coordination with the chopper.'

'Forget the chopper.'

'It's laid on. The crew has been training.'

'Training's never wasted. But the way it's going to be now, the chopper's out.'

'We agreed on a chopper extraction.'

'I've got a better method.'

'Then lay it out for me.'

'Sure,' Durman said. 'As much as I can. Remember the rule—need to know.'

Anton remembered it. And spoke about it at length. Durman was more curt. When he had finished, Anton said: 'Appendicitis can't be that easy to fake.'

'I told you,' Durman said. 'In 20 percent of the cases, the operation's not really necessary.'

'The doc won't go for it.'

'You mean you don't go for it because you still want it to be wham-bam.' Durman poured himself a second cup of tea. 'Believe me, if I thought wham-bam would work, wham-bam it would be. But a gaol like that. Shambolic. No way you can plan for contingencies. It's all bloody contingencies.'

'The prison doctor.'

'Come on. He's yours. Tell him you'll move him to the top of the immigration list. Tell him he's covered by the margin for error.' Anton drained his glass. Durman poured him another. 'You said yourself, the executioners have a vested interest in keeping the condemned healthy. And after the frog OD-ing, the Thais won't want to see another farang cheating the machine-gun.'

Anton's sea-blue, sea-deceptive eyes fixed on Durman. 'Simple. Very simple. And very risky.'

'But based on your intelligence.'

'Indeed.' Anton was coming round. 'First, Ig has to get sick, you say.'

'Nauseous. He complains of being nauseous. And of a pain in his abdomen. Right side.' Durman dug his fingers into the appropriate spot.

'You right, dear?' the waitress said. 'I can get you a Quick-Eze.'

Durman laughed. 'I'd rather have the apple crumble.'

Anton wanted only coffee.

‘Okay,’ he said as the waitress departed. ‘The doctor relays the symptoms to Ig.’

‘Not him,’ Durman said. ‘He’s got to have room to believe the symptoms might just be genuine. Better use your other contact. And don’t forget, there’s only a Thai and a Chinese between Ig and the gun now.’

‘I’m not forgetting. The signal—I will see to it—goes today. The news of Ig’s illness will be leaked to the media at the right time. The more pressure on the Thais the better.’

‘The media’ll still be there?’

‘It’s death-watch time. Those bastards are rats.’

Who could be useful, Durman thought. And said: ‘I’m going to need a couple of Thai auxiliaries. Preferably ex-soldiers who know Bangkok and vehicles and can handle themselves. You see to their paperwork, tickets, passports.’

‘No problem.’

‘And a new passport for me.’

‘Is that necessary?’

‘Stop piss-farting around. You know it’s necessary. If the computer shows me on another visit so close to the first, someone could start checking.’

‘I’d better get myself another one as well.’

‘No need. You’re not going back in with me.’

‘I must.’

‘No way. I need you to make sure the final withdrawal is solid. I don’t want anyone getting toey because I’m a bit behind schedule.’ Anton was about to protest again when Durman added: ‘If the op goes wrong, you’re a direct link to the government and bang goes deniability.’

Anton’s eyes shifted from Durman’s. ‘You’ll use the new passport to exit Oz after the op, I suppose.’

‘You’re ahead of me.’ Durman took out his wallet, extracted a passport photo of himself and handed it to Anton. You bastard, he thought, not far enough ahead. Exiting on an Anton passport would give him the chance to program a computer trace that might lead to the one safe place.

Nothing the old Anton liked better than digging up secrets. Except maybe burying them. The earlier exhilaration was still on his face. Now Durman recognised it as something else. A line from Eng. Lit. 1 came into his mind: ‘… the lineaments of gratified desire.’

# 6

The police station had the appearance of a suburban, red-brick villa. It was shabby and run-down compared to the surrounding homes, all painted to within an inch of their mortgages in burnt umber, sludge green, pink, white, terracotta, and seeming to stand on tiptoe for a view of the precious sea.

Silvertail country, Durman recalled. But Sergeant Jack Sands was no silvertail. He was a big Mick who looked as if he was wearing some kind of new-fangled body armour beneath his blue uniform shirt so mighty was the carapace of his chest and belly. Above the left pocket of his shirt was a purple and green ribbon which Durman recognised as that of the General Service Medal. The shirt was knife creased, as were his blue uniform trousers. His eyes were equally sharp.

He led Durman past a charge room, decorated with WANTED and REWARD posters, a map showing the city's patrol areas and a busy-busy of cops, to an inner office. He cleared a chair of manila folders for Durman before seating himself behind a desk, a manoeuvre that caused much creaking of his black gunbelt.

Economical with words, Sergeant Sands. He used the same ones he'd used in telephoning Durman at his hotel. 'I have reason to believe you know and/or were known to Bart Costello.'

Durman had already pleaded total ignorance of Bart Costello. He had also said his lawyer was in London, which had caused Sergeant Sands to throw in a 'sir', like a bone to a dog of uncertain temper, while insisting quietly that he come to the station.

'There's a lawyer here who used to act for me,' Durman said. 'Maybe I should give *him* a call.'

'Suit yourself.' Sergeant Sands threw in another 'sir'. He opened a folder in front of him. 'But if I was you, I would save my dough and just tell me what you make of this.' He handed Durman an envelope.

One of the telephones on the desk rang. Sergeant Sands lifted it and began to take notes. 'Yeah, yeah … three of them, you say … red T-shirts … okay.' He yelled as he put the telephone down. 'Won't be a tick,' he said to Durman and yelled again.

Two constables came into the office, one male, one female, both fair and so young they might have been given their uniforms for Christmas.

'We've got three shoplifters heading this way,' Sergeant Sands said. 'Kids wearing red T-shirts.'

The constables turned for the door. The female paused and her hand touched the revolver on her hip.

Little hand. Big gun.

No toy. Glock automatic.

'What did the little bastards take?' she asked.

'Red T-shirts.' Sergeant Sands sighed. When the constables were gone, he said: 'What d'ya reckon? Some of the blokes call them Ken and Barbie after the flamin' dolls. Me, I say they're Hansel and Gretel in the Wicked Wood.'

He grinned, showing a set of teeth he would undoubtedly put in his pocket before arresting anyone with a punch. Durman thought he had him made: a veteran coming up to retirement, stretching to cover what he was supposed to cover but trying for a quick wrap, snapping his fingers and pointing at the envelope. 'So what do you make of it?'

Durman had made five things of it: it had been in water; it had been dried; it had been posted to Bartholemew Costello at an address in Surry Hills; it carried the return address of the Australian Credit Assessment and Recovery Company—a PO Box in North Sydney—and his own surname and the name of his hotel were scrawled on the back.

Durman handed the envelope back. 'I thought I told you. I don't know this Costello. As for my name, why don't you ask him?'

'That's something I always wish I could do in these cases.' Beneath Sergeant Sands' sun-dried Sydney cockney accent lingered an Irish cadence which increased as he went on: 'But I have to tell you that Bart… Bart Costello went off the Gap last night.'

The Gap, the city's favoured death-lover's leap.

'Poor bastard,' Durman said. 'Australian Credit Assessment—a debt collecting agency?'

'The deceased was a booze-artist *and* a freelance journalist—a terrific recipe for any amount of money troubles.'

Durman saw a way out. 'A journalist? He might've written my name down because he wanted to interview me.'

'You said you were here on business.' The butt of Sergeant Sands' gun seemed to be causing him discomfort. He shifted in his chair to ease the pressure. 'What sort of business?'

None of yours, you Mick bastard. Durman handed Sergeant Sands a card.

Snobbery is a conditioned reflex in cops. Sergeant Sands tested the card's engraving with his thumbnail. 'International Sports Promotions Limited.'

'We did start in general sports promotion. Now our focus is on acquiring rights to sports events. I'm here to look at prospects.'

Durman's training had conditioned him not to volunteer more cover than absolutely necessary. He waited for Sergeant Sands to ask what prospects and was ready to answer. But all Sergeant Sands said was: 'Could be. The deceased was always fossicking for traces of colour.'

Fossicking—searching. Colour—gold. 'But not getting much?' Durman said.

'He wasn't that desperate. He did well enough to keep himself half-pissed most of the time and totally shickered on special occasions.' Sergeant Sands put Durman's card in the folder. 'I'll keep this, if it's okay with you.'

'No problem.'

Nor would it be. If this Mick Sherlock rang International Sports Promotions in London he would be told that, yes, Mr Durman was employed by ISB and was in Australia on company business. The Boss? Mr David Parrick was out of town at a conference. Could he return the call? For ISB, Suzie Downie, the secretary receptionist would do what she was employed to do for all the one-man-bands-of-hope in Grantham House.

Outside, the sun beat down so hard that the ocean roar seemed to be rising from the earth itself. From somewhere at the rear of the station came the smell of barbecuing meat.

Durman had come in a taxi. Sergeant Sands offered him a lift back to the city in his prowl car. He turned into Old South Head Road and drove up the hill. 'Look,' he said, 'why don't I show you where the silly coot went off?'

He parked near a board which bore the deeply incised name: The Gap Park.

Prettiest suicide spot in the Southern Hemisphere, Durman thought, as Sergeant Sands led him along a path which twisted among rocks and shrubs to the booming ocean cliffs. A pine-log, post-and-rail fence ran parallel to the cliff edge. Sergeant Sands clambered over it where a beak of rock jutted out over the ocean.

Durman followed him over the fence and joined him at the point of the beak. The Pacific rollers broke below in sounding foam. 'He was pissed,' Sergeant Sands said. 'Way over .05. A rum drinker. Bundy. He was spotted a fair way out. So I reckon he didn't only jump, he did a running jump.'

'Pissed?'

'Well, maybe it was more of a stagger than a run.'

'How old?'

'Too old for chasing around. Nudging sixty.' And as if to prove he was still full of beans, even though he was of similar vintage, Sergeant Sands ran to the fence and vaulted over it.

Durman took a final look at the rollers breaking below. Sixty. And still fossicking for colour. No wonder the poor bastard went off.

Sergeant Sands drove on up past the South Head lighthouses, new and old, chatting.

'Funniest thing I ever saw in my life,' he said as they drove through the Rose Bay shopping area. 'A Rolls-Royce floating down this road. Yeah, floating. But sinking slowly. Happened in the floods a few years ago. The driver refused to leave. Must've wanted to go down with his Rolls. A bloke in one of the shops threw a rope to him and they managed to moor the Rolls to a verandah post.'

Durman was revising his opinion of Sergeant Sands. He might be a veteran close to superannuation and he might be tempted to go for a quick wrap. But he wasn't going to leave any loose ends that could turn into fuses.

'Do you mind?' Sergeant Sands said. 'There's something I've got to do first, then I'll drop you at your hotel.'

When Durman said he did not mind, Sergeant Sands seemed to decide he was on official business. He switched on the prowl car's siren. Its banshee wail cut the traffic ahead and where it did not Sergeant Sands' driving skill took them inside as well as outside vehicles. 'Fifteen years with the Highway Patrol,' he said at one point.

Durman did not doubt it.

It was not until they hit Broadway that he began to suspect what Sergeant Sands had to do first. When they screamed from Broadway into the start of Parramatta Road, he knew.

He knew because it was a journey he should have taken years ago, a journey to a long, low-set building of dark brick, lying like despair across the road from the mock Gothic of the University of Sydney.

'Depot 83,' Sergeant Sands said.

He drove round to a rear entrance. 'You want to come in?'

Durman did not. Yet he did, the past and the present compelling him to enter the City Morgue.

From somewhere in the building came the whine of an electric saw.

On bone? Durman waited while Sergeant Sands conferred with a white-coated attendant.

Years before Durman had given up nicotine as one drug too many. Now he felt the need of a cigarette to kill the taste of what he could smell: formaldehyde and flesh.

'Since you're here,' Sergeant Sands said, 'you may as well have a squiz at him.'

The body of Bartholemew Costello lay under a green sheet on a trolley in a closed room. A sealed observation window gave on to the room.

His face was clay-pale, bruised and with a tinge of green to it. From the rocks and the sea?

Alone.

So alone.

Durman heard himself saying: 'If he hasn't got anyone, I'll see to the funeral.'

'He's got a union,' Sergeant Sands said. 'The secretary's already been here. And there's next of kin to be notified.'

Durman continued to stare through the window at the body of Bartholemew Costello. Not the first he'd seen. Nor the twenty-first. But it reminded him of the third.

How could it be—a booze-artist like this, reminding him of his comrade-in-arms as Anton called her? How could this booze-artist be like Helen?

Little hand. Big gun.

The same, still dignity of the face, holding a lingering trace of shock.

But Helen had not expected death whereas this booze-artist had gone to meet it.

'You don't know him,' Sergeant Sands said.

'No, I don't know him,' Durman said, turning away.

The exact truth. Not the whole truth, for he recognised him. Bartholemew Costello was the beer-bellied guy who'd followed him after he left the *Norn*. The beer-bellied guy he'd taken for one of Anton's heel-shits. The beer-bellied guy he'd kidney-punched. The guy who'd tried to speak to him. Was the bruise still there? And what had Bartholemew Costello wanted to say to him?

Maybe he was saying it now, his dead silence more eloquent than his punch-cut words.

'How good was he?' Durman said. 'I mean at his job.'

Sergeant Sands held the door open. 'I told you—a …' He broke off as if Costello's dead silence had spoken to him. 'Stupid bastard was down on his luck—desperate enough to try for a job writing the words that keep the twats apart in *Stud's Eye*. He broke off again. 'Ah, Jesus,' he said. And his tone caused Durman to glance at him but his face was rigidly under control.

'I had to see the editor—Eric Ramsay. His name was on another of the deceased's envelopes. That's all he had—old envelopes and scraps of paper. Ramsay told me the deceased had been after him for a job on his magazine. Magazine! Dunny door. A real plummy pom, Mr Ramsay. Years ago, I could've put the bastard in. Now… Shit, I don't know.'

Nor did Durman. He did not know whether Costello had been after the covered-up story of The Unit's *coup d'etat* exercise that had gone wrong—oh, bloody wrong—or the op that was on.

Sixty. Old enough to have been around for the exercise. Sixty. Too old to be chasing the story of the current op.

Half-wrong, half-right: his fate.

Bart Costello had been after both stories.

And more.

## 7

The Regal Tower Hotel clearly impressed Sergeant Sands, but he was nonplussed by the ragged and brightly patched beggars who clustered around its entrance, so nonplussed that he refused Durman's offer of a drink and wailed off in the direction of his station.

Durman's own puzzlement turned to amusement when one of the beggars in jodhpurs, riding boots and a paisley silk dressing gown held out a slouch hat and said: 'Spare a million for an old colonial?' He had a wrinkled bald head and a fringe of beard which gave him the look of one of those kids' puzzles that made a funny face either way up.

He grinned, exposing blackened teeth. 'Or if you haven't got a million, fifty will do—cheques acceptable, made out to SAD—Sydney Against Drugs.'

Durman gave him 50.

'Dollars, I meant, pal,' the beggar said. 'Not cents.'

He didn't mean pal.

Inside the hotel, there were more jolly beggars. These ones were mingling with guests in black tie and blinding ballgowns. All were strongly scented with a variety of alcohols taken externally and internally.

Durman checked at reception for his package. It had not arrived, a Swiss-movement flunky said. There *was* a message: 'He said to say a gentleman was waiting for you in the bar.' Simultaneously, the flunky contrived to make it clear that the he who had left the message was *not* a gentleman, and that Durman was a cretin. 'That's the Rum Corps Bar, sir. Through the archway and to your left. You can't miss it.'

There were enough archways for a Gothic farce. Durman chose one. Had they decided to hand-deliver the package? Keep the finger on him? His anger rose. He had specified an official envelope and registered airmail.

He found himself in an empty reception room, about-turned and tried another archway, conscious of the flunky enjoying this. But the flunky was right—you couldn't miss the Rum Corps Bar. It was done out in scarlet and brass with a row of bass drums for its counter and individual drums for tables.

Durman spotted Jerry Telfer before Jerry spotted him, and was about-turning again to leave when Jerry hailed him.

Jerry was impeccable in black tie, set off by a top hat that looked as if it had been kicked into unconsciousness and barely revived. He wanted Durman to join his table. Durman said he wasn't dressed for the occasion. Jerry guffawed. 'When did you last look in the mirror?'

'This morning.'

It wasn't the answer Jerry had wanted so he supplied it himself. 'Talk about the great white hunter.'

Durman was wearing his bushjacket. Jerry took his arm and led him through the multitude, most of whom he seemed to know, for he greeted them loudly and cheerily by their first names while muttering to Durman, 'Rentas. Bloody Rentas.'

'Sounds like one big happy family.'

'Rent-a-crowders. They're everywhere. Remember when this town had real society?'

Durman could not. Nor did he see how Jerry could. True, Jerry's Dad had been known as 'Champagne Charlie,' but that was because of the number of empties he collected on his bottle-o round in Bellevue Hill.

When he was introduced to Jerry's table, however, Durman was given an idea of Jerry's social aspirations. And Syl's. She was dressed as a beggarmaid, her ragged silk gown patched with sequins where it wasn't patched with gold lame. As she moved to kiss Durman's cheek, the silk of the gown rustled like autumn and she gave off the scent of summer, confusing him so that he couldn't quite believe the name of the second woman, the Princess Celia Von Kronberg. He caught only the third woman's first name, Caro. He was still concentrating on the second woman's bushranger outfit—all white leather from slouch hat to stockwhip coiled on her shoulder to gunbelt to boots in startling contrast to her oiled mahogany tan. When he gave his attention to Caro, he could scarcely keep his eyes from frying on her breasts, caught in swags of flame-coloured velvet.

A rare trio of women. But Jerry's pride came through most strongly when he introduced a tall, sinewy guy in a sinewy black shirt, sinewy black strides and sinewy black boots. He had worked on his handshake. And his voice. It was basso-bosso: Mervyn Vesmar.

He didn't look as if he needed a minder, even one like Anton. Under dark, silver-winged hair, his eyes were hard—a raptor's calculating the degree of resistance in a prey.

Jerry said: 'You missed each other at our Sunday brunch so I thought…'

'I was there. And I'm here.'

This voice was high with pretensions to mightiness, and smoothly plummy compared to the raw falsity of Jerry's, 'Sorry, buddy.'

He went into a send-up introduction: 'Eric Ramsay, editor-in-chief of *Stud's Eye*, our most phallic but not fallacious organ.'

During this, Ramsay stood fingering his bowtie. 'Not bad,' he said. 'Not bad at all—as long as you don't mind that since you're a PR, I think of you as an authority on the fallacious rather than the phallic.'

Score one for the poncey Pom, Durman thought, as Caro giggled and Jerry yelled, 'Waiter!'

Unnecessarily.

A waiter was already dancing attendance on them.

Literally.

A young guy with plastic vine leaves in his hair was cavorting around dispensing wine from a goatskin. Durman got a whiff of it as the waiter squirted a glass full for him.

Retsina.

'Shit,' he said to Jerry, 'whose idea was *he*?

'Mine,' Jerry said. 'A Greek tourist tie-in.'

His tone was that of a kid watching his sandcastle threatened by the tide. Durman said no more. Ramsay, having taken a sip of the retsina, proceeded to piss on the sandcastle. 'I'm sure it was retsina the Athenians gave to Socrates. The poor chap died of terminal hangover, not hemlock.'

Jerry affected to ignore the remark and the laughter it caused. Other people were dancing attendance—though not quite as literally as the waiter, and not on all of them, only on Mervyn Vesmar. Jerry kept greeting these people in a way that kept most of them dancing. From time to time, a favoured individual or couple would be allowed to linger and talk to Vesmar.

During one such audience, Jerry muttered to Durman: 'Your lucky night. Miss Stud's Eye of the Year.'

'The decade.'

'The century.'

The breasts were saying breathlessly: '… bought it for 400,000 just nine years ago, and it's now worth nine mill.' Durman found himself nodding as she went on. 'One of those rare convict sandstone places. Accommodates 300 for dinner. Seated.'

There was longing in her voice. They were standing in an anteroom as the dance of attendance on Mervyn Vesmar continued. A sideshow to Durman, Miss Stud's Eye was his main event. Time for the basic chat-up.

'You're not from Sydney?' he said.

'Not originally, no.'

'Anyway congratulations.'

'On not being from Sydney?'

'On winning.'

'Not you, I hope.'

'Miss Stud's Eye of the Year.'

Durman might have found it funnier had he not been so embarrassed. She tugged at the swags of flame-coloured velvet and her breasts disappeared.

'That's rich,' Eric Ramsay said. Possibly too rich. On his face disgust mingled with surprise. 'How on earth did you get the impression my wife …'

Durman knew. He couldn't say. He couldn't say he was confused by Syl, by the dance around Mervyn Vesmar, and by the words that came from the hubbub like desperate messages heard through static. '… skiing's a thought' … 'big nose, flinty palate' … 'yacht'…

Jerry thought he knew and was delighted at the chance to score when two points down. 'Come on, you're always saying you married the most beautiful woman in the world. Why wouldn't you want to let your readers have a sight of Caro since you show them the twat, the whole twat and nothing but the twat of other women?'

'The fee would break my budget.' Ramsay put his arm round Caro's shoulders and kissed her. 'Wouldn't it, darling?'

The spin on this recovery shot beat Jerry. It did not beat the green-head who joined them. 'My fee certainly didn't break your budget,' she said. 'So where the hell's my cheque. And if you tell me it's in the mail, I'll bite your balls off.'

'Big mouthful.'

The green-head's eyes widened. They matched her hair as her lipstick matched her language. 'Can't say, I remember taking frigging measurements but my impression was two dried peas and a matchstick. Yeah, a burnt-out matchstick.'

Simultaneously, Caro said: 'Eric!' and Jerry said: 'Bit early for this kind of show, Patsee.'

'I suppose. But I felt so down I gave myself a toot in the toot.' She sniffed. Not sadly. 'Where's this mate of yours, the dude from overseas?'

Durman found he was the dude from overseas and she, according to Jerry's introduction was, 'Miss Stud's Eye of the Year, Patsee Urquhart, Master of Arts of the University of Western Australia with a major in Speech and Drama but not spelling—she spells her name with two Es.'

The configuration of the group kept changing, Mervyn Vesmar providing its constant focus. Two towering monoliths had left him, their places having been taken by Syl and the Princess Celia Von Kronberg, with Ramsay and his wife awaiting their opportunity to attain the presence.

The plastic-vined wine-bearer stopped cavorting to offer Patsee retsina. A more conventionally attired waiter offered her Bollinger. She decided to have both. In the same glass. Durman's glass was still full. As Patsee announced that she'd invented 'Bollocks Fizz,' Durman drifted towards the Ramsays. Behind them was a door. He did not know where it led. But anywhere would have to be better than here.

The Ramsays, focused on the irresistible object Mervyn Vesmar, were not disposed to move. Durman was trapped. Syl must have said something in praise of Sydney, for the Princess Celia Von Kronberg was saying to her: 'Of course, Sydney's colourful. Of course, it's getting bigger and more sophisticated but so does a pimple when it turns into a carbuncle.'

Mervyn Vesmar liked that. He said so and Ramsay said: 'Sydney, the sophisticated carbuncle.' He sniggered. 'On the backside of the world.'

Courtiers, trying to catch the eye of their king. Syl was trying. She said to Ramsay: 'Well, I suppose backsides are something Poms are authorities on.'

Vesmar liked that, too. His hand, brown and hairy-backed, appeared on Syl's shoulder like a spider, causing her no distress. Nor did Jerry seem disturbed as he manoeuvred a new couple between Vesmar and Celia, remarking—jokingly, Durman thought—'Excuse I, Your Royal Highness.'

The couple appeared to be well-known to everyone except Durman and Jerry didn't introduce him to them, although the woman did glance in his direction. Durman wondered where he had seen a similarly tentative smile before.

'Look at the poor dear,' Caro said.

'Yeah,' Ramsay said. 'She'd be much happier under her Hill's hoist.'

'With the sheets flapping and the nappies bleaching.'

'But she married a trade unionist whom the bowel-movement of the Labor right deposited in a safe parliamentary seat.'

'With a parliamentary allowance to cover the cost of natty gent's suiting.'

The guy *was* natty in a dinner-jacket that hadn't been cut with an acetylene torch. His dark hair was quiffed up at the front and he seemed to be standing on tiptoe to further enhance his height. His wife had hold of his arm as if seeking to take the strain off him.

The Ramsays were back on the subject of Sydney. 'You must admit, it is an open city,' Caro said.

'Absolutely,' Ramsay said, 'if you mean every acquaintance is a friend until proven inadequate to deliver, at which point he becomes a recyclable mate.'

'How do you describe two guys linked by a dead man?'

Durman's question surprised Ramsay as much because he had been focused on Vesmar as because of its import. 'I'm not into riddles,' he said. 'At least not before the passing of the port.'

'Bart Costello. He wrote your name on the back of an envelope.'

Durman passed his business card. 'And mine.'

Ramsay had been still half-focused on Vesmar, waiting for the moment when the natty Labor politician and his wife should leave his side. Now he gave Durman's card his complete attention as he told him what Durman already knew: Bart Costello had been seeking work on *Stud's Eye*. With equal smoothness, he elicited from Durman the reason Costello had made a note of *his* name.

'You're fortunate, he didn't get to you.' Ramsay passed his wine glass to his wife while he read the card. 'I don't know how I survived his breath.'

'Boozy, eh?'

'And Hawke.' Ramsay chuckled although Durman couldn't see why. 'I spent some years in Fleet Street,' Ramsay went on. 'I've seen some soaks. Costello was positively the Empty Quarter—the Great Thirst.' He examined the card again. 'Perhaps I could have one of my people have a chat to you.'

'I'm flat out for the next few weeks.'

'Oh, it shouldn't take long. I'm not thinking of a major feature you understand.'

'No, I don't think so.'

'It might help you to make local contacts. You'd be surprised who reads *Stud's Eye*—or perhaps you wouldn't since you've met Mervyn and me.'

'Don't push, Eric. I'm sure Mr Durman has more important things to do than be interviewed by one of your hacks.'

Mervyn Vesmar's basso-bosso silenced Ramsay.

Trumpets blared. A wall of the anteroom folded in on itself to reveal the splendours of a banqueting room, dotted with round tables covered in red and white gingham from which grew gumtree branches with hurricane lamps hanging from them.

A booming, disembodied voice announced: 'Your Royal Highness, my lords, ladies and gentlemen, in keeping with the free and easy spirit of the occasion, there are no formal table settings, so take your places as you will.'

At the far end of the banqueting room on a raised platform was a Jaguar XJS, sleek and glittering in a spotlight which also lit the Ali Baba's cave of consumer goods behind it—television sets, video-cassette recorders, cases of wine, huge bottles of scent, food hampers and refrigerators.

Over this display was a silver-on-black banner:

SYDNEY AGAINST DRUGS.

Pandemonium—no less so for being ruthlessly polite—as guests manoeuvred for position. Durman stood back, noticing that the Labor politician's wife had found another woman to talk to, and was moving with her towards the tables.

The Labor politician, while continuing to chat to Mervyn Vesmar, reached out and grasped a handful of his wife's dress, and possibly her bum. This halted her as her companion was swept ahead by the flash flood of other guests.

Durman's eye caught the eye of the Princess Celia Von Kronsberg. 'Egalitarianism,' she said. 'It's simply too wonderful for words.'

Mervyn Vesmar, his spider hand still on Syl's shoulder, led an entourage consisting of the Labor politician and his wife, the Ramsays and any number of jostling hopefuls towards a table on which Jerry and the green-head Patsee had already established squatter's rights and from which with cheery squatter's abusiveness they were diverting claimants.

The prospect of troughing added a shrill quality to the hubbub. In the midst of it, the dead silence of Bart Costello spoke to Durman again. Durman was a loner who sought in group action a substitute for the only ties that freely bind: the familial. He was suddenly aware that in Bart Costello—*I've got to talk to you*—he had lost a possible friend—even a brother.

He was still holding the glass of retsina. The Princess Celia Von Kronberg had been engaged in conversation by a tall guy rigged out as a Scottish Highlander in white lace jabot, plum velvet doublet and the kilt. Durman had learned the tartans, and wondered whether the guy knew he was wearing that of the robber McGregors. Persuasive bastard anyway. She was taking his arm. As she did so, she looked over her shoulder, smiling. Rescue me. Durman raised his glass of retsina to her. And downed it for Bart Costello.

Mate, he had said. I've got to talk to you, mate.

And Mervyn Vesmar—the way he'd said, *sure*. And *more important things*. Had the old Anton, his bodyguard, been talking to him?

# 8

In his room, Durman changed into his jogging gear. As he ran through the darkened streets near the hotel, a newspaper poster caught his eye. It said:

> BIG IG
> DEATH CELL
> HEALTH CRISIS

Durman increased his pace. Bloody brilliant.

The car was parked as agreed in Olympic Drive outside 8 Wyatt Park and the Auburn Swimming Centre, when Durman came out, stuffing his towel and still-wet bathers into his haversack. He'd opted to jog 25 k's by a roundabout route to Lidcombe and do 50 lengths of the pool, despite Anton's offer to pick him up at the hotel. Further training, he'd told Anton. It wasn't simply training though. It was not wanting to be driven past the City Morgue where she had lain. It was not wanting to take the risk of Anton rubbishing him about her, his comrade-in-arms, Helen.

The car was a Lancia, white and highly polished. Anton himself was similarly well turned out in a cream, raw-silk jacket, dark blue shirt, matching trousers and black moccasins.

Raw-silk shoulder holster? Durman wondered. Or black leather like the moccasins—with tassels? He took a walk round the Lancia, kicking the tyres which were freshly blackened. 'Not exactly government issue,' he said.

Anton pointed a remote control at the car to unlock its doors. 'We leave government issue to the dodos who think they're running things.' One of The Unit's jokes, meaning the politicians and the mandarins of the bureaucracy. Durman noted the licence plates were standard issue and not marked with the red C denoting a Commonwealth vehicle. He mentioned this to Anton.

'New operations protocol,' Anton said. 'Like the Lancia. Too many sticky beaks have been blowing the whistle on fat cats using C-cars privately.' He eased the Lancia into the traffic flow. 'They caught one supreme nong using his as a courtesy car for the brothel his lady was running.'

'Lady?'

'As in wife. De facto variety. Absolute knockout. Celia …'

'Von Kronberg. The Princess Celia. Is that for real?'

'Real enough for Sydney.'

'She sounds so Aussie. Posh with dosh but Aussie.'

'Don't say that. You'll have her mum doing as many turns in her grave as she did in bed. Her family were in line to be part of the bunyip aristocracy and you know what happened there.'

Durman did. The notion of a local hereditary peerage had been laughed out of the country. 'So how did she get the Von handle?'

'Von a German fizz-salesman.' Anton liked a rare joke. 'She kept the title when he divorced her after discovering she'd turned pro.'

'Forget the bordello reminiscences,' Durman said. 'What I'm trying to establish is whether this op's still on.'

'On? It's countdown time. The other Thai has had his nirvana ticket. The Chinese is next. He's for the high jump in a week.'

'Nice to have inside gen.'

'Only if it's put together right. I established a pattern from the Thai executions. There's a three-week interval and our Thai mates love their rituals. They strip and clean the machine-gun exactly a week before an execution is scheduled. I reckon four weeks to go for Ig.'

'All he's got to do is be sick.'

'He's coming along nicely there.'

'I'm not feeling so hot myself,' Durman said. 'Touch of leak fever. You know I can scrub if there's a leak. And without penalty.'

Anton braked although he could have beaten the traffic lights ahead. 'Leak? The only leak's in your mind, mate—a touch of operational paranoia.'

'Could be. So why not try to clear it up by telling me what it was like working as minder for Mervyn Vesmar.'

'I've told you.' Anton accelerated on the green light. 'It was a one-off. I'm a mercenary. Like you, mate, like you. He was a … a paymaster.'

'Not to mention a media proprietor.'

Anton laughed and flipped his sun visor down. 'You think media proprietors are into broadcasting everything they know. The whole point and power of being a media proprietor is in *not* broadcasting what you know, in concealing not revealing.'

'So he does know.'

'I didn't say that.' Anton flipped his sun visor back up. 'I was making a general observation. You've given it a particular slant. Paranoia, mate. Paranoia.'

*Could be,* Durman'd said. *Could be,* he meant. Paranoia, he knew, was the inevitable result of his kind of work: impossible to live a deception, without coming to believe people are out to expose you. 'Mervyn Vesmar,' he said, 'You've got to admit he doesn't look like the kind of guy who needs a bodyguard.'

'He doesn't. Not normally. But when he took over Ausgravure Holdings not everyone was totally happy.'

'Something illegal?'

'Buggery's not illegal between consenting adults and that's what a take-over can be. It doesn't necessarily leave everyone totally happy. Some nuts were very unhappy. Some hard nuts.'

'You settled them?'

'They weren't *that* hard. They were money hard. When they got theirs—end of job. I picked up my money which I can tell you was less than theirs. And that was the last I saw of Mervyn Vesmar.'

'The last?'

'Come on. You know how it is—after a really shitty job, the paymaster doesn't want to be seen with the guy he hired to clean the latrine.'

'Maybe.'

'Dead set. Have a squiz at the paper on the back seat.'

It was a copy of *AllDay*, its front page headlined THE ALLDAY VIEW. Beneath the headline was a boxed editorial:

> Disgraced ironman champion Ian Graeme is a convicted drug trafficker.
>
> That is, a dealer in death.
>
> No more.
>
> No less.
>
> It is within this context that the hysterical campaign in some quarters to ensure that Graeme gets treatment for what appears to be appendicitis must be seen.
>
> In this context, the campaign is sentimental.
>
> It is also impertinent.
>
> And outrageous.
>
> If the Thai authorities should advance the date of Graeme's execution, who would blame them?
>
> Certainly not *AllDay*.
>
> But *AllDay* believes in the democratic right of its readers

> to have their say on whether or not Graeme should receive treatment…

Two telephone numbers followed to enable readers to register a vote for or against treatment.

Durman said: 'What's Vesmar trying to do?'

Anton shrugged. 'He's not trying to do anything. He doesn't have to. He's a self-made shit who loves only his maker as you would know if you'd ever worked for him.'

Durman stared at the picture of Ig alongside the editorial. In contrast to the earlier cheesy-grin picture, this one showed Ig unshaven, shifty, his eyes dark-ringed. He tossed the paper on to the back seat. 'There's something else.' Anton was silent as Durman told him about the phone call from Sergeant Sands and about Bart Costello.

At the mention of Costello's name, Anton laughed. An exhilarated laugh. A laugh with the relish of the ridiculous in it. 'He's a joke.'

'Was.'

'Is—the joke goes marching on.'

'So how do you know him?'

'Everyone knows him. When Vesmar took over Ausgravure, Costello was one of the journalists agin' him. That's how I got to know him—or of him. Spent most of his time talking about stories he'd done—except he hadn't quite. Like a fisherman. The bigger the stories were the closer he was to getting them. But not quite. Never quite. All chat—plus an empty notebook.'

Durman had been thinking how much Anton's jeering tone matched Eric Ramsay's. 'Empty notebook?' he said. 'Old envelopes. I only mentioned old envelopes.'

Anton gave the horn and the finger to a grey trundler in a Mini-Minor. 'Empty as in empty head, mate. Meta-bloody-phori-cally empty.' He swung out to pass a cabin cruiser towed by a 4WD. 'As for Sergeant Plodd, you can't be worried about him.'

Durman did not reply. They were running between the car-yards of Parramatta Road, mile after mile of multi-coloured cars with multi-coloured plastic pennants chattering multi-lie prices.

'Old vehicles never die,' Anton said. 'They only come here to be flogged to the next dill with a credit rating.'

'The cop,' Durman said. 'He's *very* worrying.'

'He wants to wrap. You said yourself you thought he was super happy.'

'At first I did. Now …'

'Listen,' Anton said. 'If you get a whisper of a leak—or even a silent fart, we scrub. Fair enough?'

The gateway to Cabramatta's Freedom Plaza was flanked by brass Chinese lions. The gateway itself was decorated with gilded fretwork in which koalas and kangaroos frolicked, and was roofed with green tiles and clad in white marble against which blazed vermillion panels, inscribed in gold with Chinese ideograms and their English translations: Liberty. Democracy. The World is for Us to Share and Respect.

Anton had left the Lancia in a car park behind a Woolworth's supermarket and was now following standard operating procedure for approaching a rendezvous—a seemingly casual stroll which gave him and Durman the chance to check whether they were being heel-shitted.

A Chinese mother was lifting her son onto a granite ox while his sister danced round the ox clamouring for a similar ride.

Durman took a silent bet with himself that Anton would point out that the ox was a symbol from the Chinese calendar—and won his bet.

Spherical, fringed lanterns and slim vertical banners added to the plaza's oriental aspect. The shops in the streets around the plaza had signs in Chinese, Arabic and Vietnamese as well as English. So, too, had the shops in the lanes leading off the street. And all the spices of the East were in the air about them. At the end of the lanes were apartment buildings. After the drive through the western suburbs with their vast herds of bungalows grazing on quarter-acre blocks, the apartment buildings created the impression of a walled, inner city.

Asian faces—Vietnamese, Thai, Chinese, Korean, Indian—abounded. It was the Euro-Australians—Irish, Italian, Slav—who looked out of place, forlorn, as if they had taken a wrong turning. It was an expression Durman had seen before. He could not place it until he and Anton were walking through a nondescript triangle of shrubs and paving named Cook Square Plaza. Then it came to him: Aborigines—the Euro-Australians had the look of Aborigines caught on the fringe of history.

The Cabramatta Inn advertised its discount liquor in English and Vietnamese. A restaurant carried the sign: Lao Thai Chinese. And the Bing Lee Centre had the slogan: BIGGEST BARGAINS THIS SIDE OF HONG KONG.

Durman remarked on all this. Anton said: 'They don't call the place Vietnamatta for nothing. The plus is you can recruit a covert-ops team for any country in Asia right here.'

# 9

Fire Base Bravo was a converted cinema, its facade sheathed in plastic panels designed to simulate sandbags. A Maori bouncer in a black T-shirt, black jeans and black cowboy boots lounged in its entrance, seeming almost to fill it, his dark stare subduing the raucousness of the young guys making their way round him into the building.

At Anton's approach, the bouncer started to come to attention, then had second thoughts. Durman did not need Anton to tell him they had reached their rendezvous.

Inside Fire Base Bravo, strobe lights flickered in the dimness and a pandemonium of battles—land, sea, air and inter-galactic—reverberated from the ranks of video machines operated by hordes of youngsters.

Anton led the way among the video machines to the rear of the building, and under a portcullis in a crenellated partition, to an area set aside for pool, each table brilliantly green under its individual bank of lights. Along the walls here ran a row of tip-up seats, probably salvaged from the cinema. Anton took one of these seats, positioning himself against the back wall, facing a table where two small men were playing pool, their faces intent, golden, under the table's lights, their dark hair gleaming, slicked back into ducktails. Elvis, Durman thought. And: Not even Charlie Chaplin had as many imitators throughout the world.

'Mongrel slopes,' Anton said. 'Stinking up the place.'

The two small men did not turn, although the one who was cueing the ball hesitated and looked sideways at his partner. 'Yeah, you,' Anton said. 'I'm talking to you. Or don't you speak English, you slant-eyed gook?'

Still sitting, Anton put the toe of his tasselled loafer against the backside of the small man who was cueing the ball. The small man whirled at this ultimate insult, swinging his cue butt-end at Anton.

That was all Durman saw, for the second small man had climbed on to the table and was coming off it in a flying leap, his foot out-thrust to kick Durman in the chest. He sidestepped and turned on his left foot, aiming to kick the small man with his right as he landed on the floor, but the small man was too quick and rolled clear before standing up, fists raised in the classic stance of muay Thai—kick boxing.

Durman circled away. Not kicks but knee and elbow strikes were the most dangerous in muay Thai.

Anton's chuckle had the quality of a wooden ratchet. The Thai he had insulted joined in with a high pitched giggle, then the Thai who had been moving in on Durman.

'Mate!' Anton came round the pool table. 'You asked for guys who could handle themselves. But you couldn't handle them.' Now he adopted the muay Thai stance and advanced on Durman who fended off the first kick, knowing Anton was seeking to show the Thais who was boss. He advanced again and caught Durman in the ribs with an elbow strike. 'No counter.'

Durman grabbed the lapels of Anton's jacket and pulled him forward. 'No counter?' he said. And head-butted him. Anton's nose gouted blood. The giggles of the Thais ceased. On their faces was a mixture of revulsion and fear. Durman had broken a sacred tenet of muay Thai and attacked his opponent's head.

He flicked a dollar coin to the Thai who had come at him and indicated a nearby Coca-Cola dispenser. The Thai brought him an ice-cold can of Coke. Durman slipped it down behind Anton's neck to stop his nose bleeding.

The treatment worked. Fifteen minutes later, Durman was wishing he had another Coke can to ram down Anton's throat to stop him talking. By then, Anton had introduced the Thais as Mongkut and Rama. At this introduction, they had smiled, but uncertainly, as if merely pretending to be amused at the outrageousness of aliases which were the names of their country's most revered warrior king. Still talking, Anton had led them beneath Fire Base Bravo to a room furnished with a formica-topped table, five chairs and a noticeboard, featuring a poster headed FIREARMS SAFETY. Alongside the noticeboard was a fridge. Next to it was a stainless-steel sink and above the sink was an instant hot-water boiler. A large tin of Nescafe and a carton of Bushell's teabags stood on the side of the sink with an assortment of cups, plates, forks and spoons.

From inside his jacket, Anton took a map which he unfolded on the table. Inside the map was a single sheet of paper which Anton set aside precisely before pinning the map to the noticeboard.

Loves a briefing session, thought Durman. Odds, he's got a telescopic pointer concealed about his person. Durman was wrong. Anton picked up a knife and used it as a pointer to follow the course of the Chao Phraya north from Bangkok to Nonthaburi. 'Objective: Bang Kwang Gaol.' Mongkut and Rama exchanged glances as Anton went on: 'Intention: To free a prisoner, namely the Australian citizen, Ian

Graeme, aka Big Ig. Method.' He pointed the knife at Durman. 'My subordinate will now advise us as to that element.'

Durman said: 'Intelligence first in this instance.'

Anton was nonplussed by this breach of procedure, as Durman had intended. His contract specified he was in charge of the operation and he wanted Mongkut and Rama to be aware of this.

Anton tried a hard look—an attempt weakened by his puffy nose and blackened eye. He swung his hand out to clear his sleeve from his wrist and checked his watch. 'Today is the third. By our best estimate, therefore, we have until the thirty-first when our subject is due to be executed. Gaol security is strict, the guard detachment is well-armed, fully trained and highly disciplined. Given the time constraints, and the need to coordinate our moves with those of others, our first effort will be our only effort and it must not—cannot—fail.' He used the tip of the knife to centre the sheet of paper. 'I have detailed intelligence on guard strengths and rosters as well as outer and inner perimeter dispositions. These, I think, would more usefully follow the briefing on method.'

Durman picked up one of the cups, put a teabag in and drew water from the boiler on to it. 'Help yourself,' he said to Mongkut. But it was Rama who got up and began making coffee. There was a bowl with only a scraping of sugar in it. Rama tipped one of the cups of coffee into the bowl, swirling it round to absorb the sugar before pouring it back into the cup and presenting it to Mongkut, who bowed when he took it. Mannerly little rascals, Durman thought. And said to Anton: 'Admin details—you may as well give us them, too.'

Anton was helping himself to coffee. 'Method,' he said. 'Method first.'

Durman shook his head. Anton set down his cup and reached inside his jacket again. Shit a brick, Durman thought, the bastard's going to pull his gun on me to make me follow procedure. He tensed himself for another confrontation. Anton drew out three white envelopes which he dealt round the table.

The first thing Durman noted on his envelope was the Australian Government coat of arms. The emu was still wall-eyed but the kangaroo had got itself a donger. Mongkut and Rama each took from his envelope a wad of American currency—$100 bills—a Thai airlines ticket, a Thai passport and an Australian passport. Rather than the dollars or their own country's passports, it was the blue plastic-covered Australian passports that fascinated the Thais. They opened them and turned the pages like children given new and exciting primers.

'We are entitled now to bring family members to Australia?' Mongkut said.

Durman, who had long ago abandoned his country, found himself moved by the eagerness of the question.

Anton said: 'You are no longer illegals, you have all the rights of citizens.' At that, Rama followed Mongkut in standing and bowing. Anton motioned them to sit again. 'For this operation, you do not use your Australian passports, you use your Thai passports which, as you can see, have been adjusted to give you an unlimited re-entry visa.'

Durman examined the contents of his envelope: an Australian passport in the name of Leslie Burnett. He smiled at the occupation: salesman. Anton was certainly remembering Unit tradecraft. Salesman was an occupation which allowed a huge variety of props to support the cover story.

Anton was saying to Mongkut and Rama: 'You will stay at a hotel of your choice and make your initial contact with me on the ninth at eleven hundred hours by telephoning the Sapphire Hotel.'

'Good idea—changing the hotel,' Durman said. 'Bad idea our friends contacting you since we agreed you're not going in. They contact me.' He pushed his new passport across the table to Rama who handed it to Mongkut. 'Method,' Durman said, giving Anton no chance to protest. 'The method comprises three phases. Phase one: extraction. Phase two: feint withdrawal. Phase three: final withdrawal.'

Mongkut translated this into Thai for Rama. When Durman finished, Mongkut said: 'Feint is false, phony?'

'Ten out of ten,' Durman said. And to Anton: 'Intelligence on phase one.'

Anton took his time about answering. 'Our subject's as sick as you could hope. Maybe sicker. I got my contact to add a little something to the last lot of vitamin supplement capsules he delivered.'

Typical of Anton to improve on a plan, Durman thought, and then to be unable to resist skiting about it. 'Yes,' Anton went on. 'There's nothing like a trace of gunpowder in the diet for raising the temperature.'

Old trick but Durman had to admit an effective one, especially when Anton made it clear that neither Ig nor the prison doctor—'Ig's friend,' as he called him—was aware of the additive. 'Ig will begin to believe he really does have something wrong with him,' Anton said. 'So will his friend. Which can only help, eh?'

'Phase three,' Durman said. 'The cigar.'

'Not on. The bluebags are fully committed. There is an alternative on which you yourself have been recently.'

Durman said: 'Has it got the range?'

'I should have given you a longer trip to show you what its Detroit GM12V92TA diesels and long-range fuel tanks can do. It's also got full satellite navigation and communications equipment.'

'A beacon,' Durman said. 'Emergency radio beacon. Can it home on one?'

'EPIRB—Emergency Position Indicating Radio Beacon.' Pedantic as ever, Durman thought. Anton was saying: 'As a matter of fact, the *Norn* is halfway there already. Singapore, waiting for me.' Anton pointed the knife at Durman. 'Unless, of course, you have changed your mind and want me with you—in which case …'

Anton was angling for intelligence. Durman was surprised. He had assumed Anton would already have deduced the elements of the method. No harm in giving him tit for tat—a teasing hint. 'Remember the stop in Bangkok that made you shitty?' Anton nodded. Durman said: 'Some outstanding vehicles.'

'An APC?' Anton said. 'Block and snatch?'

'Something like that.' Durman handed Mongkut the business card he had been given by the car dealer in Bangkok. Mongkut examined it carefully and turned it over. On the back, Durman had printed: ACQUIRE AMBULANCE. Mongkut's expression did not change as he slipped the card into his pocket. Durman's mouth twitched. Mongkut was his man, however much Anton might posture as team leader.

"You will still need tools,' Anton now said.

'Yeah, bungers and bones,' Durman said. 'I got the impression when we discussed tools before that you might have a friendly fairy who could bag them in.'

Anton rinsed his cup in the sink while considering the suggestion that he had a member of the Department of Foreign Affairs who would use the diplomatic bag to convey weapons into Thailand. He turned to Durman, smiling. 'I don't know how you got that impression,' he said. 'But it is wrong. Our fairies are not like that.'

Bastard, Durman thought. He did give me the impression. And said: 'Okay, we'll find another way.'

Mongkut said: 'Bones are guns?'

'And bungers are grenades,' Durman said. 'Stun grenades, not fragmentation.'

‘Such grenades …’ Mongkut waggled his fingers. ‘Maybe, but guns, they can be acquired’—he glanced at Durman—‘In Krung Thep.’

‘Bangkok’s true name,’ Anton said. ‘It means City of Angels.’

Durman ignored the lecture and said to Mongkut: ‘There’s a dealer you know personally?’

‘Heckler and Koch,’ Mongkut said, ignoring in his turn Durman’s indiscreet question. ‘Sterling, Skorpion, Uzi.’

‘Gun that won the West Bank,’ Anton said.

‘No sub-machine guns,’ Durman said. ‘Pistols.’

‘Revolver?’ Mongkut said. ‘Automatic?’

‘Automatic.’

‘Walther 9 mm. Beretta 9 mm Brigadier, Heckler and Koch VP-70, Colt .45 Commander, Little Tom 7.65 mm. Browning GP-35 9 mm.’

‘That’s the one,’ Anton said. ‘The Grand Puissance—greatest handgun of them all. Right, mate?’ He was rubbishing Durman again. But he was also serious. Deadly serious. He went on: ‘Those APCs in Bangkok were not armed. We should refit ours with a heavy-calibre machine gun.’

Durman realised he had gone too far in teasing Anton and told him what the method would really involve.

‘It will not work,’ Anton said. ‘The time frame is too tight.’

‘That’s why it will work,’ Durman said. ‘No one will expect us to use a gap of only fifty-five minutes.’

He then proceeded to a full briefing on the method, detailing for Mongkut and Rama the part they would play and emphasising to Anton precisely what he was to instruct ‘Ig’s friend’ to do.

Mongkut again translated for Rama. Neither made any comment. For them it was not a risky operation, it was an opportunity to transform their lives and the lives of their families.

Anton had to make a contribution. ‘Clear communications are essential,’ he said. ‘I can lay on army walkie-talkies, of course. But I suggest mobile phones will be more effective as well as less noticeable.’

‘Agreed,’ Durman said.

‘It can work then, but there is a high probability of bang- bangs so …’

The sandbags beneath Fire Base Bravo were real, squared off, whitewashed and held in place with chicken wire. They formed the walls of firing ranges, radiating north, south, east and west from a central, fluorescent-lighted square of thick pine firing benches, built over locked olive drab, steel cupboards, each range having its own target-control panel.

The range supervisor was Roy Rankin. It said so on the name tag he wore on his dark brown uniform shirt which was also badged with a red V balanced on a black boomerang inscribed 'Vigilanz' in red.

Rankin personified the badge—blocky build, purposeful strut, eyes missing nothing yet at the same time detached, calculating your next move and his counter-move.

'Laser or live, sir?' he asked Anton.

'Live. Nice toys those laser pistols but there's no comparison between firing them and firing the real thing.' Anton held up three fingers. 'Brownings—GPs.'

Rankin did things by the numbers. One, he pulled out a bunch of keys on a chain. Two, he selected a key. Three, he unlocked a cupboard. Four, he took out three 9 mm Browning GPs. Five, he went to a nearby safe and twiddled the combination lock, saying, 'How many clips, sir?'

'One each, Mr Rankin. It's only a refresher.'

Anton took off his raw silk jacket. Durman's second guess had been correct. Anton's shoulder holster did not match his jacket, it matched his shoes. And his weapon was equally modish: an Austrian Glock. Seventeen 9 mm round capacity compared to the thirteen rounds of the Brownings which Rankin was issuing. Yes, issuing, writing down Mongkut and Rama's names as he handed them each a pistol and ammunition clip. He did the same with Durman and as he did so Durman caught a whiff of his aftershave: citrusy, spicy, leathery, incongruous amid the smell of mouldering sandbags and burnt cordite. The mix, by some kink of memory, brought to Durman the scent of a banked peat fire, waiting to be blown into the flame of a new day.

Rankin had been watching as Mongkut and Rama snapped the clips into the butts of their Brownings. 'Okay,' he said. 'But it's a dark night. The wind's howling and it's pissing with rain. Do it again. Eyes shut.'

Mongkut and Rama did exactly as they were told. Durman eased the top round from the clip and, keeping the spring depressed, put the point of the round between his teeth to test it before re-inserting it in the clip which he then snapped into the pistol butt. When he opened his eyes, Rankin was staring at him and he was not impressed. Anton laughed. 'Old superstition, eh, mate? But maybe like French letter after the abortion. Too late, eh?'

He was already at the firing bench alongside Rama who was to fire first, Rankin said: 'Distance, sir?'

Rankin pressed a button on the control panel to bring a man-sized target at the far end of the range whining towards them.

'Thirty,' Durman said. 'Thirty's plenty.' Rankin ignored him. 'Thirty,' Durman repeated. 'If it goes to hot, it'll be even closer.'

Rankin looked questioningly at Anton who nodded and passed a pair of ear protectors to Rama. Rankin said: 'If you're likely to go to hot, anyone can concentrate with ear muffs on. It takes a pro to concentrate when all hell's breaking loose.' He pressed another button on the control panel.

Suddenly, all hell was breaking loose: the rumbling thunder of heavy artillery. The screeching passes and crumps of close-support jets. The over-arching whistle and thump of mortars. The rip-rip of machine guns. The brush-fire crackle of small arms.

And above, under and around them, the screams and the bubbling groans of wounded and dying men.

Rama, ready to fire, looked at Mongkut who said, 'Mai pen rai'—It doesn't matter. This seemed to steady Rama. He fired two shots. One hit the target.

Rankin shouted: 'You're trying too hard, old son. Pistols are more instinct than anything else. Relax. Imagine your hand can kill when you point it at your enemy. If in doubt, aim for the balls.'

Mongkut translated this, giggling. Rama did better with his remaining shots. When his target was brought in, he had a gut shot and a chest shot.

Mongkut got seven from his possible thirteen: Three heart, one head, three gut. Anton patted him on the back as he himself stepped up to the firing point.

Always the stylist, Anton. He brought his Glock to bear two-handed as he crouched to fire—only nine rounds from the magazine's seventeen.

When his target was brought in for inspection, he had four head, three heart and two gut. He gave Durman a beat-that grin.

Durman, crouched at his firing point, got off his shots, saw them strike, heard Anton say: 'Still the ace of hearts, mate,' and straightened up to watch his target coming in.

Only it was not his target.

It was his comrade-in-arms Helen, running across the greensward of Kirribilli House. His comrade in arms, Helen, bulky, sexless, in black body armour running zigzag and being jolted to a staggering halt by the three armour-piercing rounds he'd fired from his silenced GP, thinking them wax-head practice rounds. His comrade-in-arms Helen staggering and—the massive black door of his dream swung open—becoming stark and agonisingly naked, blood from her severed aorta flowing in the valley between her breasts down to the delta of her being.

He was shaking, shaking sober as he had so often shaken drunk, shaking as all-hell-let-loose continued on the sound system. And in his mind.

Rankin was shouting to Anton: 'You're never sending this guy operational, are you? He should be RTU-ed.'

Returned To Unit. Durman whirled and thrust the Browning at Rankin's stomach. 'Go on,' he said. 'Have first shot, you mug.' Rankin's hand did not reach for the pistol holstered on his belt. Nor did he back away. Durman could feel the hardness of his stomach muscles against the muzzle of the Browning. Rankin was a pro. He had been counting Durman's rounds and knew he had one in the chamber which Durman's dying reflex would put into his gut. Yet Rankin was grinning. And Durman knew that Anton had told him—told him as one pro tells another pro of a third's balls-up: how Durman, pissed, had mistaken a live-round clip for a practice-round clip.

Rankin reached over and switched off the all-hell-let-loose tape. The sound of the videogame intergalactic battles came to them like distant memories—or remote prophecies. Durman turned away and laid the Browning on the firing bench. Rankin said: 'You're on my A-list, old son.'

## 10

Outside Central Station was a news vendor's hut and an *AllDay* poster, black on yellow in the strident sun:

> BIG IG
> POLL RESULT

The result was on page 3: 49,755 readers were in favour of Ig getting immediate treatment for his appendicitis and 21,371 against. Below the result was a box headed *ALLDAY* SAYS …

> 'In view of this result, AllDay now adds its voice to those calling on the Australian Federal Government to make urgent

representations to the appropriate Thai authorities about initiating treatment for Ian Graeme …'

When he looked up from reading this, Durman found himself in the Plaza Iberoamericana, according to the plaque, dedicated to the Spanish and Portuguese explorers of the South Pacific. Dotted about plazas were a number of bronze statues and busts.

There were other bronzes, living bronzes. A group of Aborigines in singlets and shorts were sitting in a circle passing a flagon. One waved the flagon at Durman in an immemorial gesture of hospitality. Durman waved a refusal. The Aborigine came over and held out a 20 cent piece. 'Flat busted, eh, mate?'

'Not me,' Durman said. 'I'm okay.'

'In that case,' the Aborigine said. 'Maybe a contribution.'

Durman handed him the copy of *AllDay* and a $10 note. The Aborigine handed him back the newspaper and returned to his group, waving the note like a small flag.

St Simon's was a gaunt, red-brick barn of a church up the hill from Central Station. Durman circled the building—to make sure he wasn't being heel-shitted, he told himself. But he knew this was not the reason. It was because he was reluctant to enter a Catholic church, particularly this one which had a pink—pink!—hearse with matching limousine parked outside.

In the church porch, a bevy of trim women in pink trouser suits waited, one of them smoking so furtively she might still have been wearing a school gym slip.

The number of people inside the church surprised Durman. Almost as many people as statues. In the pulpit, a priest was reading. Something about a centurion. Another surprise, the priest—not one of the big, thick Micks Dad said were bred to be wallopers or bible-bashers or crims or both. A midget in white, reading with the slow care of a child how the centurion had asked for Jesus to give only the word and the centurion's servant would be healed.

The church reeked of what Dad called 'the poncey stink of incense'. Candles flickered before the statues and on the altar and round the coffin of Bart Costello which was draped in the stars and jack of the Australian flag.

When the midget priest left the pulpit, his place was taken by a guy with the gait of a slackly strung puppet. His face was a droll's—a droll sacked for terminal cynicism. But his voice was nervous. 'For those who don't know me,' he began, 'I'm Normie McLaine. At least, I was until I got up here. Now I'm just a friend of Bart's.'

The phrases, 'Good mate', 'great bloke', 'fought the good fight', 'real pro', 'kept the faith' recurred with the hopeful monotony of the best line in a rock ballad.

Then the priest was back again. Without even an encore, Durman thought. And so small he peered over the edge of the pulpit as if looking for a box to stand on.

'I would be doing less than justice to Bartholemew Michael Costello and to the Catholic Church of which he was a lifelong adherent were I not to deal with the manner of his death.

'Officially, there are said to be no suspicious circumstances. This is, of course, an early example of the kind of correct phraseology which in our morally bereft world enjoys a vogue, semantics as it were substituting for ethics. What it means in effect is that Bartholemew Michael Costello committed suicide but we are too genteel to say so lest we offend his shade. Those of us who knew him are aware that he always called a spade a spade and on occasions a bloody shovel.' A ripple of laughter broke over the priest's next remark: 'Not that he did commit suicide ...'

How many others had caught the remark, Durman wondered. Typical. The priest was saying: 'The Church now takes a less rigorous view of suicide, believing that as Jesus Christ, walking on the waters, saved St Peter at the extremity of his faith, he continues to walk on the waters of time, saving others at the extremity of their faith.

'Say but the word! Say but the word!'

Typical. Durman watched the priest descend from the pulpit. Really typical. Can't face the reality that one of his Micks, far-gone in booze and debt, offed himself.

Bells rang. Durman did not attend their message. He was visualising his moves, linked to those of Mongkut and Rama at Bang Kwang gaol.

Some words of the priest, he half-heard and couldn't believe them so apt were they to his visualisation.

Once when the bells rang more loudly, Durman looked up irritably, as at a too insistent stranger, and saw the midget priest at full stretch holding up what appeared to be a white disc of bread.

Durman returned to his visualisation. Its clarity was fractured by the worry that there might be a leak on the op, that Bart Costello might have left some record as to what he'd been investigating. Or had Anton been correct when he called the leak fever operational paranoia? Back and forth Durman sifted the matter before switching to the checklist of tools for the op. Mongkut had acquired the bones and hungers. He himself had bought an emergency radio beacon the day before and telephoned Anton in Singapore to give him the beacon's frequency. A-okay tools. Yet something was nagging there, too. Some simple thing he'd forgotten.

The rattle of what he took to be a tin roused him. He looked up to see the midget priest moving round Bart Costello's coffin declaiming more prayers about Jesus and Resurrection and rattling a metal container on chains from which blue smoke rose to reinvigorate the stink of incense.

Down the aisle of the church came the bevy of pink-suited ladies, pushing a chromium-plated trolley. As they neared the coffin, Sergeant Jack Sands rose from a seat. He was wearing a dark tweed jacket over his uniform shirt and tie but he was all cop in the implacability with which he faced the women. There was a moment of stretched embarrassment, then Normie McLaine joined him and another guy and another till there were five around the coffin. To his astonishment, Durman found himself going forward to join the impromptu bearer party along with two other guys.

He was paired with Sergeant Sands as Sands said, 'Raise him' and the members of the bearer party lifted the coffin and Bart Costello on to their shoulders.

They began to move up the aisle. The midget priest announced a favourite hymn of Bartholemew Michael Costello's: 'St Patrick's Breastplate.' The priest led the singing in a voice of fog-horn resonance. Durman did not know the words. Nor, it seemed, did many of the congregation. Normie McLaine, behind Durman, did and joined his rasp to the midget's foghorn.

A strong tune.

And stronger words about rising through the strength of heaven … splendour of fire … swiftness of wind … depth of sea … firmness of rock …'

Soon the strong tune and the stronger words were carrying the congregation:

'Christ be beside me, Christ be before me,
Christ be in all hearts thinking of me …'

Durman had his right arm across Sergeant Sands' shoulders in carrying the coffin and felt them shaking.

With laughter.

For Normie McLaine, the droll, had rasped: 'All blokes drinking with me …'

Outside the church, the pink ladies regrouped and insisted on loading the coffin into the pink hearse.

Sergeant Sands said to Durman: 'A veteran cop once told me, "Always go to the funeral, you never know who'll turn up."'

Durman said: 'If you mean me, it was … well … I don't know.'

But he did know. He knew the silence of Bart Costello was still speaking to him. His worry was what the silence might be saying.

To him.

And to Sergeant Sands who was pointing at Eric Ramsay, editor of *Stud's Eye*, hurrying down the hill. 'Looks like a journo who's heard something interesting,' Sergeant Sands said.

The remark set off another spasm of leak fever in Durman, intensified when Sergeant Sands introduced him to Normie McLaine and McLaine said 'Durman?' As if he knew the name.

The pink hearse and the pink limousine were drawing away from the church.

Sergeant Sands said: 'You blokes okay for the cemetery?'

'Wish I was,' McLaine said. And laughed. 'Wake. There's a bit of a wake for Bart, and I've got to be there for the jump off.'

Durman, alert to check whether Sergeant Sands was on to him, said he would go to the cemetery.

The outside of Sergeant Sands' Subaru four-wheel drive was covered in red country dust and the inside full of music from the same area.

He had switched on the car radio as soon as he got on the tail of the cortege that formed behind the pink hearse and pink limousine.

Durman recognised the singer and the song: Smoky Dawson and 'The Fierce Red Steer.'

The country music, the dusty Subaru, the dark tweed jacket signalled that Sergeant Sands was off-duty. Except cops are never off duty. Sergeants Sands said, casually—too casually—'So how's the hunt for video rights going?'

'Football's no go. League, union, soccer—all tied up.'

'Wasted trip, then?'

'No way. I've got an appointment with the guy who runs eighteen-footer sailing.'

And he had—just as he'd had telephone contact with the football authorities in case some smartarse like Sergeant Sands should decide to check on him.

Durman smiled. 'Come on,' Sergeant Sands said. 'It's a funeral. Share the joke.'

Durman couldn't. The joke was on him. He'd been smiling because he'd realised he'd promoted Sands from 'thick Mick' to 'smartarse'.

Persistent smartarse. 'Wouldn't've thought there'd be much interest in eighteen-footer sailing overseas.'

'You'd be surprised how much interest can be generated,' Durman said. 'Those eighteen-footers—fantastic, bloody fantastic on a spinnaker run. Like marlin with wings. Promotable, very promotable as Sydney Harbour's third icon along with the Bridge and the Opera House.'

Sergeant Sands was silent as he followed the pink hearse and the pink limousine along Anzac Parade. Baffled by the bullshit? Durman wondered. Or thinking of another line of questioning?

The car radio was halfway into the news bulletin before Durman became conscious of it: '… the increase in the petrol price was in line with a rise in distribution costs,' the spokesman said, 'and was not designed to increase the profit margin.

'In Canberra today, the Thai Ambassador Mr Prasart King-petch, was called to the Department of Foreign Affairs. Subject of the visit is believed to have been ironman champion Ian Graeme, known to fans as Big Ig, now on death row in Bangkok for drug-smuggling.

'Graeme is suffering from a life-threatening condition and a senior department official is believed to have urged on the ambassador the necessity of immediate treatment…'

Not too immediate, Durman thought, as Sergeant Sands growled a laugh. 'How would you be, facing lead poisoning from a machine-gun and then getting a life-threatening condition.' He blasted his horn at an overtaking motorist who had slipped into the gap between the Subaru and the next vehicle in the cortege. The motorist could have got no more than a glimpse of Sergeant Sands' uniform shirt and tie but his middle-finger salute changed to a placatory wave and he pulled out to pass the pink limousine and pink hearse. Sergeant Sands growled another laugh. 'Life-threatening condition. Life's a life-threatening condition. Ask the crims in the Bay.'

They were passing the perimeter fence of Long Bay Gaol. Durman noted an outbuilding angled to the fence—gatehouse. He had a flash of a furniture van halting opposite it and a prisoner jumping from the roof of the building over the fence, on to the roof of the van—and the van speeding away.

Sergeant Sands was saying: 'Katingal's where the bastard ought to be, appendicitis or no appendicitis.'

It was Durman's business to know about places like Katingal—maximum security facilities. This one so inhumane even by the standards of a country founded on penology that it was not being used. 'Katingal,' he said. 'Sounds Aboriginal.'

'Yeah, it means hell in concrete. And that's where the bastard ought to be, doing life in solitary with nothing to watch except videos of heroin addicts going mad for a fix. I've seen them—seen what they do. Rip off their own mother. Sell their own kid.'

Durman said nothing, waiting for Sergeant Sands to question him about Katingal in particular and gaols in general. No way he would—could—resist it if he was on to Durman and the op. But Sergeant Sands was silent, too—Durman and him, linked by the silence of Bart Costello.

A forest of old gravestones from which rose a panoramic blue sky where seagulls flew, seagulls that were in the process of becoming angels as dolphins, grinning, leapt to meet them from white-capped waves.

In his travels, Durman had carried that memory of Botany Bay Cemetery. The panorama had been painted on the curved side of a huge fuel tank with the eye-cheating simplicity of a theatrical backcloth.

Now Durman was back at Botany Bay Cemetery. Real seagulls still cried over the bay. But the painted panorama seemed to have vanished. Disoriented, he turned to ask Sergeant Sands about it only to see him break into a head-down run as if he were going for the line with a rugby ball in the crook of his arm. It was not the line he was going for, it was the pink ladies who had obviously moved with some speed themselves and were already pushing Bart Costello's coffin on their trolley up a slope. Ahead of them was the midget priest and behind them a straggle of mourners.

One of the pink ladies looked back, saw Sergeant Sands and must have said something to her colleagues for they began pushing the trolley so quickly that they passed the midget priest and disappeared over the crest of the slope.

When Durman reached the crest, the pink ladies and the trolley and Bart Costello's coffin were speeding down the reverse slope. Sergeant Sands was closing the gap but the pink ladies might have won the race to the open grave had the nearside front wheel of the trolley not stuck in a pothole, slewing the trolley round and sending the coffin crash-sliding on to the pathway.

'See what you've done,' one of the pink ladies said. And her voice was hard enough to have incised the words on the nearest tombstone.

Sergeant Sands did not reply. He lifted the coffin upright and, uncannily, from inside came the sound of Bart Costello's feet thudding against the end as if he were trying to kick his way out. Sergeant Sands got the coffin up on his shoulder. It see-sawed and Durman put out his hand to steady it, then shouldered it and walked in lockstep with Sergeant Sands.

Planks had been laid across the open grave. Sergeant Sands and Durman placed the coffin on the planks as the midget priest began another prayer of which Durman caught … go forth Christian soul…' and thought of a tireless kelpie yapping at a recalcitrant sheep. Too much.

He moved left, up and over another slope, to where graves were slipping inexorably towards the sea in drifts of sand.

Among the graves he found those of his parents, Mum's marked with black granite and Dad's with what he'd always called 'the Gallipoli Biscuit'—a slim, official slab of sandstone which did resemble a giant version of the hard-tack biscuits that had been part of the ration on Gallipoli. On Dad's Gallipoli Biscuit was the eagle insignia of the Royal Australian Air Force.

Durman tugged out a clump of dandelions on Mum's grave and noted that erosion had undercut Dad's Gallipoli Biscuit. It shook on its foundations when he touched it.

Shit, he thought, it'll go over like Dad, poleaxed so swiftly by the heart attack that he had time to gasp only one word while Durman thumped furiously at his chest in a futile attempt to revive him.

One word.

Jahbulon.

The Sacred Word to Keep in Dad's Masonic belief, a belief and a practice that had taken Dad off to Lodge with his black attaché case so regularly and so discreetly.

The black attaché case, the secrets of which Durman had unlocked:

the lambskin apron with its rosette decorations, the white gloves, the insignia of office.

And when he'd asked Mum about them, she had smoothed her own apron and said proudly: 'Dad's Grand Master of his Lodge—Lodge Intelligencer.'

Lodge Intelligencer, named in honour of Baron Philip Von Stosch who spied for the Hanoverians against the Jacobites in Florence in 1731. Durman was attracted by the secret romance of it all—and as strongly repelled because it took Dad away from him. Yet he had to admit to himself it had influenced him to join The Unit—more secret, more exclusive than any Lodge.

He searched until he found a piece of rock and wedged it under the Gallipoli Biscuit to steady it. For the time being.

A sudden wind gusted up off the bay, the kind of wind that had caused Captain Arthur Phillip to order the convict transports of the First Fleet to up anchor and sail round to the sheltered waters of Port Jackson for the landing and the orgy that established the penal settlement of Sydney.

As Durman came back over the slope, he saw that Sergeant Sands was standing alone by the still-open grave and halted in the shadow of a stone angel. Sergeant Sands threw something into the grave, crossed himself and marched away as if on a parade of his own.

Two grave-diggers had started to fill the grave in when Durman reached it.

'Thought the big bastard was never going to move,' one was saying.

'I didn't hear you call *him* big bastard,' said the other.

On top of the coffin amid the first shovelfuls of sand was a purple and green ribbon. Durman had seen it before. It was the ribbon of the General Service Medal from Sergeant Sands' uniform shirt.

The ribbon.

The bearer party in the church.

The look on the face of Sergeant Sands as he got the coffin on his shoulder, the look not of a cop on duty but of a man intent on a gesture, no matter how ridiculous he might appear to others.

Whatever tick was into Sergeant Sands, Durman knew now for sure it was not the op. It was something between Sergeant Sands and Bart Costello.

Alone.

The wind brought from the bay the sound of breaking surf. In his mind, Durman heard a mightier surf, booming on the peerless white strand of the one safe place, the booming counterpointed by the frail bell-like cries of oyster-catchers.

He knew he would be back there.

Sooner—if he had to scrub the op because the way Normie McLaine'd said 'Durman?' meant there was a leak.

Or later—if McLaine checked out and the op was on.

## 11

The Journalists' Club, remembered as blue-tiled like a lavatory turned inside out, was what Durman had expected. Instead he was in The Shakespeare where Bart Costello's mates were going at it hard enough to justify its nickname, The Shakey.

Durman tried to edge past a couple of guys, one a lean rake: 'Read your Sunday piece about the Greedy Society, Ray.'

And the other a smooth paunch 'Well, mate, I thought it was about time someone said something. Everyone's been smoodging round the subject.'

'Smoodging? I like it. But I was sorry you didn't get down to personal examples.'

'Mate, do I have to tell what the libel laws are like. Yeah, and the lawyers, vulture-eyed mongrels.'

'I know. I know. Still you can't libel yourself, can you?'

'Don't follow you there, mate.'

'Of course, you do. Weren't you the guy who floated your bullshit mine of a media monitoring agency when the feeding frenzy was at its height?'

The smooth paunch waved. 'Sorry, mate. I've got to talk to someone.'

The lean rake turned to Durman 'Four million. Four,' he said 'Wouldn't it?'

He didn't seem to expect a reply and moved away himself into the raucous melee giving Durman a chance to advance towards the bar.

From the besiegers of the bar itself, Normie McLaine emerged with a beer, not his first, for he said to Durman: 'You've got some catching up to do. What'll it be?'

When Durman asked for ginger ale, McLaine's face became less droll. 'You're sure that's what you want? It *is* a wake, you know, not an AA meeting.'

'It's not what I want,' Durman said. 'It's all I can have.'

'Quack, right? Mine tried to scare me a couple of months ago. Said I showed signs of portal hypertension—condition indicative of liver damage.' He raised his glass. 'Here's to us, let's liver little and hope we die before they lay us out on the back lawn of the old folk's home to hose the shit off us.' He expected a laugh from Durman and when he didn't get one supplied it himself before swallowing half his beer in a gulp. 'Knew Bart well, then?' he said.

Durman explained as he had explained to Sergeant Sands how he thought Bart Costello might have been aiming to interview him, adding, 'Maybe he mentioned my name to you.'

McLaine gulped the other half of his beer. 'Not to me. Or anyone. Absolute no-no with Bart, talking about a story before he did it. Afterwards? Yeah. You couldn't stop him talking with a load of wet concrete. Dopey bastard chased all over the world.'

'Freelance, wasn't he?'

'There's nothing free about necessity. The poor bastard didn't have a pot to piss in. The number of times I told him to get a slot.'

Durman had seen drinkers who overplayed the extent of their drunkeness. McLaine, he suspected, was one. 'Sounds as if you've got a slot yourself,' he said.

'Yeah. And did Bart ever rubbish me about it.' McLaine tightened the loose strings on his limbs and straightened.

'Associate Editor (Standing Features) *AllDay.*'

'What're they,' Durman said. 'Features about rail commuters?'

'Funnee.' McLaine gazed into his empty glass. 'Enclose a stamped, self-addressed envelope and I'll send you a big guffaw by return.'

'Sorry,' Durman said. 'But what are they?'

'Executive peanut's term for the comic strips, the competitions, the fucking readers' letters, yeah and the non-fucking readers' letters—they're the worst, wowsering on about programs they couldn't bring themselves to switch off. Then there are the jokes, the word games and the crossword puzzles. I had Bart doing crosswords. Under a pseudonym because the bastard's *AllDay* file was marked, 'Never to be employed again.'

'Sounds interesting.'

'Sounds terrible. My appointment was a sideways promotion to make way for the new wave—the blow wave, the permanent wave, the affirmative-action wave. Should've told them where to stick their promotion. But I need a bit more superannuation to do what I really want.' He glanced right and left. 'Antiques,' he said. 'They're getting less old all the time. And royal Australiana's going to be so big in the republic. I've got a place down on the South Coast and the wife's already into collecting. We build on a gallery and live behind it, looking out over the bush and drinking red until the bell rings to announce another fat cat from Canberra spending his fringe benefits.'

He held up his empty glass and stared at Durman, daring him to laugh—or to refuse to buy him a drink. And Durman knew he wasn't as drunk as he appeared. Pisspots tended to buy their rounds.

The scrum round the bar was so fierce that it took Durman all of ten minutes to fight his way in and out of it with the drinks.

When he got back to Normie McLaine, she was there: the impossible stranger who, even as he took in her dark, upswept hair, her face—honey-coloured?—and her flowing slimness, he had a sense of knowing forever, a sense similar to the sense of coming home he had felt when he first came to the one safe place. It was a sense that held him unmoving.

She was saying to McLaine, her voice soft against the raucous mourning of the crowd: 'He rang me only two weeks ago.'

'Pissed?'

'He'd had one or three. Or maybe five. Told me he was going to make it up to me.' She smiled. A white starburst. 'Drinking my party shoes.'

McLaine misheard. 'He drank from your party shoes?'

'Not from. The shoes themselves. Silly. Very silly. I used to whinge about having to wear my school lace-ups with my party dress.' Tears were close. 'He didn't say goodbye. You know how people are when they're drunk.'

'No.' McLaine's droll face went deadpan. 'How are people when they're drunk?'

Her white starburst smile came and went again. Lightning through summer rain.

'Oh, you know, circling back on what they've said, saying things out of context. It's hindsight, bloody hindsight but I have the feeling he knew. Just before he hung up, he said, 'Listen to the silence.' Except he didn't hang up, he dropped the phone. And I didn't go round to his place, did I?'

McLaine reached out and took his beer from Durman. 'Glass of

White for the lady. And not the Chateau Cardboard, mate, the Tyrells chardonnay.'

'Normie!' she said.

McLaine remembered his manners and introduced them. Maree Costello, Bart Costello's daughter, her dark eyes bright with tears, regarding Durman so intently he could've sworn she knew what he was wondering: how could the beer-bellied, the bruised and sea-battered Bart Costello have begotten this shining senorita.

He pushed through the bar scrum again. When he returned with her wine, she had gone. So had Normie McLaine.

Listen to the silence, Bart Costello had said to her. And Durman himself still sensed the silence of Bart Costello speaking to him amid the raucousness.

At the far end of the room under a mirror-facetted globe, a guy was singing in a fractured baritone that he had done it his way.

Two other guys were dancing in close embrace. At least Durman thought they were dancing until they broke from their clinch and began trying to punch one another.

'Give them a paper bag each,' someone yelled.

It was Jerry Telfer, the last person Durman expected to see. He did not say so. Jerry beat him to the remark and chided him for leaving the charity-do early. He explained he was there because Bart Costello had been one of his writers and introduced his companion Ray Turnbull, adding, 'You used Bart, too, didn't you?'

'Once,' Turnbull said. 'It was disastrous—utterly so.' His voice had a plum-in-mouth quality. 'Dreadful man.' His suit was lightweight Prince of Wales check, set off by a white shirt, pink tie and matching pocket handkerchief which was for show not blow. 'Truly dreadful.'

'Come on,' Jerry said. 'He wasn't that bad. So he put round the story of you, Richard Thirding and one of your Pink Ladies over a coffin. But he also did a brilliant article on them.'

Ray Turnbull grimaced as if the plum in his mouth was sour.

'He could be of use when he wanted to be.'

'Of course he could. And was—otherwise you wouldn't have arranged the 10 per cent discount on his funeral.' Jerry's wig gleamed.

Cunning bastard, Durman thought, you oil your wig to make it seem more natural. He raised the full glass of wine when Turnbull offered him another drink. Jerry was having another and when Turnbull went off to get the round in Jerry said: 'Did you cop the accent? Bart always said it sounded like a cross between the Widow Twanky in a pommy panto and Dr Arnold of Rugby. But he's an operator, Ray. The amount of media he gets for the Pink Ladies—phenomenal. And all for 150 an hour plus disbursements.' He leaned closer to Durman. 'We're discussing a merger.'

'Doctors?' Durman said. 'And undertakers?'

'The synergy's there. Demand-driven, both of them.' Durman stared at Jerry. Was he joking? But Jerry was serious. 'Syl has done the numbers. The bottom line is fantastic. We ought to get together again soon—you, me, Syl—maybe Merv. You made an impression there. He kept asking me about you. Old times. Let's do lunch. Soon.'

'Yeah, soon,' Durman said. Merv, he was thinking, Mervyn Vesmar. But he was moving too fast to think it through. He had remembered the simple thing he'd forgotten.

A cab was decanting a passenger outside the club. Durman got into the front passenger seat. 'Nock and Kirby,' he said.

The driver was Chinese. 'No Nock and Kirby,' he said.

Durman twisted round in his seat. 'What do you mean, you don't know Nock and Kirby?'

'No Nock and Kirby,' the driver repeated.

'Let me out and I'll get someone who does know.' But the driver smiled and kept weaving through the traffic.

'Big shop,' Durman said. 'Hardware shop. On George Street.'

'No Nock and Kirby.'

Time: 16.35. He had to make it before closing time. 'Hardware. Nock and Kirby sells hardware. All kinds. Hammers, saws, screwdrivers.'

'No Nock and Kirby.' The cabbie pulled up and gestured. 'Hardware shop.' He scribbled a receipt when Durman paid him what was on the meter.

The receipt carried a motto: 'We help the stranger.'

## 12

In a darkened room on the third floor of the Sapphire Hotel, Durman was listening on his NEC P5 mobile to Anton being as cheery as a postcard: wishing Durman was there, how incredible the weather was, really incredible. Like Queensland with sex appeal.

Amid the postcard burbling, Anton was conveying crucial gen. 'What a view. We can see the lights of Chon Buri. Hard to believe they're six k's away. But the air's so pure here. And the sea—fantastic. The place to visit is the Marine Science Centre Aquarium. What a trip.'

'Half your luck.' Durman played along. 'I'm stuck in my hotel with another meeting scheduled. But save a couple of long, cold ones. I should be there soon with a friend.'

'Not the guy with the unhealthy interest in the crazy vehicle.'

'The same.'

Durman broke contact.

Time: 23.30.

But not time for the old Anton to know there was now a second—and even crazier—vehicle involved in the withdrawal.

Durman had the map of Thailand clear in his mind. Chon Buri was just over 100 k's from Bangkok, say 90 minutes drive. And the *Norn* was six k's offshore. His sea-entry point was near the Marine Science Centre Aquarium.

From the corner window of the room, Durman surveyed Nonthaburi's traffic. Quieter than Bangkok's bedlam, and further muted by the closed window, so that its noise blended with the benign hum of the air-conditioning system which, by design or accident, was recycling the smell of lemon grass from the hotel's restaurant on the fourth—top—floor.

That smell was the reason Durman could not stomach Thai food. It reminded him of the lemon-scented Fairy liquid his Mum had used in washing the dishes. So he had added to his reputation as a mad farang by getting room service to make him a Thai version of steak sandwiches. He was finishing one off. Another lay on a hotplate trolley—a round of crusty bread big enough to accommodate a brace of sirloin steaks side by side.

From the window, Durman also had a view of the floodlit main gate of Bang Kwang Prison. He raised his Zeiss Jenoptem 8 x 30 binoculars—a souvenir of Berlin—and focused them. Anton had been right: the Sapphire was an ideal Forward Command Post. And right again: the journalists were death-watch rats. They maintained an informal but constant presence at the gates.

One of them spoke into his mobile. Trying to persuade a replacement from too long a meal break in one of the local floating restaurants? Urging a colleague to come from the Tiara? Or simply reporting, nothing doing?

Another looked up towards the Sapphire. Durman stepped back from the window. Those guys were rats all right.

Sharp.

Ever alert.

And about to be offered a bait.

'Call, you bastard,' Durman said to the empty room. 'Call.'

And yawned.

There was a reading lamp over the bed. On the bed itself was a packet of blue duct tape. Durman lay down beside it. Scattered on the green-carpeted floor were other packets, red, yellow, green from the hardware shop, samples for his cover as a salesman. And a radio scanner, bought locally. Not a sample. A diversion.

The P5 rang again. 'Mai pen rai,' Mongkut said. It's all right. And broke contact.

Time: 23.35.

Mongkut's call signalled that he and Rama were cruising in the ambulance through Nonthaburi's traffic, waiting for Durman's word. And he in turn was waiting for the prison doctor's word. 'Call, you bastard,' he said to the empty room again. 'Call.'

And yawned again.

Not tiredness.

Fear.

He took a deep breath. It helped. But not enough.

He needed more than oxygen.

The bar fridge gleamed.

He needed a shot of alcohol.

In the white light of the opened fridge, an array of miniatures glittered: gin, whisky, brandy, rum and saki.

Whisky, the warrior's drink—even samurai salarymen admitted as much, passing their personal bottles in the bars of Tokyo.

But rum was tinctured with the courage of those who'd gone over the top and walked into hell on earth.

Rum.

He touched a miniature, and slammed the fridge door shut on the memory of his comrade-in-arms Helen running slap-bang dead into his drunken bullets.

The deeps of her.

All honey.

All gone.

The fridge rocked and rattled when he gave it a kick.

Time.

He resisted rechecking.

But you cannot recheck your weapons too often.

Hard-angled across his spine between his black T-shirt and the waistband of his black tracksuit pants, the Browning GP-35 Mongkut had procured for him. In the black, rubber-lined bumbag two bungers. He tightened the bag's belt. And felt its steel-cable core bite against his body.

Right-handed he cleared the GP-35 from his waistband and crouched before a big gilt-framed mirror, designed surely to reflect lovers in passion, and dry-fired two-handed at his own image. The feel of the butt was not quite right. From the pocket of his tracksuit top he took a roll of black gaff tape and bound another layer of it round the butt.

Better.

Only then did he go to the bedside table and take the clip of bullets he'd polished and repolished and snapped it into the butt of the GP. Safety on, he returned the GP-35 to its position hard across his spine.

And old John Thomas was with him. He yawned. The condemned man had a hearty hard-on. Inspired by the memory of his dead comrade-in-arms, Helen?

The P5 rang three times. Durman ignored it and switched on the radio scanner. The P5 rang again three times. Again Durman ignored it. The agreed signal.

Time: 23.50.

The prison doctor had summoned an ambulance for Big Ig.

Now was the time of instinct—Durman's instinct against the traffic tides of Bangkok and the response times of its military ambulance crews.

Nearly two million wild vehicles snarling at each other in wide expressways, narrow sois and concreted-over klongs. Not so much traffic as a plague on wheels, each vehicle farting leaded carbon monoxide into the lungs of eight million residents and the umbilical cords of uncounted foetuses.

From 05.30 hours to 10.30, the traffic built towards daily gridlock. At 11.00, it eased and then began to build again at 15.00 hours, continuing this pattern until 24.00 hours.

Average speed: eight kilometres an hour.

Except early on Sunday mornings.

The window he was aiming for.

As he began to sound like Anton.

Durman blanked his mind.

And she was there.

The impossible stranger.

So still.

Yet so vibrant.

Querida.

A word from Rio.

The word for her.

Darling.

Now.

Durman tapped the key for the Tiara number he had stored in the P5. 'Let me speak to Ric Wyler-Star. It's urgent.'

'Sorry, old boy. He's not here.' English voice. 'I'm a friend and if it's really urgent, I'll be happy to take a message.'

I bet you will, Durman thought. And said: 'Tell him a certain sick ironman's been smuggled out of Bang Kwang and is now on his way to Don Muang to catch a flight for Sydney.'

'How very interesting.' The English voice was bored. 'I'll let him know.'

Very bored.

Too bored.

The Englishman would now be moving away from the phone slowly and even more slowly heading towards the exit and then going hell-for-leather to Don Muang airport.

Solo.

Time: 23.59.

Durman waited.

Yawning.

Time: 24.02.

He called the Tiara again.

This time the voice was Australian. Durman said: 'Shit, mate. I can't believe it. I'm out here at Don Muang waiting for a flight to good old Sydney and a decent feed and who should I see being unloaded from an unmarked van but Ig. Big Ig. He's on his way home.'

No affected boredom in the Australian voice. 'Ig's at the airport, you say. Thanks a million, mate.'

'Should I give you my name and address?' Durman said. 'You know? So's you can send me something.'

There was no reply. But whoever had answered left the receiver off the hook and Durman heard the yells and the rush as the Tiara emptied.

He moved to the corner window and raised his binoculars. One watcher was talking on his mobile as he ran. He was followed by a TV-cameraman who had his hand-basher on, taping the running watcher. Behind the cameraman was a squabble of journalists.

Time: 24.05.

Durman tapped Mongkut's number into the P5. 'Paz,' he said. Go.

*'Ja, pai,'* Mongkut said. Will go.

Near the door of the room was a black webbing sports bag. Durman wrapped the steak sandwich from the hotplate in a towel and put it in the bag with what was already there: Thermos of brew, emergency radio beacon in its padded satchel and the absolutely essential tool he'd almost forgotten to bring.

He returned to the window.

A military ambulance was pulling up to the main gate of the prison.

Time: 24.09.

Too soon.

He'd briefed Mongkut and Rama not to rush it, to wait at least ten minutes before making their approach.

The main gates were swinging open and the ambulance was driving in.

An ambulance that had happened to be in the vicinity when the prison doctor put in his emergency call?

It was an eventuality Durman had taken a chance on. And the chance had gone against him.

Scrub!

Scrub! He was alive because he knew when to scrub an op.

But if he scrubbed, he would forego his completion payment. And he needed that to make the one safe place his forever more.

Time: 24.12.

'Move!' he shouted. 'You're standing there like a pig shitting razor blades.'

A jibe of Anton's.

Durman picked up the sportsbag. No matter what, he had to snatch Big Ig. He took a final look round the room. Radio scanner still on. As if left behind in a hurry. And Mongkut and Rama's gift was on the floor at the foot of the bed: an olive drab U.S. military-issue flak jacket.

Since the shooting of his comrade-in-arms Helen—all armoured, all dead—he had not worn a flak jacket, preferring to work with the odds in favour of death.

But Helen was gone.

And she was there.

The impossible stranger.

Querida.

Waiting.

All encompassing.

The one safe place made flesh.

He stripped off his black tracksuit top and put on the flak jacket before resuming the tracksuit top.

The lift dropped groundward, rattling against the shaft. Durman exited, a bearded, tall, strong farang with a black sportsbag slung casually over his shoulder, the bag complementing his tracksuit and his boots.

He turned right out of the hotel, jogged easily across the road, through a busy soi to a position from which he had a view of the main gates of Bang Kwang Prison.

Neon light pulsed to the beat of rock music, contrasting with the eerie silent glow of the prison security lights.

Durman shifted the sportsbag so that it was slung knapsack-style on his back by its handles, one end sticking above his head.

Time: 24.21.

The prison gates began to open.

Durman yawned.

And gulped in the night air like a swimmer preparing to dive from a high board.

The ambulance emerged from the prison and swung right. Durman began to jog. He had decided to stick with the first phase of his original plan: go in from the rear. And after that…

For a moment Durman lost sight of the ambulance in a late surge of traffic. Then its horn sounded. Mongkut. Mongkut was driving. The Thai showed no emotion but he did raise his thumb in the, ancient Roman sign for survival, and then two fingers.

Two guards. Durman had been hoping for one.

He had briefed Mongkut and Rama that he would make his move beyond the Museum of the Department of Corrections where

Nonthaburi's street lights petered out.

Mongkut slowed the ambulance as it hit the darkness.

Time: 24.32.

Taking a bunger from his bumbag, Durman closed the gap between himself and the ambulance. Its rear door opened easily on the dimly lit interior. He pulled the bunger pin, popped the bunger inside, closed the door on its stunning thud and drew his GP-35.

His first shot would be Mongkut's signal to go like the clappers. Thirty seconds, he'd said. Inside 30 seconds.

Light flared in his eyes. 'Here,' a voice called. 'Here.' Durman put his gun hand up against the light. 'Great,' the voice said. 'Great.'

Beyond the nimbus of light, Durman could make out a dark figure, deformed by a monstrous growth from which a glinting eye stuck.

Cameraman.

The pack was chasing a false scent. But there's always a lone wolf. This one was advancing, grabbing Durman's face to bounce off the world's satellites into Sydney, Belfast, Rio, Berlin and all parish pumps in between. Yet Durman could not take him out with a shot. Not unless he wanted to send Mongkut and the op to hell and gone. He crash-tackled the cameraman low, clubbing at him with the GP-35.

There was as much outrage as pain in the cameraman's, 'I'm only trying to do my ...' Durman did *his* job and knocked him out, pulled the camera from him and, in a sudden blare and veer of vehicles, sprinted towards the ambulance.

It was crossing a klong bridge when he reached it. He hurled the camera from him into the klong and the splash coincided with the cameraman's wailing like a woman bereft of her child, 'My camera. Oh, you bastard, my camera.'

The second bunger was in Durman's hand, pin pulled, safety lever down. He opened the ambulance's rear door and popped the hunger in.

The reverberation of its stunning thud was still in the air when he reopened the rear door, expecting to see two guards reeling in shock. One was. The other was bringing an Uzi to bear on Durman who let out a fearful wordless roar as he leapt into the ambulance. Not his roar but his silhouette, the end of the sportsbag sticking above his head, confused the guard. His first burst ripped into the top of the bag. He did not have a chance to get off a second burst. Durman's first shot hit him in the arm and sent him spinning back against the for'ard partition of the ambulance. He was catapulted off the partition when Mongkut hit the accelerator and the ambulance surged ahead.

The guard had no time to recover. Durman cuffed him on the side of the head with the full weight of the GP-35, knocking him cold.

The other guard was on his hands and knees trying to get to his feet—like a boxer who'd taken a combination of brain-scrambling blows.

A game boy, the Thai.

He managed to get his Uzi up one-handed. Only the first round of the burst punched against Durman's flak jacket, high on his shoulder, the rest missing and piercing the roof of the ambulance as the unsteadied Uzi climbed on its own muzzle velocity.

Durman put him away with a kick to the chin.

He whipped out the roll of gaff tape and used a length of it to bind the guard's wrists together, then his feet, biting and tearing the tape to length. He used another length to gag the guard. As he bit, panting, at the tape, he looked and sounded like a beast savaging its prey.

Yet in his mind, he was repeating over and over.

Querida.

Querida.

The first guard, he bound and gagged in similar fashion. The earphones connected to the Walkman on the guard's webbing belt were still giving out the sound of the heavy-metal rock that had saved him from the worst effects of the hungers.

Time: 24.43.

Durman slumped, panting, to a sitting position. First part of feint withdrawal complete in 53 minutes—two minutes inside estimated time frame.

'Took you long enough.' Big Ig's complaint ended in a groan as he writhed under a drab green sheet and webbing straps on a tubular stretcher. In the dim light, his face was greyish-green and sweat-slick.

Durman, high on close-combat adrenaline, peered at Big Ig. Great. A subject supposed to be malingering who'd got really sick. Automatically, Durman began to modify the feint withdrawal phase.

All the way by vehicle.

Stretcher Big Ig.

Call Anton to bring the *Norn* inshore.

Durman unslung the sportsbag.

Only then did he remember Anton's ploy of putting gunpowder in Big Ig's vitamin capsules and asked Big Ig whether he'd been getting the capsules, explaining about the additive.

Ig groaned and kept gulping for air. 'They're all I've been getting. The doc's had me fasting for the operation. Dopey slope.'

Clever slope, following correct procedures. Durman opened the sportsbag and took the Thermos out. 'Stick your fingers down your throat,' he said. 'Try making yourself sick.'

'Never been sicker.' Big Ig groaned.

Durman poured a cup of hot brew from the Thermos and held it while Big Ig drank. He then had a brew himself and was preparing to pour another for Big Ig when he heard the most beautiful sound.

A fart. A mighty fart. Appropriately modulated, it would have provided the opening for a new Trumpet Voluntary.

Big Ig began to laugh. 'Gunpowder,' he said. 'Did you say gunpowder? Well, don't put a match to this one.'

And farted more mightily.

Durman turned his head away. Big Ig said: 'What's the difference between a dead guy's pong and a live guy's?'

Durman didn't know and didn't want to know. Big Ig told him anyway. 'A laugh,' he said.

From the sportsbag, Durman took what had been his almost forgotten yet most essential purchase at the hardware store: a pair of heavy-duty bolt-cutters. He undid the straps that held Big Ig and pulled back the sheet.

'*Scheissen,*' Durman said. Big Ig, wearing only a drab green surgical gown, patched with sweat, was unfettered. Durman dropped the bolt-cutters. Big Ig kicked at the sheet. His left ankle was handcuffed to the end of the tubular stretcher. He leaned from the stretcher, got a hold of the bolt-cutters, set their jaws on the handcuff round his ankle and applied full pressure. The jaws snapped through the hardened steel of the cuff. Big Ig swung his feet to the floor. 'Okay,' he said. 'What else do I have to do?'

Durman pushed the sportsbag towards him. 'Get into the running gear.'

Big Ig began taking cotton wool plugs from his ears. The prison doctor had certainly earned his place high on the immigration list.

'Hurry,' Durman said. 'I won't be waiting for you.'

'Pig's. Old dag like you waiting for me.'

The contrast between Big Ig's genial cheek and his earlier groans made Durman realise how young Big Ig was, young enough to be his son. Yeah, if he'd fired for effect like Big Ig's father before he'd gone to Vietnam to die.

The ambulance swayed and rumbled, making good time: 60 maybe 70.

Big Ig pulled on a running vest. 'Where the hell are we?' he said, as his head emerged from the vest.

Time: 01.03.

Durman knew they were clear of Nonthaburi and heading into the outer limit of Bangkok's sprawl. Where exactly they were, he didn't know and there was no communication window to the driver's compartment. He *could* pinpoint their location by calling Mongkut on the P5. But he wouldn't.

He had calculated for ten minutes' confusion after the arrival of the authentic ambulance at Bang Kwang. Plus another ten caused by the media pack at Don Muang, baying for Big Ig and interviews. He wasn't relying on that extra twenty minutes. Effectively, he was now in a Code Red and inside the radius of the first search cordon. As part of the search, the Thais would be making scanner sweeps.

All they needed to pick up was a farang and a Thai exchanging signals about their exact whereabouts.

Durman said: 'Where we are exactly doesn't matter. All you need to know is you're going home.'

'Winki Pop, here I come,' Big Ig said and, seeing Durman's mystification, 'Hell surfing break over at Manly.'

He grinned at the prospect. His mood changed again when he took out the running shoes Durman had provided. 'Dunlop KT 26s,' he said. 'What about Nikes or Reeboks or Adidas? Or even a pair of old Uncle Herb's Pumas?'

It took Durman a few seconds to work out that old Uncle Herb was one of his boyhood heroes, Herb Elliot, Olympian and greatest middle-distance runner of his generation. 'Cheeky bastard,' he said. 'Put them on.'

Big Ig didn't. He sniffed suspiciously at the shoes. 'They're not even new. How tight can you get.'

Few will admit to tightness about money. Durman was not one of the few. Nor was he prepared to admit he had worn the KTs on his training run to Bondi, decided they weren't for him but would do for Big Ig who was rummaging in the sportsbag. 'Any socks?' he was saying.[s]

'Should be a pair there.'

'Shit, they're not new either. I could get athlete's foot. Or something.'

Big kid. listening to him, Durman found it easier to believe that the five keys of heroin had been planted on him. Not that it mattered. Durman likened himself to a lawyer. A lawyer aimed to get his clients off, guilty or innocent. Durman aimed to get his clients out.

Big Ig completed tying the laces on the KT 26s. Double knot. He looked up at Durman as if expecting praise for his cleverness. When he didn't get it, he eased open the ambulance door and had a piss.

Great, big kid. Young enough to be his son. Definitely. And hers—Helen's. She'd wanted a child. He hadn't.

Career prospects.

Durman got the first guard by the shoulders and began to pull him towards the stretcher Big Ig had occupied. Big Ig got the guard's feet and they lifted him on to the stretcher. There was another stretcher along the opposite side of the ambulance and they lifted the second guard on to it.

Big Ig helped himself to a bottle of distilled water from the rack Mongkut and Rama had been briefed to fill. 'Do I have to survive on this?' Big Ig said. 'It's as bad as a dingo's breakfast—a piss and a good look round.'

Great, big, silly kid.

Durman indicated the sportsbag. 'If you hadn't been so busy sniffing shoes, you'd've smelt it. In the towel.'

Big Ig unfolded the towel and took out the steak sandwich. 'Not very hot.'

'There's a portable microwave oven in the bag,' Durman said and, as Big Ig's hand moved. 'We'll stop the ambulance so's you can plug it into the battery and the Thais can find you having munchies.'

'Dag.' Big Ig bit into the sandwich. Durman took a bottle of distilled water. 'Maybe I should've brought you something to read,' he said. '*Stud's Eye*, say.'

'That wanker's rag. I wouldn't use it to wipe me arse if I had the squitters in a high wind.'

'But you had a copy when you were arrested.'

'Not to read the bloody thing. I had it for the address—you know?'

The first guard moaned behind his gag. Durman took the gaff tape off, gave him some water and redid the tape. Blood was seeping from the wound in the guard's arm. The bullet must've struck bone to send him staggering the way it had.

On the front partition of the ambulance, there was a locker with a red cross on it. In it, Durman found some field dressings and, rolling back the guard's ripped and bloody sleeve, bound a field dressing on the wound with gaff tape.

The ambulance slowed.

'Road block,' Big Ig whispered.

Durman heard the snap and rattle of an Uzi being cocked and whirled, clearing his GP-35. Big Ig had the second guard's Uzi trained on the rear door of the ambulance. 'Cadet camp,' he whispered. 'Guys from a skid school were there and they had one of these.'

Skid. Yid. The ambulance swung hard left and Durman lowered the GP-35. You beat racist insults out the front door and they returned by the back, lightly disguised and more contemptible than before.

The ambulance bumped along a surface rougher than the one it had been speeding on, then came to a halt.

Footsteps and Thai voices.

Durman returned the GP-35 to his waistband and grabbed the Uzi from Big Ig. 'Hell're you doing, man?'

The rear door opened and Mongkut and Rama were there, grinning and beckoning, as a myriad of birds twittered and sang.

Durman laid the Uzi alongside the guard. He would be in enough trouble without losing his weapon.

Time: 01.29.

Feint withdrawal complete.

He tapped Anton's number on the P5. 'Get those beers on the ice,' he said. 'We're on our way.' He broke contact and put the P5 into his bumbag.

## 13

The birds were in cages, bamboo cages, a wall of them at the far end of the long, wide aluminium shed where Mongkut had driven the ambulance, its headlights creating the false sunrise which had caused them to sing.

In a near corner of the shed was a shrine to the Buddha, lit by tapers, their flicker reflected in the shiny black bodywork and bright chrome of the crazier vehicle—the hearse from the same yard as the ambulance—and its optional extra.

Durman grinned his appreciation of the way Mongkut and Rama had acquired the elements needed for a modification of his plan. He had calculated the Thai response time in relation to the optimum possible speed of the ambulance and decided it might just clear the first security cordon but certainly not the second, and that another vehicle was necessary.

This he explained to Big Ig as he led him towards the hearse. Beside it, lying across the blades of a forklift truck, was its optional extra, the massive coffin.

He explained to Big Ig about the coffin. Big Ig did not grin. More than ever like a kid, resolute for his irresolution, he baulked. 'I don't mind the hearse,' he said. 'But I'm not having a bar of any coffin. I've been dreaming coffins for the last seven months.'

Durman felt a flick of anger. Cold anger. Anger directed as much at himself as at Big Ig. Durman knew he had probed too far, and the great, big, silly kid had said too much.

*I had it for the address—you know?*

Durman didn't know. He could guess. A call girl's? A hotel? A restaurant? Guesses only. He didn't need to know. Just as he didn't need to know whose shed it was—although he could guess again: relatives of Mongkut's and Rama's, creating an obligation in anticipation of the rewards that would flow from their settling in Australia.

All Durman wanted was to get Big Ig back to Australia and earn the completion slice of his fee. 'You don't have to worry,' he said. 'The coffin lid's drilled for ventilation.'

'I don't care if it's tapped for Fosters. I'm claustro-you-know?'

Great, big, silly, cunning kid.

*I had it for the address—you know?*

Durman snapped a cold, short left to Big Ig's body and struck a right on his chin as his head came forward. Big Ig went down and Durman, working with the speed of a bulldogger, trussed and gagged him with the gaff tape as he had the guards.

Mongkut helped Durman carry Big Ig to the coffin. Massive though it was, they had to turn Big Ig on his side with his knees bent and his head hard against the end before they could get the lid on him.

Rama manoeuvred the forklift so that Mongkut and Durman could push the coffin feet-first on to the raised platform inside the hearse.

All this time, Durman sensed that they were being watched—by the relatives who had allowed the use of their shed?

Rama ran a Mo-Ped up a plank into the ambulance. Mongkut closed the ambulance doors as Rama climbed into the driver's seat and reversed out of the shed, raising his thumb to Durman to signal that he remembered his briefing and would carry it out. 'Sydney,' he called, pronouncing it Sid-en-ee. Like an incantation of good fortune.

At the withdrawal of the ambulance headlights, the birds fell silent, the flickering Buddha tapers their roosting light.

Mongkut had changed from military uniform into a chauffeur's dark suit, complete with peaked cap. Durman tweeked the edge of a fold of white cotton in Mongkut's breast pocket. The little bastard hadn't forgotten a thing. And had even thought of things for himself. Durman watched as Mongkut fetched a dozen of the bird cages and placed them on top of the coffin to conceal the ventilation holes.

Such cage birds Durman had seen Thais buying in Bangkok and then releasing them to gain merit.

Mongkut waited. Under the raised coffin platform was a zinc-lined space, the original purpose of which Durman could only guess at. Storage of funeral implements? Or ice to preserve the corpse? He shoved the sportsbag in, then tried to get in himself, feet-first. Im-bloody-possible. Mongkut tapped the flak jacket. Durman took it off. Even then it was such a tight squeeze that he also had to take off the bumbag and remove the GP-35 from his waistband. Mongkut shut the little doors that closed off the space and put a caged bird in front of the crack, leaving Durman in darkness, the luminous face of his watch gleaming like a tiny green asteroid.

The hearse's engine roared, surprisingly powerful. Durman felt the vehicle move out of the shed on to the rough track and bump out the paved way, heading for Sukhumvit Road, Thailand's longest.

Or the nearest police post.

Nothing to stop Mongkut driving Big Ig and him straight to a police post to claim indemnity and a reward.

Nothing except the lure of Sydney, the city Durman had learnt to hate.

Durman thumbed the safety off the GP-35. The bird beyond the door shifted in its cage.

Was that why Mongkut had placed it there—as a sign to hunters?

The hearse slowed and came to a halt.

Roadblock.

But the search that followed the halt was so cursory it caused Durman's paranoia to lift like mist before summer sun and persuaded him that the hunters had been deceived by the feint he'd briefed Rama to carry out: abandon the ambulance on a back road near the chopper pad 35 kilometres from Nonthaburi, then withdraw on the Mo-Ped.

As the hearse rolled on, Durman became so convinced that his surmise was fact that he did what he'd been trained to do in situations where there was nothing to be done: he had a Winnie—Unit slang for a Winston—a kip, a snooze, a zizz, a sleep.

And dreamt.

He was flying above the one, safe place.

The long island.

Its peerless white beaches.

Its raw silk seas—summer, blue and green, winter, grey.

Its heather honeyed air.

Becoming her.

The impossible stranger.

Lying, silken, honeyed, ready to receive him.

Querida.

The jolt of the hearse braking awoke him.

Roadblock.

But this time, the search was not cursory.

Mongkut's voice protesting. The insistent voices of the hunters, made more menacing by the thud of paratrooper boots on the road.

The rear door of the hearse opened.

And the caged birds sang in the false dawn of the roadblock floodlights.

A torch into the crack of the doors to his space and Durman—dill! dill!—too late! too late!—buried his face in his arms.

Mongkut continued to protest, the hunters to insist. The driver's door slammed. Mongkut getting out reluctantly to help the hunters.

Durman risked a look. The bird in front of the doors was fluttering and chirping along with all the other birds.

Beyond the bird was a Thai officer. Durman needed only a glimpse, he had seen the type before. In South America. In Germany. In Northern Ireland. He himself had been the type after completing The Unit's killing course: young, piss-proud and shit-hot to impress. Not least himself as the Thai officer was, gesturing with his pistol and issuing a command to Mongkut.

Durman could not understand the Thai of the command. He could interpret the pistol gesture: open the coffin.

Mongkut made a final protest in a torrent of Thai, taking from his breast pocket the fold of white cotton. The Thai officer's voice rose as

Mongkut unfolded the cotton.

And fell.

The cotton was a surgical mask.

The Thai officer asked a single question. Mongkut replied, equally curt. Again Durman did not understand the Thai, he remembered what he'd briefed Mongkut to say: the body in the coffin was that of a gem dealer who'd died of AIDS, homeward bound for a funeral in Chantaburi. From his inside pocket, Mongkut was taking the documents to prove this. The Thai officer waved them away as if they carried the disease. His voice rose again—a mixture of revulsion, fear, plain anger and anger about being fearful—and the fluttering and chirping of the birds rose with it.

The P5 rang. Anton, Anton ringing for a sit-rep. I'm at a meeting, you bastard, Durman thought. Piss off. The P5 rang again, its sound was muffled by the bumbag. But the Thai officer must hear it. He brought his pistol up. Durman did the same with his GP- 35. The bloody bird. It kept fluttering in its cage, preventing the single, clear shot Durman needed.

BANG.

The officer's shot cracked and thudded into the head of the coffin. And all the caged birds went mad in panic.

The Thai officer waited until they were quiet, waited listening.

The P5 was silent. But the Thai officer was not listening for its ringing. He was listening for a sound from within the coffin.

As was Durman, his own heart drumming.

And Mongkut.

Listening for the thump of Big Ig, trying to kick his way out of the coffin.

Silence.

BANG.

The Thai officer's second shot sent the birds into another wild panic. Again he waited, listening.

And again silence.

This time it was broken by Mongkut shouting, as if the farang acronym were more terrible than its Thai translation: 'AIDS!'

BANG.

The Thai officer's third shot crack-thudded into the head of the coffin. He did not wait, listening. *'Pail,'* he shouted. *'Pail.* Go! Go!'

Mongkut went. Durman thumbed the GP-35 safety back on.

The hearse rolled forward and Durman could hear, muted, the blare of Bangkok's traffic and the rock-and-roll of its nightlife. Then the hearse swung left—Sukhumvit Road, otherwise known as Highway 3, which ran all the way to the east coast of Thailand and the Gulf of Siam.

But Durman could not lull himself to sleep. He knew he would not be getting the completion slice of his payment which would have made the one safe place his forever more. He knew because under the terms of his contract he had to deliver Big Ig alive and well to Australia.

Above him, Big Ig, icon of his generation, was trussed and gagged.

And dead.

Great, big, silly, cunning kid.

Yet he had an amiability, a sunniness about him.

Her amiability and sunniness.

His comrade-in-arms, Helen's.

Big Ig was like the son she could've had.

His son.

And he had trussed and gagged him.

So that he could not call out.

And had been killed.

As surely as if he had faced the ceremonial heavy machine-gun in the killing yard of Bang Kwang Prison.

Both Durman and Mongkut reeked of sweat and fear. But when Durman pushed the coffin lid aside, the stench was so terrible that Mongkut replaced the surgical mask. Then with his help, Durman eased the lid right off, uncovering Big Ig.

Great, big, silly, cunning, stinking kid.

Durman breathed through his mouth as he cut the gaff tape away from Big Ig's wrists. He then had to turn Big Ig over to get to his ankles. Only then did he rip the gaff tape from Big Ig's mouth.

Wrong order.

He should've left the wrists till last.

'Mongrel,' Big Ig yelled. 'I shat meself.'

And grabbed Durman by the throat. He felt the surge of Big Ig's angry strength and for a moment his coolness was swept away by the primeval fear of the older bull, the older stag, challenged by a younger. Then his fists went inside Big Ig's wrists to break his grip.

'Silly old bastard.' Big Ig varied the insult as he pulled himself over the side of the coffin and began crawling from the hearse.

Mongkut had pulled deep among the outbuildings of a roadside petrol station—another property of his and Rama's relatives?

'Shat meself *and* pissed meself.' Big Ig's tone, childishly rueful, and incongruous compared to the magnificence of his physique, made Durman smile.

'Your pecs are okay. But you'll have to work on your sphincter.'

'Yeah? And what about this?'

This was a bump on top of his head. Durman held out the towel from the sportsbag. Big Ig said: 'Stick it where the movie star stuck the gerbil.' But he took the towel and went towards a water point.

Working under an inspection light, slung from a tree, Mongkut was unbolting the hearse's lamps, preparatory to stripping the vehicle to its chassis and transforming it into a flat-bed truck.

Mongkut paused in his work to point to the bullet holes in the wood exterior of the coffin. He had pulled away the quilted interior lining and Durman saw that the coffin was lead-lined, the lead carbuncled from the impact of the bullets fired by the Thai officer, one where Big Ig's head had rested.

No wonder the kid had shat and pissed himself. The bullet's impact must've felt like sudden death.

Mongkut handed Durman a bottle of distilled water and he took a grateful swallow of it. Anton had certainly known what he was doing when he bribed Mongkut and Rama with Australian citizenship papers.

Durman stripped off his tracksuit top and pants and strapped on the bumbag containing the P5 mobile. He slung on the satchel containing the emergency radio beacon. A give-away if he and Big Ig were stopped. But a necessity. Unlike his binocs and the GP-35. He gave them to Mongkut who, smiling, offered Durman one of the caged birds in return. He took it and held the bird to calm it before throwing it upwards. The bird circled the inspection light and Durman found himself trying to remember the words half-heard at Bart Costello's requiem.

Time: 03.35.

The bruise on his shoulder where the bullet had struck the flak jacket was blue-black and throbbing.

Big Ig had cleaned himself up and was swigging from a bottle of distilled water. There was something forlorn in his stance and Durman said: 'You going to be able to make it okay?'

Big Ig laughed. Durman yelled: 'Move, you bastard. Move.'

He held his lead for three minutes, then Big Ig passed him running with a peculiar gait. Durman let him get ahead before lengthening his own stride to catch up with him and as he passed him said: 'You're waddling along like a kid who's just pissed and shat in his nappy.'

This time he held the lead for seven minutes. But again Big Ig passed him, running with his peculiar gait, and said: 'No I'm running like you—an old fart chasing his ball on the bowling green.'

And so they went. To peasants moving into the early fields and to drivers of passing vehicles, a couple of mad farangi out for a run, passing and re-passing each other, the younger yelling to the older: 'You going to be able to make it okay?'

Mostly Durman let Big Ig run ahead. A kid thinking he was leading but in reality being shepherded.

When Durman heard the thunder murmur of the sea and felt its breath salty on his face, he ranged himself alongside Big Ig and passed him, saying: 'Can't stand running in your smelly slipstream.' He led all the way into Chon Buri.

Big Ig caught up with him as he passed the Marine Science Laboratory and turned for the beach. 'Like being in a senior citizens' gala.' He pronounced it galah.

Great, big, silly, cunning, stinking, cheeky kid.

They went shoulder to shoulder down the beach, the roar of the sea their crowd.

Time: 04.45.

They would catch the ebb.

Big Ig pulled off his running shoes, socks and vest and left them lying on the grey sand of the beach. 'Come on.' He kept running towards the sea on which a far line of light shone, and returning. 'Come on.'

Durman had conditioned himself to slow down in response to impatience. He took the emergency radio beacon from its padded satchel. He replaced the beacon with his running gear and Big Ig's, adding handfuls of beach sand to weight the satchel.

The beacon's frequency had been pre-set. Durman switched it on. He tapped the P5: Anton's number. 'Where the hell've you been?' Anton said. 'I tried to make contact.'

'When you shouldn't have,' Durman said. 'I was at a meeting. A very sticky meeting. I've just sent a signal.'

'Yeah, we're getting it.'

'Then it's me for a swim. And don't forget two coldies.'

He broke contact and jammed the P5 into the satchel before adding another handful of sand.

'Come on.' Big Ig was fairly dancing with impatience. 'Come on. Did I say senior citizen's gala? Make that geriatrics'.' He ran towards the sea.

'If you don't wait, you'll be the lost kid at the gala,' Durman yelled. 'Yeah, the lost kid in the smelly nappy.' He held up the emergency radio beacon and its signal beep was echoed by a bird of dawning, soaring in the onshore wind.

Big Ig ran back from the sea. 'Let me have it.'

Durman kicked the satchel full of gear towards him. 'Dump it when you're in deep.' He clipped the lanyard on the beacon to the belt of the bumbag.

For all the childishness of his behaviour, Big Ig had been reading the sea with a knowing eye. 'Rip,' he called. 'There's a rip here.' He lifted his legs high to clear the first waves, timed one, dived into it and came out of it on his back, the satchel of gear clutched to his chest, and kicked like a stern-wheeler until he was far enough out to jettison the satchel and turn over to settle into his crawl.

Durman could not match him, only keep sight of him in the risky exhilaration of the rip—the deeper channel of water moving out even faster than the ebb.

They had caught it. Durman increased his beat. They had caught it as they had caught the traffic tides of Bangkok.

The wind began to get up against the ebb, causing a relentless slop through which they ploughed, the beacon bobbing alongside Durman.

They were a couple of k's out when it happened.

Durman had been ignoring the pain of his bruised shoulder. But this pain could not be ignored. It blitzkrieged its way out of his heart, seized his solar plexus in an armoured hand and knotted his arms and legs. He turned on his back, fighting panic, telling himself it would only make the cramp worse, yet knowing it was more than cramp.

Big Ig had something of a fish's instinct for panic. He swam back to Durman. 'Old bastard,' he said. 'This is too gnarly for you.' He began to unbuckle the bumbag belt. Durman, thinking he meant to take the beacon and leave, tried to stop him. But Big Ig only shifted the belt so that it passed bandolier-fashion over Durman's chest and shoulder. Turning Durman on his back, Big Ig got a grip of the belt one-handed and began towing him.

Not back to shore.

Out to sea.

The emergency radio beacon was sending out its signal. Durman could sense the pulse of it through the pulse of pain while Big Ig swam on through the rising wind and waves as steadily as if he were equipped with a lifesaver's belt and line and was being hauled in by team-mates away in Australia.

Away.

Away.

Durman drifted away on the pain.

And drifted back.

And Big Ig was chanting, timing the chant to his arm-stroke.

'Cherry Venture… Tea Tree… Boiling Pot…'

An incoherent litany to Durman.

'Kirra… The Pass… Pippies… Spookies… Speedie's Reef… Old Bar… Seal Rocks… Treachery… Hawk's Nest…'

The *Norn*? Durman wondered. Where was the *Norn*? Anton was supposed to order its skipper to home on the beacon.

'Samurai Point… Ghosties… Norah Head… Pelican… Crackneck… The Wedge… Avalon… Crosswaves… Butter- box… Curl Curl… Winki Pop… Bondi.'

Bondi was Durman's key. Big Ig was chanting the roll of beaches and breaks he had surfed round Australia.

'Mackenzie's… Tamarama… The Toilet Bowl… Voodoo… Cronulla… Peggy's… The Farm… The Boneyard… Bombo… Dum-Dum… Corsair… Vera Lynn… Marengo… Castles… Joanna… Point Danger… Granites…'

Snafu, Durman thought. Situation Normal All Fucked Up. Mal-bloody-function aboard the *Norn*. It wasn't picking up the beacon signal.

'The Coorong… Moana… Trespassers… Point Avoid… Venus Bay… Supertubes… Crushers… Caves… Castles… Cactus… Witzigs… Cottesloe… Bullet Reef… Cathedral Rock… Head Butts…. Coronation… Jake's Point… Turtles… Barnyards… The Quarries… Lighthouse… The Other Side of the Moon…'

The *Norn's* not coming in.

'Peabrook… The Gallows… The Guillotine… Margaret River… Mandalay Beach… Foul Bay… Anvils… Crazies…'

The *Norn's* not coming in.

'Seamander… Tamashanta… Beerbarrel Beach… Dave's Place… Tessos… Lumpeys… Marraway… Cherry Venture… Tea Tree… Boiling Pot… Kirra… The Pass… Pippies.'

Durman, half-conscious, realised Big Ig had started his beach litany again.

'Cherry Venture… Tea Tree… Boiling Pot…'

He'll abandon me, Durman thought. Has to. Operational necessity.

## 14

On the cream-painted bulkhead of the *Norn's* main cabin, a fret of light, reflected from the sea, danced to a crystal chandelier's tinkling which was backed by the bassline of the vessel's twin diesels as it headed south.

The click of Anton's Nikon was metronome to this music. The bastard's overdoing his cover, Durman thought, taking in Anton's blue-striped Breton shirt, wide white canvas trousers and blue espadrilles. Amazing, he's not wearing a blue beret.

Through the waterbed on which he was lying, Durman could feel the motion of waves like gentler memories of the relentless slop through which Big Ig had towed him. He won the first part of one of his silent bets with himself when Anton said 'Sumatra to starboard, Java to port. End of the Sunda Strait coming up.'

He had a porthole opened and was focusing his Nikon through it. The second part of the silent bet Durman also won when Anton continued the commiseration about his collapse, a commiseration which had been part of their daily routine since they'd cleared the Gulf of Siam and headed for Singapore to top up the *Norn's* fuel supply before sailing on.

'Could've happened to anyone,' Anton said in tones of shallowest sympathy. 'Right, Doc?'

Doc, washed out jungle greens on which the name Monroe could be read, blimpish face—steel-grey hair, moustache stained khaki with nicotine—said: 'Yeah, I've seen it happen to the fittest. Suddenly—kaboom—the body goes, "enough of this shit already" and shuts down.'

From Durman's upper arm, he unwound the collar of the sphygmomanometer he'd been using to get a blood pressure reading.

'Not bad,' he said. 'Not bad at all, considering what you've been through. But maybe you should see a doc when you get back to Oz.'

'You're not a doctor?'

'Crikey, I've been wondering when you'd recover brain function.' Monroe returned the sphygmomanometer to its case and snapped the case shut. 'No, mate.' He glanced at Anton. 'I thought you knew who I was. Me, I'm a paramedic. Doc's a nickname.' He took out a packet of Drum tobacco and cigarette papers which he offered to Durman and Anton. When they refused he said, 'Mind if I do?' and before they answered rolled and lit a cigarette.

The smell of the tobacco made Durman realise how hungry he was. He mentioned this to Monroe.

'No problem. This is the original good ship lollipop.' At the door, he said: 'Another day or so in bed. Then light duties. But no active service.'

'Hold it.' Anton knocked off a shot of Monroe and after he'd gone focused on Durman. 'Forget the happy snaps,' Durman said. 'The state of the game's what interests me.'

Anton lowered the Nikon. 'Well, as you know, the media went galloping off in all directions after the wild goose chase you sent them on. Now they've settled down to the old mystery-surrounds-the-present-whereabouts-of-Aussie-surf-icon-Big-Ig.'

No need for Durman to ask where Big Ig really was. From the deck came the sound of his laughter, punctuating his attempt to sing his list of surfing beaches to the guitar accompaniment of a woman who kept joining in. Obviously, Big Ig was enjoying another part of the *Norn's* cover: Miss Stud's Eye, Patsee Urquhart.

'Government reaction?' Durman said.

'Ours or theirs?'

'Ours.'

'Same as theirs. Nothing—officially.'

'Unofficially?'

'Still nothing—but those in the know are chuckling quietly. Not least because extradition cuts both ways. Ig couldn't be extradited from Thailand to Oz and he can't be extradited from Oz to Thailand.'

'He could be charged in Oz.'

'No DPP would bring a case.'

'You know that for sure?'

'As surely as you know public prosecutors are totally independent of political pressure.'

Anton's irony further convinced Durman that his ultimate paymaster was the Australian government. He said: 'The Thais could mount a counter snatch.'

'They could but they won't. Which is why they're saying nothing. Not a whisper about anything—the duplicate ambulance extraction—anything. But there's a fair amount of high-level you-know-that-we-know-about-your-coup-de-main.'

'The gaol doctor.'

'In the clear. Absolutely. The radio scanner you left in your hotel was a nice touch. It fooled the Thais into reaching the brilliant conclusion the emergency call to the ambulance depot was monitored.'

'Mongkut? Rama?'

'You worry too much, mate.' Anton turned at the door. 'You ran a classic op—your collapse doesn't detract from that—as I said in my assessment.'

'Your assessment?'

'Routine, mate. Routine. You know how those Canberra desk rats love crispy-crunchy paper. Completely routine. It was no more your fault you collapsed than it was mine when the Thai navy patrol boat came alongside us hove-to in the rendezvous zone waiting to zero on your beacon. Luckily our cover held. The Thais were bug-eyed.'

Suddenly, the head of Patsee Urquhart was framed in the porthole. Conservative kid. Her lips and her hair were still blue to match her lingo. 'The romp shots of me and Ig, you said you wouldn't be long, you prick.' Anton strode across the cabin, his Nikon coming up to focus on her. He knocked off a series of shots as she mugged and smiled and licked her lips before disappearing.

'You said the Thais were bug-eyed.' Durman grinned rarely. 'What about their ears?'

'Fried. Fried to a crisp. But while they were hanging around, we couldn't go in-shore for you. We had to go through the motions of sailing off before fetching a circle to zero on your beacon.' From the deck came another burst of Big Ig's laughter, starting deep and ending high pitched. 'You owe that kid your life,' Anton said. 'He must've swum ten, fifteen k's towing you.'

It was a remark to go on. And Anton did—with a parting grimace of sympathy.

Durman turned over in bed to face away from the door. No wonder a man was depressed. Anton's mock sympathy. The memory of the blitzkreig of pain. Doc Monroe's remark: 'I've seen it happen to the fittest. Suddenly—kaboom—the body just says, "Enough of this shit already" and shuts down all systems.' The one safe place. Now more than ever, Durman knew he must get back to it.

The chandelier chimed as it tilted to port—the *Norn*, clearing the Sunda Strait and coming on to a fresh south-west bearing, its twin diesels which had been throttled back in the strait roaring to full power for the run across the Indian Ocean to Australia.

The sea-fret danced on the bulkhead. The chandelier tinkled on the bassline of the diesels, and was joined by the tinkling of ice in a jug as Her Royal Highness, the Princess Celia Von Kronberg, entered. The jug contained fresh lime juice. With it on a silver tray were plates of sliced salami, black olives, onions, red and green sliced peppers and segments of melon and papaya.

On the tanned Princess Celia was a black bikini which was a triumph of eroticism and engineering. Human beings are not machines. But they do have triggers. Black silk on brown skin was one of Durman's. He sat up to eat and drink. As he did, hungrily, he found that he wanted the food more than the drink and her more than both as her bikini bottom joined her bikini top on the deck and her breasts came sweeter than the papaya.

She was as brown as a trout and as supple but by no means as cold. Yet detached. 'Light duties only, I believe.' And efficient. She broke from his kiss, laughing, to roll over on top of him. 'No active service.'

Sex as short-arm thrill drill.

Afterwards, they slept, spooned together.

And Durman dreamt.

Variations on the death of his comrade-in-arms Helen and his meeting with Bart Costello's daughter.

'Querida.'

Wild variations.

The wildest.

The massive black doors swung open.

And he was flying above her.

His comrade-in-arms Helen.

Lying naked, blood from her severed aorta flowing in the valley between her breasts down to the delta of her being.

And becoming the one safe place, its dark lochs lily-starred and its burns trout-glinting.

And becoming Bart Costello's daughter.

‘Querida.’

Running like Helen into gunfire and emerging bleeding.

Every drop of her blood a tinkling crystal.

Silence.

Black silence.

He awoke, sweating.

Every dream has elements of reality. Radium in pitchblend. Gold in sand.

Gunfire was one element of reality here.

And silence. The chandelier no longer tinkled. The bassline of the diesels was gone.

The *Norn* was dead in the water.

Durman rolled out of bed and hit the deck running—wobbly—wobbly after his days in bed—but responding to the gunfire.

And the silence.

The silence of Bart Costello.

Behind him the Princess Celia said: ‘Querida? Who is she?’

Durman thought he knew.

In the saloon, black velvet curtains were drawn. Lights were focused on a section of red leather-padded bulkhead which had been swung open and Anton was issuing weapons and magazines of ammunition to crewmen while Big Ig hovered, a kid eager for a picnic.

The crewmen loaded the weapons in trained silence as they headed for the upper decks and the gunfire.

Austeyr F88s, Durman noted. Australian Army issue automatic assault rifle.

‘Never fear,’ Anton said. ‘The Jocks are here.’

Durman had kilted a gaudy towel round himself and, as he stepped over the saloon door combing, Big Ig said to him: ‘Okay, Dad?’ Beneath the sarcasm was concern. Durman thought to thank him for the rescue and compliment him. But hesitated. His compatriots were as touchy about thanks and compliments as they were about criticisms.

The moment passed as life passes.

And Big Ig was saying to Anton: ‘The next, I’ll have the next.’

Anton gave the next rifle and ammunition to a crewman and reached another from the racks. Big Ig grabbed it and a magazine of ammo. Durman had seen Anton deal with amateurs and pros more formidable than Big Ig and waited for the kick or the chop that would put him away. But Anton only said: 'If you're sure you can handle it, the flying bridge is your best possie—portside. Wait for my word. The bastards can't know we've got bones. They'll be aiming to board us after softening us up. Then …' He handed Durman a rifle and ammunition. 'Pirates.'

'You're playing sitting duck to bring them in?'

Anton stared at him.

Eyes sea-blue.

Sea-deceptive.

'Doc said you'd recovered brain function. I'm not so sure. We've got a ruptured cooling pump line which I wouldn't be surprised to learn is down to someone in Singapore, who also tipped off our friends that we'd soon be easy pickings.'

Durman locked a 30-round magazine on to the Austeyr. He'd test-fired its prototype, the Steyr, in Austria, its country of origin. 'Pity we don't have something with more range.'

'We do.' Anton held an M7 2rocket launcher. Loaded and armed. 'Bastards won't know what hit them.' He led Durman from the saloon. On the way to the upper decks, they passed the Communications Room. 'One sec,' Anton said. 'Got to check on responses to our Mayday. You get topside—bow. And repeat my order, No firing till I give the word.'

When he reached the top deck, Durman's first thought was: dark of the moon, ideal ops night. He was to recall the thought.

The *Norn* was hove to, rolling slightly in a gentle swell, its navigation lights off, the only light starshine and phosphorescence. As he got his night vision, Durman could see a crewman crouched in position behind the bulwark, rifle ready. He passed Anton's word about not firing till ordered. The crewman passed it on. Beyond him was Doc Monroe. And Patsee. Her whisper was unmistakable, vitriolic, intrepid. 'How the hell can I fire if I haven't got a gun. And I'd rather have one than bandages if you don't mind.'

Durman gazed out over the bow. No sign of the pirate vessel. And its guns were silent. Maybe its crew had intercepted a response to the Mayday and sheered off.

A flash caught his eye. And another. A succession of flashes as the pirate vessel appeared to be circling the *Norn*. Amid the hissing immensity of the sea, the brush-fire crackle of small arms—rifles, carbines, burp-guns, sub-machine guns—was incongruous.

Wildly incongruous.

So much noise. So little effect. The bastards were firing high and at a target beyond the range of most of their weapons. Only a few rounds wheep-wheeped overhead.

Anton was right. The bastards didn't know the *Norn* was armed and dangerous. They meant to board and were aiming high as a softening-up tactic without damaging the *Norn*. Bugis from Indonesia? Malays? Chinese? A mix?

A mad, bad mob whoever they were. Their weapons went silent again.

On the flying bridge, Big Ig was in position—portside as ordered—crouched behind the safety rail, rifle ready. Anton emerged from the wheelroom, crouching, and spoke to him.

The brush-fire crackle of small arms began again. And the wheep-wheep of stray rounds. The bastards were circling for sure.

Clockwise.

And closing in?

Durman watched the flashes, listened for the wheep-wheeps and estimated the range at 1,200 metres.

Still too far for the Austeyr. Its designed maximum range was 800 metres. But not maximum effective. At that range it couldn't knock the cream off a Sachertort. Six hundred more like it. And not against Kevlar body armour. Say 400.

The pirate guns were again silent.

He cocked the Austeyr for instant fire.

Anton was beside him. 'Right. You'll be able to hose the bastards away like cockroaches with live steam after I've crippled them.'

He raised the M72 to his shoulder and peered into its sight.

From the flying bridge, Big Ig yelled, voice parade steady: 'Pirate at 9 o'clock.'

Anton swung the M72 on to that vector. Durman glanced up at the flying bridge. Big Ig was standing by the wheelroom door which was open. Clever dick Anton. The wheelroom crew were giving Big Ig a radar fix on the pirate and he was relaying it.

'Pirate at 10 o'clock. Range 1,000.'

But Anton did not fire.

'Pirate at 11 o'clock. Slowing.'

The M72 on Anton's shoulder had a quality of sculpted menace intensified by his whistling quietly.

Durman said: 'Now.'

Anton ignored him and traversed the M72 to follow the target.

'Pirate at 12 o'clock. Stopped.'

To put a rubber-duckie overside and send in a boarding party?

The renewed brush-fire crackle of small arms might have been designed to answer Durman's question.

Anton fired. As the rocket flashed and wooshed from the launcher, the crew of the pirate vessel increased the intensity of their small-arms fire.

And fired a salvo of flares.

The vessel itself was lit up by the flares, riding sleek and black and lethal but untouched by Anton's rocket. Close but no hit.

Peering through the Austeyr's sight, Durman spotted a blue rubber duckie alongside the vessel. He had been right, the bastards had stopped to send over a boarding party.

Into the brushfire crackle came the roar of the vessel's engine restarting. The bastards were turning away from the threat of further rockets. Durman loosed off a burst from the Austeyr. But there were no more rockets. He loosed off another burst.

Under the flares, the vessel was heading back towards the Sunda Strait, its crew continuing to give it unnecessary covering fire.

On the *Norn* there were cheers and louder bursts of gunfire.

Anton looked up at the flying bridge and turned back to Durman. 'You're fault, mate,' he said. 'I did not give the word. You should not have fired your weapon.'

'If you'd fired yours sooner, we would've had the bastards.'

'That was not our main objective.'

Anton's face was exhilarated as it had been at the Australian Imperial Forces Club.

The lineaments of gratified desire.

## 15

In the Chinese Garden, rocks as grey, wrinkled and rounded as elephant hide loomed against the blue enamelled sky and the grey tiled roofs of quiet, timbered pavilions rose from the verdant droop of willow trees.

Durman crossed a humped bridge beneath which carp swam in a pond system fed by a waterfall and rivulets and climbed a twisting rocky path to a three-storey pagoda roofed with mustard-coloured tiles which turned golden in the sun as he approached.

Up there, overlooking the perimeter wall of the garden, the music of the waterfall and rivulets, designed to complement the quietude of the garden, was overwhelmed by the cacophony of the city's traffic, ear-deafening and brain-poisoning.

Outside the pagoda, waiting as he said he would be, was Sergeant Jack Sands.

Thick Mick had been Durman's instant judgment on him.

Then: smartarse cop.

Now, seeing him where he couldn't be taped or surprised, Durman's judgment was: pro.

There was a constant drift of camera-toting tourists around and through the pagoda, Chinese and Japanese in suits and dresses, Australians in T-shirts and shorts. Sergeant Sands led Durman to a small, three-sided pavilion in which were benches set at right angles to each other. 'Used to bring one of my dogs here,' he said. The oldest interrogation move in the book: truth has its own force field—reveal a truth to attract a truth. Durman knew the counter-move. Sergeant Sands took his silence for ignorance and went on: 'Dog—fizzgig, grass, dobber, stool-pigeon, informer.'

Durman said: 'You told me you were ex-highway patrol.'

'And so I am.' On Sergeant Sands' left temple were what looked like a couple of white warts. So far from home and Micks were still in strife. Skin cancers. He touched one of the cancers. 'He was a good dog, that dog—the best. I bent some rules for him and he turned on me.'

'Tricky.'

'It was. That's why I'm also ex-Drug Squad.'

'Trickier. I mean, the name's so ambiguous.'

'Don't try to bullshit me, mate.' The final word was spat out. No friendliness in it. Only menace. Sergeant Sands opened his dark, tweed jacket. The jacket was civvy. The .38 Smith and Wesson beneath was not. 'You've been away?'

Definitely a pro. Enough of a pro not to ask a question unless he knew the answer already. Durman said: 'Yeah, I got back from Perth a couple of days ago. Flew the red eye.' The truth. But not the whole truth. Durman had come in transit through Perth from Broome, the old pearling port in Western Australia which Anton had said was a more discreet landfall than Darwin where the grog-happiness had been spiked with suspicion by illegal Indonesian fishermen and all-sorts of boat people.

'Perth?' Sergeant Sands' tone was sceptical. The scepticism of a Sydneysider dealing with any other Australian city? Or that of a pro interrogator?

Despite the warning he'd been given, Durman tried a measure of bullshit. 'Fantastic place. Incredible. Makes you realise Sydney's the backside of this continent. Perth's the front door. The future—Byzantium to Sydney's Rome.'

Sergeant Sands was no more impressed by this than Durman himself had been when he first heard it from Anton. 'Perth,' he repeated. 'What took you to Perth?'

'Hockey,' Durman said. 'The best players, the best games are over there. And there's a market for them in India and Pakistan. Not big but growing and it all adds up.'

This answer wrong-footed Sergeant Sands. Durman had come prepared. He held out the padded postbag he was carrying. 'Videos—picked them up in Perth. *Olympic Glory—The Golden Years*'.

Sergeant Sands gave the contents of the bag a cursory check. 'Five?'

Durman pressed his advantage. 'Yeah, terrific archival footage. I'm sending them to London to see whether they want to negotiate rights.' But Sergeant Sands wasn't to be diverted. 'Remember the priest at Bart's funeral?'

*Bart's*, Durman thought. And said: 'The midget?'

In the heat of the day, Sergeant Sands shivered. 'The midget was a priest forever—Father Voitre Solovjev. He was killed the day after Bart's funeral.'

The day Durman had flown from Sydney. He didn't ask the precise time of the priest's death. He said: 'Car accident? Or what?'

'Golden bullet.'

'What?' Durman said—although he knew the meaning of the term.

'Heroin overdose. In his case, pure heroin.'

'He was a user?'

'There was a needle in him—vein between his toes.'

'Obviously a secret user.'

Sergeant Sands shook his head slowly, painfully. A front row forward biffed in a scrum. 'No way. There's no way—I can't believe it—no way—he was a user.'

Priest-ridden Mick. Durman's mouth was dry. He can't believe a priest could be a user. He'll be telling me next they don't drink. And heroin was more powerful than grog. Some addicts claimed a heroin rush was better than sex. Which was why after a while, they weren't interested in sex. What's more natural than someone who wasn't getting sex turning to heroin? 'Come on,' Durman said. 'The way he lived, he wasn't getting any.'

The laugh which Sergeant Sands started ended in a sigh. 'How is it I'm always running into guys who never seem to have done without it, who have it every day and twice on Sundays with women who always have orgasms, never headaches? How is it?'

The rendezvous point. The tweed jacket. The fact that Sergeant Sands was working without an offsider. This wasn't official. This was wild card—with Sergeant Sands playing it to get back on the Drug Squad. Durman stood up. 'I'm sorry to hear about the priest's death but when you rang me you said you wanted to see me in connection with Bart Costello's death.'

Sergeant Sands sat where he was. Durman was conscious of the cop eyeing his crotch. That's where the Mick bastard'll grab me if he gets any madder. He took a step back. Sergeant Sands said: 'It is connected, I'm sure of it. And so should you be. You heard …' He stood up. 'You heard Father Solovjev saying he knew Bart didn't kill himself.'

'Only because he didn't want to admit one of his people had committed suicide.'

'No.' Sergeant Sands buttoned his jacket as if putting away an impulse to pull his gun. 'It was because Bart had gone to him in confession, told him what he was involved in. Whoever offed Father Solovjev didn't believe in the seal of confession.'

Durman said—and knew it was too late, too weak: 'I don't know what all this has got to do with me.'

'Common factors,' Sergeant Sands said. 'I'm eliminating common factors. Everyone connected with Bart who was also connected with Father Solovjev.'

'So eliminate me.' Durman turned from the mad Mick's madder eyes and walked away. 'I flew out the day after the funeral.'

'Maybe.' Sergeant Sands was behind him on the twisting, descending pathway. 'But you didn't fly *to* Perth.' Not a question. The statement of a pro who'd done his homework.

Durman kept walking. 'I came here because you said you wanted to see me in connection with Bart Costello's death.'

They were passing through another pavilion and Sergeant Sands ranged himself at Durman's side. 'Only kids try to make lies believable by repeating them,' he said. 'You flew out to Bangkok. And you came here because you wondered whether I might've put two and two together about why you were there.'

Durman had another ready answer: 'Muay Thai.'

But Sergeant Sands was not a pro you could wrong-foot twice. 'Muay Thai, eh? And I suppose you discussed a rights deal.'

'Worldwide.'

'Yeah, I'll bet. But maybe you found time for another kind of business.' Durman got a laugh going. 'Since when has it become a crime to have a massage in Bangkok?'

'Since it became available here.' Sergeant Sands strode on. Durman turned into the souvenir shop near the Chinese Garden exit. His aim was to shake Sergeant Sands off. But after browsing among the T-shirts and postcards and other merchandise, he did make a purchase.

Sergeant Sands was waiting for him by one of the stone lions which guarded the garden. He suggested they have a beer in the nearby Pump House Tavern. Durman refused. But he could not refuse the clutch of newspaper clippings Sergeant Sands thrust into his hand. Even before he unfolded them, Durman knew what they were.

Reports about Big Ig, datelined from round the world.

Aspen, Colorado: He had been seen snow-boarding there, wearing a ski-mask to hide the scars of recent plastic surgery…

Honolulu, Hawaii: He had been spotted riding the Banzai Pipeline, his blond hair dyed black, his style undisguisable…

London, England: He was working as a surf lifesaver in Cornwall.

Other datelines on the cuttings were in France, Switzerland, Morocco, New Zealand, South Africa, Spain.

The clippings Durman read as he and Sergeant Sands walked in the Darling Harbour precinct, its convention centre like a circus big top in steel and glass, its restaurant and shopping complex like a giant conservatory. But largely deserted. Like an overblown film set waiting for Central Casting to send in the crowd extras.

Durman said: 'I remember this as a railway goods yard. Derelict.'

Sergeant Sands ignored the obvious attempt to divert him. 'When a guy like you returns to work in his home town, he can have problems,' he said. 'Cover. No point in using a work name when you're likely to run into old mates.'

Durman handed back the clippings. 'I don't know what you're talking about.'

'No more do I—yet. But I did run a security check on you.'

'Okay. Okay. I'll go quietly. You discovered the unpaid parking tickets I left behind.'

Sergeant Sands put the clippings into the inside pocket of his tweed jacket. 'I discovered your name was in a security-barred file,' he said. 'Top security. Crypt. And I don't have to tell you—do I?—what that means.'

He didn't. It meant he knew that Durman had been some kind of spook and that he was deducing a linkage with Big Ig's escape.

'I'm not looking to arrest him,' he was saying. 'It's just I've got a feeling in my water that Bart's death and Father Solovjev's are down to a drug deal and Ig may have a lead he doesn't even know he has.'

Durman laughed at that. But not in amusement. Sergeant Sands had swallowed the newspaper garbage about Big Ig's escape.

They were passing under a flyover which carried a rumble of traffic above the precinct. On trapezes suspended from the flyover girders, a quartet of acrobats were in rehearsal—juggling clubs, blowing up balloons, clowning. The trapezes were so counter-weighted that when one acrobat rose another was lowered.

Sergeant Sands said: 'You ever have a mate who helped you when it was life or death and then when he needed help you weren't around?'

It was another, more powerful, invocation of the field force of truth. Durman countered again with silence. 'That was Bart and me,' Sergeant Sands said. 'Guess who helped and who mongreled?'

Durman handed him the paper bag containing the purchases he'd made in the shop. 'If you want to see me again, make it the police station. And give me more notice so's I can bring my lawyer.'

'The government's lawyer, you mean.' Sergeant Sands opened the paper bag. 'Well,' he said. 'My favourite police commissioner's.'

He did not move when Durman did. And when Durman looked back Sergeant Sands was under the flyover watching the acrobats raising and lowering each other by their contortions.

Heaven. Durman was in heaven—fisherman's heaven. All the fish he'd tried to catch as a boy were swimming around him, their mouths opening and closing as they spoke their names in childish voices: 'Bream, Leather jacket, Flathead, Mullet, Yellowtail, Whiting, Red Morwong, Rock Cod, Snapper, Rabbit Fish, Pig Fish, Blackspot,

Trevally, Beardie, Tailor …'

The water was crystal to the silver of the fish and he was gliding in it, towed by Big Ig.

Durman knew it was Big Ig because he was chanting the litany of his surf beaches: 'Cherry Venture… Tea Tree… Boiling Pot… Kirra… The Pass… Pippies… Spookies…'

Like some weird angel, the white face of a stingray—flattened, clownish, grinning—passed over Durman.

The crystal water went murky and all the fish vanished—except for a black and white pilot fish.

And it was swimming close under the hungry belly of a shark torpedoing towards him out of the murk.

Murk he knew then was blood.

Blood that flowed from his comrade-in-arms Helen and the delta of her being.

Blood from which came Big Ig, continuing to chant his surf beach litany: 'The Gallows… The Guillotine… Margaret River… Mandalay Beach… Foul Bay… Anvils… Crazies…'

The beach names linked now by an astonishing word.

And the shark was upon Durman, its assassin teeth flexed out to take him.

Durman said the word.

And woke, soaked in sweat.

The sun was stabbing through the curtains of his suite at the Regal Tower. On the bedside table was the bottle of Oban he'd used to drink himself to sleep. He took a pull of it as a heart-starter.

And a memory starter.

Wrong memory.

He rolled out of bed. In the bathroom, the face that stared back at him from the mirror was as pale beneath the beard as the stingray. What he'd remembered was the pain that'd clutched at him in the Gulf of Siam. He grinned against the memory. Sprint or marathon, doc or no doc, life was a dead heat.

Dreams. Durman recalled a lecture by a trick-cyclist, part of a Unit training course. Dreams, the trick-cyclist said, tended to increase in intensity under operation stress and were the means by which the mind dumped unwanted material in a process of psychological prophylaxis.

Early though it was, Durman was not the only hotel guest leaving for a morning run.

Whatever happened to bloated capitalists, he wondered, following a brace of lean executives in jogging gear through the hotel's revolving door.

The run downhill to Circular Quay burnt off the worst of his hangover and he turned towards the Opera House as the sun ricocheted from its cowls.

An early-bird yacht, sails set, got a hoot of encouragement from an incoming ferry and at Man o' War Steps a water taxi was picking up a passenger.

Farm Cove glittered and slapped against its stone retaining wall as he headed along the crescent path to the lookout point of Mrs Macquarie's Chair where a mobile caravaner was brewing up and frying bacon on a portable gas cooker.

Gulls lifted and cried over Garden Island and the numbered, gray hulls of Royal Australian Navy vessels—a patrol boat, two missile frigates and a corvette.

Where were you? Durman asked. Where were you when we needed you?

Wild questions.

Durman was back aboard the *Norn* at the moment when the pirate vessel sheered off.

Summoned to the flying bridge by Doc Monroe's cry: 'Ig! Mate! Son!'

With Anton ahead of him.

Cool Anton.

Durman, running now on the perimeter of the Domain, the common where early settlers had held grazing rights, threw a flurry of furious punches. But he'd thrown none at Anton aboard the *Norn*.

Only nodded.

So where was Anton?

Still going over his op assessment with the Boss Cockie?

Sweet-talking the bean-counters about payment?

More likely rooting himself silly while awaiting their final decision.

Durman let-go another flurry of punches.

On his left, walled off from Woolloomooloo Bay, was a swimming pool—the Andrew Charlton Pool. 'Boy' Charlton, another of Australia's golden swimmers, Olympian peer of Johnny Weiss-Muller and Buster Crabbe. Clarence Buster Crabbe.

Already swimmers were ploughing their ritual morning laps in the salt water of the pool.

Durman had an impulse to join them. He did not. He knew if he did, he would hear again Big Ig's voice, chanting his surf beach litany.

And the word.

Too much.

Sooner he was back in the one safe place, the better.

No rush.

Rush equalled mistakes. Mistakes could be fatal.

The State Art Gallery was as he remembered it: a stolid pile of Victorian classicism, alien in the bright sun, looking as if it had been shipped from Manchester or Birmingham and was waiting for its fog to arrive.

In the portico of the gallery a woman was standing.

A woman sculpted by sunlight from shadows.

A woman in yellow.

Waiting.

But not her.

And not for him.

He'd sought her everywhere since his return.

Querida.

## 16

Durman hadn't handed in his room key before leaving for his run and was by-passing reception.

'Your package, sir.' It was the same Swiss-movement flunkey who'd greeted him on arrival. 'The package you've been expecting, sir.' His smile had lost a degree or two of its permafrost.

Outside Durman's suite the shoes he'd left out for cleaning had been returned, the laces possibly ironed, the arches of the soles definitely polished. Beside the shoes were the morning newspapers.

The package was registered and postmarked New Zealand. Inside it was another registered package, postmarked New York. Inside the second package was a third, postmarked Dublin. This one contained a green Irish passport in the name of Brendan Coyle. Occupation: chartered accountant. The photograph was of Durman. Clean-shaven. He rubbed his beard. Time enough to shave it off when he had assembled the rest of the Brendan cover.

And a bolt hole.

He took the passport and its wrappings into the bathroom. The passport, he tucked into the recess behind the toilet roll, the wrappings he ripped before flushing them away in the lavatory.

His room service breakfast arrived: 'The Bushman's Delight'.

T-bone steak and two eggs. Toast and tea. Billy tea, according to the menu, but served here in a silver pot.

He had to search *AllDay* for the latest on Ig.

> QUEEN GOES TO
> BAT FOR BIG IG
> LONDON: The Queen has intervened on behalf of champion ironman Ian Graeme, known to millions as Big Ig, said a report in the *Daily Mirror* yesterday. According to palace sources quoted by the newspaper, the Queen has made a monarch-to-monarch plea to Thailand's King Bhumipol about Big Ig, now on the run from a Thai gaol. While the outcome of the royal plea is awaited, Big Ig is believed to be hiding in Paris.

The *Sydney Morning Herald* carried a similar story, sourced to a London tabloid but at greater length than the *Telegraph*. The version in *The Australian* was again similar. It also had a long comment piece by someone called Adam Courtney about the unprecedented nature of the intervention and how it was part of a strategy to slow, if not halt, Australia's rush to republicanism.

Durman threw it to the floor with the other newspapers. Garbage. Long or short—all garbage.

He unfolded *AllDay* expecting more of the same.

> WORLD EXCLUSIVE
> PIRATES
> KILL
> BIG IG

Durman crumpled the newspapers into a ball and drop-kicked it into the far corner of the room.

He took a last gnaw at the meat on the T-bone and went to the far corner of the room. He smoothed out the copy of *AllDay* and began to read it, standing.

> Ian Graeme, aka Big Ig, it can now be revealed, was killed after his daring escape from death row in Bangkok. Graeme, 20, died in the finest tradition of Anzac during a stand-off against pirates when his escape vessel broke down off the coast of Indonesia on its voyage to Australia and home …

Durman found himself sitting by the window.

The impact of the truth.

As emphatically the truth as the picture of Big Ig accompanying the report.

Big Ig, head as bloody in death as it had been at birth, lying on the flying bridge of the *Norn*, to which Durman had been summoned by that unforgettable cry of Doc Monroe: 'Ig! Son! Mate!'

Cool Anton in front, knocking off the picture. As cool and quick with the words: 'Stray round. Crazy stray. Mongrel pirates—couldn't hit a door if they had it by the handle. Now this.'

Cool. So cool.

Ordering Big Ig's body over the side.

No flag.

No coffin.

Only the splash of Big Ig's going, with six fifteen-kilo weights from the *Norn's* gym roped to his body.

A bird skimmed the sea as Big Ig went in. For a moment, Durman had wondered whether it could be the bird he'd released. And he tried to recall the words that had startled him during Bart Costello's requiem.

Prisoners. Something about prisoners. Couldn't be.

Doc Monroe's memory was better. He'd recited Laurence Binyon's stand-to verse as the *Norn*, pump line repaired, got under way again.

'They shall not grow old, as we that are left grow old,
Age shall not weary them, nor the years condemn,
At the going down of the sun, and in the morning,
We will remember them.'

Durman remembered then: 'To prisoners freedom.'

And the rest: '… A man like us in all things except sin. To the poor he proclaimed the good news of salvation. To prisoners freedom. And to those in sorrow, joy.'

The midget priest, like a tireless kelpie. A Jesus kelpie. Cool, calculating Anton.

'What this does to your final payment, mate, I don't know. Your contract specifies delivering Ig safe and sound to Oz.' Patting Durman's arm. 'You know I'll do what I can to make the bean-counters see sense. I mean, one stray round. Pirates. Not your fault, mate. You got him out.'

*AllDay* had a spread of pictures and words, recalling Big Ig's ironman and surfing triumphs.

No mention of the *Norn.* Or Anton. Or himself. Now Durman knew where Anton was and what he was doing.

He could see Anton meeting with The Unit's Boss Cockie in The Dingoes' Den to prepare a briefing paper. He could see Anton and the Boss Cockie lunching at the Australian Imperial Forces Club while the contents of the briefing paper were selectively leaked.

The television set confirmed Durman's belief. A reporter was conveying the gist of the *AllDay* report with the barely suppressed excitement of someone who'd just learnt to read.

On the radio, a woman reporter had advanced the story. 'So far the Australian government is refusing to comment on the sensational report, although a source close to Foreign Affairs in Canberra indicated it was substantially correct.'

A source close to Foreign Affairs.

Anton in balls-up control mode, purveying disinformation. Shovelling bullshit to the mushroom media.

Durman, showered and shampooed, got on the telephone to Qantas to confirm his prepaid seat for London.

'I don't want to find myself bumped because of overbooking,' he said.

'Bumped,' the clerk said as if he'd just realised what an obscenity was. 'Overbooking. In first?'

'Bloody oath.' Durman slammed the receiver down.

That clerk would remember him.

When the telephone twittered, Durman assumed it was Anton and yelled: 'The hell do you think you're playing at?'

'Mystery weekend.' Not Anton—Jerry Telfer with an invitation Durman felt he could not refuse.

Not given the possibility that the balls-up control, as it frequently did, stirred the media, including the international pack who would be sure to hit town.

And others.

Sergeant Jack Sands with his two-and-two about Bangkok and his suspicion about what the Crypt file entailed.

Doc Monroe with his eyewitness knowledge of what had happened on the *Norn*.

Patsee Urquhart.

Doc Monroe had needed to sedate her after Big Ig's death.

He would not be able to sedate the media if she talked.

Miss Stud's Eye Ironman's Last Love.

Her Royal Highness, the Princess Celia Von Kronberg.

The international pack would go ape over her.

Durman packed a weekend bag.

All he needed was to run into the tubby guy he'd met in Bangkok who thought he remembered him from Berlin.

Shit-fan time.

Durman knew his native city as only a lover turned hater could. He went to Bondi—by underground train and cab, the easier to shake off possible heel-shits.

Streets of low-set bungalows from a spacious dream of seaside suburbia following the contours of primeval sand dunes and contending against narrow-gutted apartment blocks, their height ratios directly proportionate to the amount of bribery involved in their planning permission.

Tang of salt and pong of sewage. White frangipani and mildewed mattresses. Purple bougainvillea and junked furniture. Pink hibiscus and plastic gutter dreck. Cockroaches and butterflies. Mynah birds and sparrows. Cockatoos and pigeons. Crows and kookaburras. Seagulls and multi-coloured kites.

His bolthole he found back from the take-away smorgasbord of the beachfront. Vindaloo and nachos. Shaslik and roast chicken. Hamburger and noodles. Tabuli and goulash. Satay and calamari. Bagels and flapjacks. Espresso and beer. Tea and wine.

A red-brick bolthole, a small motel which should've had an inferiority complex, huddled as it was next to a luxury, all-suite hotel that looked as though it had been hand-carved from an escarpment of cream marzipan by an artist crazy for balustrades. But the motel retained a certain jauntiness, table parasols and palms outside, a coffee lounge inside and a discreet side entrance.

He paid a week's rent in advance. In the wardrobe of his room, he left the suitcase and clothes he'd bought at the nearby St Vincent de Paul centre—a couple of pairs of jeans and a leather belt, three shirts and a windbreaker—the kind of gear a bushie might carry on a trip to beautiful Bondi.

Good old St Vinnies.

One of the few quarrels he'd ever heard Mum and Dad have was over their local St Vinnies. Mum for. Dad against. 'Typical. Typical. Rags and cast-offs for the poor. Silk and satin for the priests.'

Mum muttering.

Dad querying.

Mum saying clearly: 'All I said was I didn't think your old suit was exactly rags.'

Dad ropable.

It wasn't all Mum'd said.

She'd muttered, 'Jahbulon.'

Not as if it was the sacred word to keep.

But like her genteel swearword: Jabberwocky.

At a newsagent's on the beachfront, Durman bought the noon edition of *AllDay.* He read it in the cab taking him back to the Regal Tower.

> The escape of Big Ig was completely unofficial and unauthorised. It was organised by an anonymous group who believed—many think rightly—he had been framed for heroin trafficking.
>
> Members of this group perished, according to pirate sources, when their vessel went down with all hands after being caught in a cyclone which ravaged the sea area.
>
> No Mayday call could be put out because the radio gear on the vessel, thought to be one of a number stolen from international marinas, had been damaged in the pirate attack.
>
> The Australian Government has assured the Thai Government at the highest level, according to a Foreign Affairs source, that it neither encouraged nor was privy to the rescue bid.
>
> While intimating this, the Government did not seek to hide its regret at the untimely death of a young hero, cut down by cowardly pirate guns, and the subsequent deaths of his rescuers.
>
> The Thai Government has made no public response. It is believed to have formed the view that Big Ig was fated by

> his behaviour to die and that his rescuers deservedly shared his fate. An indication of this view came from a senior Thai official who made anonymity a condition of his being quoted.
>
> 'There is a higher, more powerful court than the Dika,' he said. 'That court's sentence has been carried out.'

The death of Ian Graeme is seen by both governments as the end of an unfortunate episode in their respective histories. Sources predict no long-term harm to the relationship of the two nations …

Anton, master of balls-up control. Durman gave the copy of *AllDay* to the cab driver instead of a tip. The driver was not impressed.

# 17

Out of Sydney in flyover leaps into its suburban dreamlands, out from them in expressway bounds, out and up into the Blue Mountains, Jerry Telfer arm-wrestled the gear lever of his vehicle.

Not the royal-blue Mercedes 260E. A gun-metal blue Range Rover. Hired, Durman suspected. Complete with bulldust.

All the bulldust was not on the outside of the vehicle. Jerry used a measure of it to evade Durman's queries as to the mystery weekender and its owner. 'Ask no questions and I'll give you no PR.' And the vehicle's radio was emitting more bulldust: a DJ who had an opinion about everything and no hesitation in expressing it to those who called him between the music and the ads.

'OTT,' Jerry said, 'Old Titanium Tonsils. King of rock'n'roll, cock'n'bull radio.'

OTT was saying to a caller. 'You may very well be right, fella. Big Ig was certainly an Elvis fan. So it's entirely on the cards, he decided he'd had enough. Let me hit you with an appropriate disc.

The appropriate disc 'Heartbreak Hotel.'

For some reason, Jerry sang the one about blue suede shoes, deepening his voice and hunching and swaying his shoulders, leaving Durman to realise he was in on a fresh offshoot of urban folklore: Big Ig wasn't dead. He'd decided to drop off the wave of fame.

Like Elvis.

If only, Durman thought, if only he could forget Big Ig's head, the exit wound of that stray round, the blood, grey brain matter and white bone fragments.

And Big Ig saying about *Stud's Eye*: 'I had it for the address—you know.'

He must've sighed. Jerry said: 'You sound as if you're not getting enough. Soon fix that.'

They were over the mountains and winding down into the plains beyond, for so long a legend of inland seas, gold reefs and boundless farmlands.

The Range Rover's engine and tyres made a rough symphony with the bitumen and the wind. Jerry seemed determined to go through the Presley repertoire. He was singing the one about the hound dog.

Out of the haze and heat shimmer of the day, a strange building appeared.

Mirage, Durman thought.

'Now that's …' Jerry eased the brim of the new Akubra that covered his wig as if coming into town from droving a thousand head a thousand k's, 'what I call a weekender.'

It wasn't what Durman called a weekender, especially with Jerry reeling off its vital statistics—'ten bedrooms, all bathrooms ensuite, reverse cycle air-conditioning'—his rhythm that of a salesman, his reverence all loyal retainer.

Durman's remembered weekender was a two-roomed corrugated iron shack where white ants rustled in the wood lining like the faintest echo of the surf beyond the sand dunes.

Uncle Ted's weekender, built originally on vacant coastal land during the Great Depression as a refuge from city rents and city hunger—fish in the sea, rabbits in the dunes—and retained, spoils of endurance like any squatter's broad acres.

This weekender was a long, low pink-tiled, white hacienda with a many-arched verandah and a tall, central tower. It was perched on a rise at the end of a broad, shallow valley so vividly green against the dusty, ragged olive drab of the bush surrounding it that its irrigation sprays could've been delivering fresh bright paint rather than water.

On either side of the hacienda's meandering, red-earth driveway, paddocks stitched together with white post-and-rail fences held horses.

More mirages.

Golden horses with flowing silvery tails. And when they whinnied the crows which had inspired the property's name, Warwarnung, gave rusty answers.

'Palaminos,' Jerry said. And again the pride of the loyal retainer made him go on about the property: 'Not huge—95 hectares—choice but—

well-watered—and rich—worth at least 3.5 mill.'

And on: 'Nice 1,880-metre private training track.'

And on: 'Stabling and grazing for 158 thoroughbreds, 96 broodmares and 59 weanlings.'

And on, teasing out the mystery of the weekender's owner. 'Works his hacks hard for all this.'

And finally revealing the name. 'Merv. Mervyn Vesmar.'

Durman's first reaction—as someone seeking to avoid the media—was to scrub the visit and do a vanish.

His second reaction was shrewder: the best place to avoid the media was at a media baron's weekender.

It rose before him. Australian suburbia's mimicry of California subsumed in a single dwelling.

Getting out of the Range Rover, Durman made one of his silent bets with himself: within the front verandah concrete peons would be guarding the doorway.

Again he was half-right, half wrong.

There were peons. But not of concrete. Flesh and blood and eager. Filipinos in white.

'Top spot, eh?' The pride of the loyal retainer was even stronger in Jerry's voice here in front of the house of his lord.

Not his master.

No way.

'Merv's a good mate,' Jerry said. 'A very good mate.'

This was not how Durman remembered Jerry's attitude to Mervyn Vesmar. He wondered what'd changed. Other birds called besides the rusty crows.

Bellbirds.

Their chiming by a trick of acoustics seemed to come from the hacienda tower. And by a trick of memory reminded Durman of the tinkling oyster-catchers on the white shore of the one safe place.

The chiming ceased.

Another bird sound replaced it.

A bird of ill omen.

Chopper.

Its whirlwind clatter sent Durman reflexively into the crouching cover of the verandah.

From there he watched it land.

A Black Hawk.

Not camouflaged for day ops.

Matte black for night.

But without its gunship armament.

As it settled, the Filipinos scurried towards it. No more quickly than Jerry, his Akubra in his hand and his wig being put to an ultimate test.

The first passengers to emerge were Eric Ramsay and Caro. The third was a Chinese who helped a woman to disembark.

The Chinese, Durman did not recognise. The woman he knew: the Princess Celia Von Kronberg, her oiled mahogany tan, gleaming in the sun.

The fifth and sixth passengers were Syl Telfer and Mervyn Vesmar.

Their arrival together made Durman think he knew what had changed. There was Jerry actually tugging his forelock. Sure, it was against the threat of the chopper's whirlwind. But Mervyn Vesmar appeared to take it as no more than the due of man who'd already enjoyed his droit du seigneur.

In the guest cabana assigned to him, Durman had a drink—Cooper's Ale—showered, ignored the bottles in the bathroom after a sniff of one labelled Stud's Eye Aftershave—citrusy, spicy, leathery—and had another Cooper's.

The sky went purple before darkness fell. The swimming pool, floodlit from above and below, shone like some gigantic, square-cut version of one of the blue sapphires to be found in the surrounding countryside.

It drew Durman from his cabana, one of half a dozen set around the pool which itself backed on to the rear of the hacienda where a bar had been set up.

Jerry, citrusy, spicy, leathery, was wearing a white tux, black T-shirt, white shorts and boatshoes which hinted he had a yachting alternative to this bush weekend. He eyed Durman's fresh blue shirt, jeans and black joggers and made no comment so eloquently that Durman said: 'Informal. You told me informal.'

'There's informal and informal, mate. Why didn't you wear bloody thongs?'

The Filipino barman saved Durman from having to answer this condundrum by asking him what he wanted to drink. Durman ordered what Jerry was having and raised his glass. 'Cheers. One thing I miss—a drop of Aussie champagne.'

Jerry didn't raise his glass. 'It's not Aussie. It's French—Roederer Cristal. And anyway there's no such thing as Aussie champagne. It's only sparkling wine.'

Only.

Jerry's Dad had earned his nickname from Minchinbury and Great Western champagne bottles. Now here was Jerry repudiating their authenticity. And further reprimanding Durman. 'Get with it, mate. Where in hell've you been hiding yourself?'

Durman surveyed his company. Not in this kind of hell. He'd thought Jerry and himself and the chopper group would make up the weekend party. Around the pool at least twenty other men and women, dressed as was Jerry with carefully outrageous informality, chatted and quaffed, grouped and regrouped, nibbling finger food and each other. Durman recognised guests from the Sydney Against Drugs bash.

'The Rentas are here,' he said.

Jerry was pleased Durman had remembered his witticism. 'Yeah, some of my A-listers. And they owe me for this one. Merv's quiet weekends are hot ticket.' Jerry's eyes'd been everywhere but on Durman's. Suddenly, he darted off.

Mervyn Vesmar, sinewy, tall was making his entrance. Jerry must've got a line on what he would be wearing: white tux, T-shirt, shorts and boatshoes. With him was Syl, similarly dressed.

No T-shirt.

Durman ordered another champagne. 'Australian.' His eyes challenged the barman to get snotty.

'If I touch you, will you explode?' It was the Princess Celia, her tanned face and body gleaming as from constant buffing with silk which was what she was wearing.

A green halter top, long, wide-cut white pants, cinched with twists of golden scarves, swirling above golden sandals.

She risked taking his arm and guiding him from the bar. 'You get around,' he said.

'But not in your dreams,' she said. 'Unlike Querida.'

Her eyes mocked him yet drew him back to their time together on the *Norn*. They were at the limit of the floodlights, looking out and over the silent sea of bushland.

The silence resonated in Durman's mind with the silence of Bart Costello, Big Ig and Father Voitre Solovjev. Was their silence saying anything more to him than the silence of the bush? He did not need to know. Or want to. But a suspicion was growing in him. He said: 'You've provided cover for Anton before?'

'You mean helped him on one of his shoots?' He nodded. She considered him for a moment. 'Once or twice. It makes a change. A woman can't spend all her life lying on her back thinking of her bank balance.'

'Miss Stud's Eye shares your sentiment?'

'Sentiment isn't the word I'd use. Ask her yourself, she's on the guest list. But don't call her Querida.'

Her title was shonky. Her power real, reminding him of Maree Costello and making him forget her.

He said: 'I'm in Cabana 5.'

She said: 'And I'm No. 7. I must tell you though, I never mix business with business.' Her head did not move. Her eyes did—to the Chinese, dazzling in red tux, red bowtie and red cummerbund. 'I'm in the book. Pleasure Dome. Every day.'

'Including Christmas Day?'

'Only for Santa Claus.' She raised her glass to the Chinese.

Durman followed suit. 'Looks as though Santa's coming early for you.'

'If only he would simply come. But he talks. And if he's as boring in Cantonese about plastic wrapping as he is in English, I pity his family. He's totally obsessed with plastic, plastic, plastic—wrapping everything and anything in it.'

'Including you?'

'Probably. And perfuming me like a magazine page.' She stopped a waiter to get more champagne. 'He's the man who impregnated the pages of *Stud's Eye* with Stud's Aftershave—now third in the market. And the man who wrapped the same magazine in black plastic, slashed to show flesh-coloured plastic beneath.' She gulped the champagne. 'There are creeps who get off on that.'

'What about the creeps who profit from it.'

'Good question. Too good. Who doesn't profit from something creepy these days?'

'Like selling stories to newspapers?'

'If you mean the Big Ig story and *AllDay*, not guilty.' Her eyes were grey. Candid. 'You can't sell a story to someone who already knows it.'

A spoon tinkled against a glass. Jerry was MC-ing the chevoo. 'Merv, our host, our mate, suggests we go into dinner.'

Durman was still absorbing what the Princess Celia had said. She was absorbing more champagne.

Jerry tinkled more loudly and yelled: 'Tucker's up.'

The Chinese had obeyed the first call and now attended the Princess Celia. He and Durman played business-card poker. Durman lost. His card from his shirt pocket had been to the laundry. The Chinese guy's was lucky red and engraved. Horatio (Horrie) Li. Vice-President PlasPacto Division. All Harmony Printing Company, Urn Stones, Taimshatsui, Hong Kong.

Kowloon-side, Durman thought. But no more.

The dining room was panelled in cedar that shone red under the light of three electric chandeliers contrived from antique brass oil lamps. Paintings of racehorses decorated the walls. Houyhnhnms at the Yahoos' feast, Durman thought, as his fellow guests jostled to read the place cards on the tables covered in white linen-and-lace cloths, through which shone dark wood of ancient grain.

To his surprise Durman found himself being helped into a leather chair at the top table by a Filipino waiter. He was between Syl who was on Merv Vesmar's right and Caro Ramsay with Jerry right-marker. On Vesmar's left were the Princess Celia, Horrie Li, a vacant place and Eric Ramsay.

The vacant place was the target of eager eyes at the other tables, set at right angles to the top table to form an inverted U. The vacant place was also the target for Vesmar's anger. Syl passed his muttered question to Durman who passed it across Caro Ramsay's marvellous breasts to Jerry.

'Dead-set bitch. I don't know where she is,' Jerry said. 'Probably so far out of it, she doesn't know what year it is, let alone what day.'

The dead-set bitch was Miss Stud's Eye, Patsee Urquhart. Durman had no need to pass Jerry's message back. Vesmar was saying in his basso-bosso: 'That's it. She's blown her chance for the *Visage* cover.'

Syl's coppery hair lifted, bird wing, as she turned to Durman. 'Merv's new title.' Her voice had a retainer's loyalty similar to Jerry's. But the look in her slumberous eyes contradicted her words. 'Launches next month. Bound to be a hit.'

'Bound to be.' Vesmar laughed, creating an expectant silence. 'Women have a thing about putting gunk on their minds as well as their faces. I'm synergising the two.' He laughed again. And his laughter was echoed at the top table and re-echoed at the other tables, most heartily by a guy Durman remembered from the Sydney Against Drugs bash. The guy with the wrinkled bald head and the fringe of beard who looked like a kid's picture puzzle.

Syl was busying herself with the entree. Some kind of seafood pie. Prawns, oysters, mussels, scallops. Durman ate the pastry. Shellfish for him was Technicolor-yawn stuff.

The puzzle-face guy must have had experience of drinking Russian-style toasts. He was on his feet raising his glass of Cristal in the direction of Vesmar. 'Here's to *Visage* and all who pale at its command.'

Vesmar responded with a toast to: 'Elliott Morgan, mightiest piece of presidential timber in the land.'

Syl joined in the toast and clapped with everyone else. 'The mightiest,' she said to Durman. 'He'd go to the opening of an envelope. And he'd certainly smooth the transition from monarchy to republic as the first presidential queen.'

'Watch it,' Durman said. 'You're tiddled.'

'Not yet,' Syl said. 'Not yet.' And turned her attention back to Vesmar.

The main course was beef. Barons of beef on silver salvers.

'Raised on the property,' Vesmar said. 'But I'll be serving horse if Trigger Finger doesn't win next time out.'

The wine was Penfold's Grange Hermitage, drunk by the other guests with a reverence that surprised Durman. He remembered Dad sticking a red-hot poker in a glass of Grange Hermitage to mull it for Mum when she had the flu while telling her that Dr Penfold himself had recommended this cure.

Eric Ramsay was on his feet for a toast, his voice English mandarin in its penetration. 'To my proprietor, Mervyn Vesmar, under whose aegis *AllDay* has secured a world exclusive of such magnitude that Fleet Street's finest…' He waved a sheet of paper … 'Have gone into their most aggressive knock-it-or-top-it mode. They seek to knock our Big Ig exclusive by saying it is a cover-up and they seek to top it by saying Big Ig was rescued by a group called Flynn's Raiders—Flynn as in Errol of that ilk—pseudonym of the group's leader.'

Durman had seen the Fleet Street pack in operation. But Flynn—in like Flynn—was too much. About three bottles.

Vesmar was responding: 'To *AllDay's* new editor-in-chief, Eric Ramsay, whom I have authorised to top any offer for Flynn's own story from anywhere and anyone, including my peers worldwide, each of whom has created his own peculiar version of news—news as instant, constant television history, news at entertainment even if it's as hokey as the Secret Love Sonnets of Benito Mussotini to Adolf Hitler, news as indiscreet Napoleonic rodomontade lightly disguised as autobiography and news as everything about everyone except oneself. Vesmar laughed. So did his guests. No one seemed surprised at his self-election to the media peerage. The lack of surprise was characteristic. Wealth in Sydney, power, could be as sudden as a gold rush and as blatant as a boot to the head.

Vesmar had an addendum to his toast. He leant forward to deliver it, his raptor's eyes passing over Durman. 'My authorisation is, of course, contingent upon Flynn being a real person and not the figment of Fleet Street's slightly Wappingised collective consciousness. If Flynn exists, he could find himself richer by not less than $250,000.'

Durman's suspicion became conviction. The amount Vesmar'd mentioned was the amount of his payment under his contract. The contract Anton was trying to get paid out in full. And where was Anton? Bedding some bean-counter's secretary most likely. Durman sensed that Vesmar expected some personal response. He turned to Caro Ramsay. 'You must be pleased about your husband's new appointment.'

How such a marvellously—such a generously breasted woman thought she could carry off haughtiness, Durman did not know. But she tried. She looked at him vaguely as if not quite sure who he was, then with definite disdain. 'Thank you … uh… It's no more than he deserves.' She turned from him to Jerry. Durman gulped at the Grange Hermitage as if it were water. And knew he shouldn't. Next op, he thought, next op I stay off the grog until I'm paid in full. Bloody woman. Just because he'd confused her with one of her sisters whose bared twat helped to pay her dress bills.

Syl was ostentatiously concentrating on Vesmar. All Durman could do was eat, drink and pretend to be merry while Horrie Li proposed a toast. 'To my mate, Mervyn—and please note the tone in which I said mate.' He then proceeded to an analysis of how the tone in which the word mate was said could alter its meaning. 'There's the tone which means, "I can't remember your name and I don't care." There's the tone that means, "Even if I remembered your name, I wouldn't use it." And the tone that means, "I'm sorry I wish I could remember your name." Tones of aspiration to friendship. Tones of condescension. The tone in which a man uses mate to a woman. Above all the rare tone in which a man addresses a true mate. That tone is pure gold.' He emptied a sachet into his glass of champagne and it glittered, golden in the light. 'I drink to it now'.

Durman joined in the toast. But something about Horrie Li's words irked him.

Vesmar was again on his feet, responding. '… No two ways about it, my good mate Horrie Li is a packaging genius, and he has subtly reminded us, with his reference to our tonal speech patterns, that we are closer to Asian ways than we think.' He raised his glass. 'To Horrie Li! We've packaged some mighty deals together, mate. And we'll package some mightier deals yet—with a little help from Abe.'

Durman got Abe this time—All Binding Enfolder. But he fastened on *tonal speech patterns.* The kind of phrase Anton would use in one of his lectures. Anton, master of balls-up control, had been talking to his old boss, Mervyn Vesmar.

And Horrie Li.

Durman waved away the waiter, seeking to serve him dessert—bombe Alaska—and the wine waiter seeking to serve him white wine. His refusal was the opening Caro Ramsay had been waiting for. 'But it's Chateau d'Yquem.' Her tone implied NQOC—Not Quite Our Class. She turned again to Jerry. 'Don't you just adore a great stickie?'

The question may have caused Jerry to rise for a toast. 'I won't keep you long. In fact, I can't. This tux I'm wearing is a Honkers special—it disintegrates if I speak for more than two minutes.' Durman wondered which of Jerry's journos'd written that for him. Jerry went on: 'It's hard to say how much I admire MV—our host, our mate, Merv. Very, very hard to say because the fact is I love him.'

Jerry's nose was getting redder and redder. Browner, Durman thought. It should be getting browner and browner. 'Yeah, I do love him. And I'm not ashamed to say it. Sure, he's the Boss. But he understands people, their deepest needs, their dreams, and I love him for it. I really do.'

Jerry downed his glass of Chateau d'Yquem. As Durman wondered whether its cloying sweetness had ever been more aptly matched by a toast, Syl's sudden hand was on his cock under cover of the tablecloth. And under cover of a raucous, Jerry-led rendition of 'For he's a jolly good fellow,' she was saying: 'If you try to pee in Merv's pocket, too, I'll break your bone off.'

It was a bone.

Hers.

At first light, she came for it again.

And again.

And again …

Bellbirds chimed the sun into the cabana as they lay on their backs under the mosquito netting of his bed, remembering their tent weekender of long ago.

'Jerry,' Durman said finally. 'He must be wondering where you are.'

'He thinks I'm serving his interests with Merv.'

'And Merv?'

'He thinks I've gone back to Jerry.' Syl rolled over so that her breasts touched him. 'Poor Merv …'

'Poor Merv?' he said 'What's that, a plea for the tax man?'

She pushed his mouth into the semblance of a smile. 'Fact is Merv hasn't got over his first. There he was, home early from the office, all eager. And there was the ride-on mower idling on the front lawn—with the gardener idling on Merv's wife on the living-room floor. Poor, poor Merv, I think that's what makes him run.'

'The gardener?'

She laughed. 'He lost his column in Merv's gardening rag, *Green Finger.*'

Durman had always remembered her left breast, its in-turned nipple. The nipple was still in-turned. 'No kids,' he said. 'You and Jerry?'

She measured him, her slumbrous eyes unsated. 'You can't conceive in your mouth.'

It was one of the bleakest statements Durman had ever heard. The bleakest was still to come. 'Not like you,' she said. His puzzlement amused her. She kissed him long and deep. 'Oh, come on, the way we … you must remember … after you ran out of your ratty condoms. Raw. You must've realised I'd fall pregnant.'

He pushed her and leant over her. 'I didn't. I had to go. Remember?'

She shrugged and her breasts came together. 'Anyway, I did what you would've wanted me to do if you *had* known.'

Durman said nothing, a cold anger building in him. All his life he'd hated Micks and yet here he was angry that Syl hadn't behaved like one, instead of having a bloody abortion. And it was in that cold, lusting anger that he entered her again.

Sex as a desperation of the flesh.

For her, an attempt to call back a simpler past.

For him, an attempt to obliterate the memory of an unknown woman.

Querida.

# 18

Under the high, killing sun, Durman lay motionless in cover.

Playing the game.

That'd been what Merv Vesmar had called it as they were having their barbecue brunch.

No axle-grease mutton chops. Or burnt sausages.

Beefsteaks cooked to perfection on gas lava-rock grills.

Waffles, eggs benedict, kedgeree and kippers.

Coffee, tea or fruit juices.

Bloody Marys.

Champagne straight. Or in Black Velvet. Buck's Fizz.

Bellinis.

'Let's play the game,' Vesmar had said.

Durman had surmised a form of charades.

Half-right. Half wrong.

It was a dress-up effort.

Australian combat camouflage uniforms.

Water bottles.

And special face masks.

'Hunt or be hunted.' Vesmar's excitment was real. 'Kill or be killed.' He'd put $100 on the table. 'Last one alive takes the pot. IOUs okay.' Durman put down cash. But IOUs predominated, some on business cards, some on scraps of paper. As many women as men had donned the camouflage gear, including Syl, the Princess Celia and Caro Ramsay. Elliott Morgan demurred. Ramsay, fastening a camouflage jacket, had said: 'As a potential Commander in Chief of the Australian Republican Force, you must be in it.'

'Fear not,' Morgan'd said. 'I shall be—as Chief Umpire.'

He'd taken the roll call of those playing and organised the Filipinos who were to act as umpires and display the casualty figures on a blackboard slung from the hacienda tower.

Twenty-two players. Or combatants, as Morgan insisted on calling them while issuing them with whistles for signalling when they were hit. *Hors de combat*, he'd said fruitily. He'd also supervised the issue of weapons. These, Vesmar being Vesmar, were expensively imaginative versions of the Kalashnikov AK47.

Durman had fired the real thing. Yet when Jerry asked him if he knew the weapon, he simply shook his head. Jerry then demonstrated his expertise—and got a laugh—by hitting the Chief Umpire on the arm. He pumped in a new round from the gravity magazine that held the weapon's supply of ball ammunition.

Paint ball ammunition.

Durman raised his weapon to his shoulder and peered through its telescopic sight surveying the terrain.

He'd gone out wide and fast to the far limit of the fence designated as marking the perimeter of the killing ground—about ten hectares of bush and rocks, creeks and ravines.

His appreciation had been that most of the kills would take place close to the hacienda. Shrieks, yells and whistle blasts told him he'd been correct. The Rentas were knocking each other off close to their champagne supplies. Already the number on the hacienda tower was down to twelve.

Durman munched on sausage and bread he'd snatched from the brunch table. The longer he lay up, the easier it would be.

He watched and waited until the figure on the hacienda tower was down to six. Then he threw a handful of dried grass in the air and watched its drift while he took a swig from his water bottle.

Now he was ready to hunt, advancing down-wind of his potential targets. As he eased out on to the wallaby track he'd decided to follow, another whistle blast sounded.

Five players left in the game.

Impossible to move in total silence across that dry-leaf ground.

The trick was to move in rhythm with the background static: the steady hum of the flies, the rustle of the leaves, the scrape of twigs and the bird calls.

Always in the bush, Durman had a sense that so much of it was still untrodden even by those who'd been there so long that their history had turned to myth.

This was a land, haunted as much by the future as by the past. A future more terrible than its past.

Another whistle blast sounded.

Four players left.

A long outcrop of rock, like an upturned boat, angled into the track.

Beyond it on the left, the terrain rose to a low, scrub-covered hill which provided a clear field of fire on to the track.

Ambush point?

Durman halted. Too far out. But he moved off the track to thread his way between the trees in a movement designed to outflank anyone lying in ambush on the hill.

The combat camouflage, mottled in shades of sand and dusty grey-green gum, was certainly effective.

Both ways.

Durman did not at first spot his ambusher. Nor did the ambusher spot Durman. But the ambusher, though he kept quiet and still, did betray himself. Durman had taken care during his advance to keep the wind in his face. From time to time, he risked lifting his face mask and caught the scent of something citrusy, spicy, leathery.

Stud's Eye Aftershave.

It was then he spotted his ambusher and got off a snap shot, ducking sideways as he did so. His ambusher returned fire. Two quick shots. Both went wide. Durman's second shot hit the ambusher smack in the heart area and he felt an irrational satisfaction at the sight of the red paint blossoming on the camouflage. Durman stayed in cover. The ambusher pulled off his face mask and began to blow his whistle. It was Eric Ramsay.

Three players left.

Durman's movement had put him under cover of a ridge, close enough for him to hear the laughter of the casualties making merry.

He reasoned that the other two players would be further out and backtracked along the ridge to where it was split by a gully, dry now but with the trees on either side of it swathed in grass swept there by the rains of winter.

Down into the gully he scrambled and followed its twisting course, halting at each bend to listen for movement.

Ahead and behind.

Nothing.

He moved on. The gully twisted a sharper angle and when he reached this angle he saw that the gully ran straight as a drain for about 100 paces before debouching into a green cup of clearing, dappled with sunlight. He was preparing to move along this straight when he caught the glinting sheen of a spider's web hung across his path.

The trick was not only in moving in rhythm with the background static. It was to move absolutely inside the intensity of the killing exercise.

Like a saint inside a prayer.

And he was doing it. For he was noticing that the spider's web was only partly hung. Someone had blundered into it and the spider was busily repairing the damage.

Beyond the web was a splash of red. Whoever had broken the web had also been shot. The red splash was fresh.

The cup of clearing ahead, and catching the last of the sun, now held menace.

Durman scrambled up the right bank of the gully, aiming to recce the clearing from the higher ground. Moving forward, weapon at the ready, he became aware that only the fly hum continued. Bird calls had ceased, to be replaced by sounds he could not initially identify so out of context were they.

Sounds of pain.

Sounds of pleasure.

By the time he was in position to survey the cup, he knew what the sounds were, yet he still could not believe he was hearing them under the vast blue innocence of the sky.

A couple.

Locked together in the green cup.

Grunting. Moaning.

The masks they wore making them appear like pigs who'd learned to bonk like humans.

The one on top, Durman recognised from his wings of silver hair: Mervyn Vesmar.

Syl.

The bastard's into Syl. Durman's shot smacked red into Vesmar's bare, thrusting backside. Durman pumped in another round and hit him in the back of the neck. Had it been a live round, his brain stem would've been cut. As it was, he lay as if paralysed. To hell with winnings. Durman withdrew, intent only on getting out of Warwarnung.

Too intent.

The round that smacked into the tree above his head was no paintball. And Anton's laugh followed it. Plus one of his lectures: 'The withdrawal phase of a successful op is the most dangerous since euphoria can induce a lack of care.'

Another round followed.. Durman doubled away. He'd been lured into a game so that Anton could play the deadliest game. The third round whipped past his leg, Anton aiming to disable him and give him another lecture before finishing him off and burying him.

Darkness: his only hope. Darkness and sending a boulder crashing down-slope from his line of retreat. He made it to the hacienda carpark. And there was Anton, loading a gun-bag into the boot of the Lancia Durman had been planning to hotwire. 'Wondered how you'd go in a live-firing exercise.'

'Bastard.'

'Come on. Sniper rifle. Three rounds. If it'd been for real I would have taken you down first shot.'

He drove Durman back over the Blue Mountains, the Lancia's headlights cutting curtains of relentless, hard rain never seen in sunny brochures of glossy Sydney. Darkness, hard rain and lightning which, as they glimpsed the distant city, appeared to be powering its monolithic towers into light while thunder rumbled like a prophecy of their fall.

'You're in shock.' Anton drove at high speed although the road ahead in the Lancia's beam and the blink of its windscreen-wipers was as slick from the rain as blackstrap liquorice.

Durman maintained his silence despite the rubbishing. He did not want to set Anton off on another lecture. But when Anton added: 'Suburban shock', he replied: 'Okay, play sophisticate but how would you feel, ex-girlfriend like Syl.'

Anton's hands came off the steering wheel and slapped down again. 'Syl? It wasn't Syl. It was Jerry.' Had Durman's silence been a knife at Anton's jugular, it would not've stopped him crowing.

'Thought you were a trained observer. Obviously, your suburban ethos blinded you to the true nature of that little close encounter. Aussies may moan and groan but only to show how much they enjoy being rogered. Why else do they have more screws—also known as warders, also known as politicians—than any other people on—or off—the planet? Essentially, this country remains a penal colony. Think of the encounter as the kind that has always been part of life in gaol.'

Forget it,' Durman said. 'I'm out of here.'

'Fancy somewhere sunny? I can arrange a contract where the locals have the time and we have the watches.'

'Out of here but not heading there.'

'Understood. Now your final payment's been okayed, you can unzip the world. Not that it was easy getting your payment through, I can tell you.'

'You already have,' Durman said. 'Twice.'

'About the bureaucrats in the Canberra foxtrot, yes—covering their arses while grasping their entitlements with both hands.' Anton's wooden-ratchet chuckle filled the car. 'The latest line is that a pair of nesting desk-rats by manipulating their maternity and paternity leave need never work again.'

'That's three times,' Durman said.

'The circumstances—I have not told you about the circumstances in which I obtained your final payment. I was also dealing with a re-jig of my special consultant's attachment. I am no longer drawing rations from Fort Fumble.' He glanced at Durman to make sure he'd got the reference to the Department of Defence.

Durman had. 'So where are you hanging your cloak and dagger?'

'Arts, Farts and Spare Parts.' The reference was to the Department of the Arts, Science and Technology. 'It is so full of dills, drongos and ratbags with private agendas, no one notices a dim spook.'

'And balls-up cover expert.' Durman was seeking a final confirmation of his suspicion about Mervyn Vesmar.

'You noticed my media strokes. It helps if you've got top contacts. A murmur from mahogany row is worth a million press releases.'

'Maybe. But you leaked disinfo to every outlet except that bastard Vesmar's rag *AllDay*.'

'I hope that's not moral censure I hear in your voice, mate. We all have our little peculiarities.

'You ought to know, you were his minder.'

'Exactly. No more. No less.'

Durman went in hard. 'You gave him the real gen. You gave it to him because he's an asset.'

'Believe me, had you needed to know, I would have told you.' They were stopped at traffic lights. Anton gave Durman a stare. Eyes sea-blue. Sea-deceptive. 'Things change. At the highest level, it has been decided intelligence should be self-funding. How better than through a servo-mechanism like a newspaper company? Especially with add-ons—radio, TV, blogs, columns by ex-pols needing extra retirement funds—even a security organisation.'

'Vigilanz?

Anton sounded the Lancia's horn. 'Better class of vehicle, terrific way of ensuring trained roughies and phonee hackers to help with L's and Q's.'

'You mean P's and Q's.'

I mean what I say: Leads and Quotes. Meat and drink to journos.'

'The twenty-five mill round-robin cheque scam—more disinfo, result of L's and Q's, right?'

Anton was genuinely surprised. 'You should've told me you'd heard that one. The true bill is there *was* a round-robin cheque for twenty-five mill but from an official slush fund and it was returned thereto.'

'Neat.'

'Mossad rules,' you might say. 'Keep things kosher. Changing objectives change methods. More and more my kind of counter-espionage relates to industrial espionage. If war is the extension of politics by other means, industry, business—now the Cold War's given way to the Warm Planet—become the extension of war by other means.'

Durman made a snoring noise. Anton was unstoppable. 'No more brown paper bags of money. The round-robin cheque is only one new method. Consider your own payment. The attraction of the Swiss piggybank I can understand, but if you'd wanted your money in a more discreet way,'

The sum of Durman's life had always been money. He asked the obvious question. Anton said: 'Simple. You're libelled—in *AllDay*, say. You issue a writ, case settled out of court on terms not to be disclosed.'

'In other words, a court-protected pay-off?'

'No flies on you, mate.'

*Mate*. Anton's tone made Durman wonder whether there *were* flies on him. Why was Anton talking so much? And about money? Durman knew his Swiss account was not completely safe. No computer was unhackable. A money trail could always be followed. Had Anton followed his? Followed the regular payments out of the Swiss bank into his other bank? So what? There was a cut-out. No bank account in the one safe place. Only a trip once a month to pick up his running expenses.

Anton was saying: 'You're still at the Regal Tower, of course?'

Durman gave him his full attention again. Anton could be on to his bolthole. 'Where else?' Durman said. 'While the bill's being picked up.'

'And happy to do it, mate.' Anton said. 'Despite everything.'

They were passing over the Sydney Harbour Bridge. To Durman its steelwork had the appearance of a gigantic dark trap. 'If you're in a rush,' he said. 'Drop me in the city and I'll pick up a cab.'

Anton was not in a rush. He insisted on driving Durman to the Regal Tower. And suggested a drink in Durman's suite with a brisk geniality that made refusal impossible. Not that Anton needed a drink. He was high again, which Durman thought was the result of the quasi-combat adrenaline of the live-fire exercise.

As he drank his gin, Anton's manner was casual. His eyes were not. Durman excused himself and went to the bathroom.

When he returned, Anton was standing where he'd been when Durman left.

A mistake.

A hurried mistake.

The door to the clothes closet was ajar. Anton had been checking whether Durman's gear was still there. He refused the offer of a second drink but asked to use the bathroom.

His parting words increased Durman's alertness. 'You have not been to see a medico as recommended by Doc on the *Norn*.'

'I'm okay.' Durman meant he would be okay when he got back to the one safe place. He knew Anton had been checking on him by heel-shitting him. And was letting him know.

Anton was saying: 'You leave next Monday?'

Durman could not resist the sarcasm. 'It's nice to have someone double-checking.'

Anton was not pleased at his slip. Durman was delighted: Anton accepted the authenticity of the booking. He was even more delighted after Anton had gone to find the bathroom had been searched. Anton had not found the Irish passport in the space behind the toilet roll, however. Durman had removed it and tucked it in his waistband under his camouflage shirt.

# 19

The house was at the bottom of a steep zigzag. In the hot sun, the red tiles of its roof and the red bricks of its walls glowed as if fresh from the kiln. It was enclosed in a thick green hedge trimmed in the shape of battlements. Behind the hedge, on either side of the front door, was a bush trimmed into the shape of a slouch-hatted soldier. The brass doorknocker was in the shape of a hand clutching a hammer. Durman, as he'd been told, struck the hammer twice against an underlying rivet and a bell clanged within.

The door opened but only to the limit of a safety chain. Doc Monroe said: 'I'm not buying. Not wine. Not religion. I'm not giving. And I'm not selling this house.' At his bare feet yapped a tiny brown terrier. Cockroach in a fur coat, Durman thought. Monroe went on: 'Down, Ace.' His voice had enough command for a rabid Doberman or a

Rottweiler. His eyes, grey and washed-out, stared at Durman with a kind of wary vacancy, which confused Durman who'd taken a cab, a train and another cab to get there at Monroe's urgent request. He reminded Monroe of this.

'When?' Monroe said.

'This morning.'

Monroe's vacant eyes lit in recognition and he unhooked the safety chain. Durman followed him down a hallway of polished wood. He was wearing an old Australian football jersey, its big gold V and green faded, and a pair of baggy corduroys which gave his backside an elephantine look.

'Beaut spot, eh?' he said as he led Durman into a living room. 'Real beaut.' His voice had a quality of reverie as if he were talking to himself.

Durman agreed. Through open French windows at the far end of the living room was a walled, jungly garden that sucked the hot sun down, turned it green and sent it in cool freshets into the room.

'Lucky, too.' Monroe was still in his reverie. 'Got it for … well, when I tell people they can't believe it. Used to be septic-tank country here until a few years back. The tanker that'd been pumping out the septics was coming down when the driver lost control. The whole shit and shebang toppled off the road onto the roof of this place.' He gave a small wheeze of laughter. 'Talk about a stink bomb.'

Durman was keen to get to whatever the point was. 'You bought it cheap and cleaned it up.'

Monroe's pink cheeks had lost their firmness. They drooped in disappointment at the short circuiting of the anecdote. 'You could say that. But it wasn't easy—even though I had plenty of experience cleaning up shit as a medic—shit and all the bloody rest.'

The living room was shining and neat. Like a barracks for a CO's inspection. Yet a faint latrine smell lingered which Durman had put down to Ace, the cockroach dog.

Monroe was continuing his reverie. 'Triage—now there's something you never see on the TV. Dividing casualties into those for immediate treatment, those for later and those for …' His voice strengthened. 'This place would've been his.' He was looking at a painting on the wall. It was of Big Ig. Blond and tanned, standing on a white beach which merged into a blue sea and a bluer sky. 'Did that before he left on his last trip.'

'He posed for it?'

'In a way.' Monroe fingered his khaki-edged moustache. 'I did it off a transparency he posed for.' He gave Durman a crafty look, as if calculating his ability to keep a secret. 'What you do is project the transparency on to the canvas and then—easy-peesie-lemon-squeezie—it's a matter of colouring in.'

On the wall opposite the painting of Big Ig was one of Marilyn Monroe. Durman said: 'You did that in the same way?'

Monroe's vacant eyes flared. Durman might just have uttered a blasphemy. 'I did that from life.' There was no reverie in his voice.

Durman had seen most of the published photographs of Marilyn Monroe. None of them was like this painting. It showed Marilyn Monroe, windswept in an orange, white patterned mini-tunic with a child upon her hip, and smiling.

A dream fulfilled.

Hers? Durman wondered.

Or Doc Monroe's?

He was insisting on getting them some tucker and Durman realised that Doc Monroe had made the climactic effort of his life in the failed rescue of his Legacy ward Ian Graeme and had been overtaken by age, even senility.

The tucker was cheese and crackers, the cheese in slivers that wouldn't have tempted a church mouse. 'I'll brew up.' Monroe's voice lifted as at some youthful memory. He plugged in a white polythene electric kettle. He got out a single teabag and used it for both cups. Durman was ashamed he'd broken the rule of the one safe place and come to a house empty-handed.

Monroe was dipping the crackers in the tea. 'There's something been worrying me. Niggling.' He held the plate of cheese and crackers out. His voice was back in reverie. 'Fire-fight. Dark as the inside of an undertaker's arsehole. Rain. Heavy rain. So heavy it feels like shit. Warm shit. Or blood. I'm beside this bloke—only a kid, a reo …' Reo, Durman thought. Reinforcement. Vietnam. 'Every kind of shit—mortars, grenades, rifles, machine-guns. Anyway, the reo stands up—maybe to go forward, you know? to show us he had it, maybe … Next thing, he crashes backwards—round in his head.'

Durman rose to go. 'You told me it was something urgent.'

Monroe said: 'Aimed round. You can always tell the aimed round when blokes are panic shooting.' He held the plate out again. 'Go on, I've got tons more.' Durman refused. 'Suit yourself,' Monroe said. And:

'There was an aimed round in all that shooting from those pirates. I know there was.'

Durman tried to achieve something he was unused to—gentleness. 'You imagine there was.'

The crafty look was back on Monroe's face. 'So what about this?' On the plate beside the crackers and cheese, he put a spent round, no longer smooth, encrusted, misshapen. 'NATO round, 7.62 millimetre.' He was trembling with the import of what he was trying to say. Durman had to help him. 'You think this was the round that killed Ig?'

Monroe nodded.

Or trembled.

'Blew away his brains before it exited. On the deck, I found it on the deck. Kept it. Kept it as a souvenir. Every time I look at it, touch it, I can hear that aimed shot. Funny, eh?—pirates using the NATO round.'

Weaponry and ammunition were the most massively traded commodities in the world. Right up there with sex, drugs and rock'n'roll. Durman tried to explain this to Monroe, tried to tell him that there was nothing unusual about the pirates having the NATO round. Monroe became as obstinate as a child. 'It's funny. Funny. Very funny.'

'Are you sure this is the round that killed him? If you're talking 7.62 millimetre, you're talking the FN SLR, and that wouldn't've had the range.'

'Too bloody right.' The archaic vernacular came out of a more assured past. 'But the Lee-Enfield—the old .303 …'

'You just said it was 7.62.'

'Right again. The old .303 was modified to take the NATO round. Sniper weapon.'

Durman walked to the open French windows to catch the full heat of the sun. The Lee-Enfield's aimed killing range, he knew, was greater than that of the SLR. Much greater. But that would need a trained marksman.

Monroe was saying: 'There was a sniper on board the pirate boat. With a nightscope, I reckon.'

The chime of their thoughts made Durman turn. Monroe was where he'd left him. But he was no longer sitting munching crackers. He was standing. And in his hands he had a .303 rifle. Durman made a couple of paces before Monroe bolted a round in and got the rifle to his shoulder.

Rock steady.

Halting Durman.

Monroe said: 'You know. I know you know. I've been told.'

Ace, the cockroach dog, had rushed to yap at Durman's feet as soon as he moved. One-handed, Durman scooped the dog up and threw it, still yelping at Monroe who got off his shot. It punched a last yelp from Ace as Durman—the crack, whine, splat of the round hitting the garden wall in his ears—drove his shoulder into Monroe, knocking him over.

Monroe's frail control broke. He began to sob. Durman unloaded the .303, including the second round Monroe had manged to put up the spout.

The rest of the house was as neat and shining as the living room. Two bedrooms. One—Ig's—had pine bunks and walls covered in surfing posters and winner's trophies. The other—Monroe's—had a single bed. Above the bed hung a slouch hat. The third room was book-lined, its walls decorated with swords, daggers, spears and a set of kukri knives. There was also a gun rack. Three sets of pegs.

Across the bottom set lay an old single-shot, lever-action Martini-Henri carbine. The .303 had obviously been kept here. Was there a third gun?

Durman returned to the living room cautiously. Monroe was still sobbing. But quietly. A kid on the verge of a long sleep after a hard day. Durman found the teabags and made a fresh brew. He also found a packet of chocolate Tim Tams and put half a dozen on a plate.

A mistake.

Monroe said: 'I kept them for Ig.'

Durman thought he would start sobbing again. But he only stared at the corpse of Ace, the cockroach dog, and supped the brew as Durman was sure he'd supped other brews with more than a dog's corpse to deal with. 'Your gun rack,' Durman said. 'Three sets of pegs. You got another gun somewhere?'

'Did have.' The vacant look was back in Monroe's eyes, the reverie in his voice.

'Nice gun?'

'Not bad. Purdey. Twelve bore.'

'Very nice.'

'Yeah, the big cop thought so, too.' Monroe's crafty look was back. 'The big cop who told me about you. Reckoned there was a mega drug deal on. Reckoned Ig knew too much and was taken out. Reckoned you know all about the deal. 'Monroe's steel-grey hair had been oiled and disciplined on the *Norn*. Now it was a mop of steel wool, magnetised by looniness. He was rummaging in a cupboard and held up an entrenching tool. 'Used this when Ig and me went fossicking for gold.'

Durman was more interested in the big cop whose name he did not need to ask. Monroe would know at least one thing: where Sergeant Sands had served. Soldiers always knew that about each other. 'He wasn't with you in Vietnam, the big cop?'

Monroe lifted Ace, the cockroach dog, by the scruff of its neck and examined it. The .303 round had passed right through it, leaving no blood. 'Shock,' he said. 'Shock killed the poor little bloke. I've seen it happen before.'

'The big cop,' Durman said.

Monroe carried the dog into his jungly garden. 'Na, he wasn't in Vietnam. He was on a winning side. The Emergency.'

The Emergency? Durman had to think for a moment. Malaya. Late Forties. Fifties. Early Sixties. Brits vs Reds. 'What about a guy called Bart Costello, did the big cop say anything about him?'

The entrenching tool rose and fell as Monroe used it to hack out a grave for his dog. 'How's that ticker of yours?' Monroe had made a connection he should've made earlier. 'We can't live forever. But there's no harm in trying. Did I tell you to see a specialist?' Durman did not reply.

He was at the door when Monroe caught up with him, and said: 'Like a mausoleum this place, isn't it?'

'No way.'

'It is—a bloody mausoleum. Know what my nightmare is?' Durman shrugged. 'That they'll find me dead in here and brick me up inside like a frigging Pharaoh. And when the last reveille sounds, I'll be trying to get out while all my mates who lie in soldiers' graves will leap up the stairs of heaven.'

Durman found himself patting Monroe on the head as if he were a child. Poor old guy. Half senile. Half love-sick for his dead fantasy wife Marilyn Monroe. And all mad with grief for his dead Legacy ward, Big Ig.

Outside with the sun hammering his own head, Durman had another thought. It was Sergeant Jack Sands who'd stirred the poor old guy up—Sergeant Sands, quietly running amok, trying to get back onside by chasing wild mega drug deals.

Durman was sure of it.

Half-right. Half wrong.

The public telephone booths alongside Bondi post office were busy. Mostly kids. Some squatting cross-legged on the street at the full limit of telephone cords, others sharing a telephone and an embrace. Durman walked away. Telephoning was a mistake. He knew it. He'd checked Anton's word. The final payment was in. For sure. And he was on his way out. Yet the closer he got to leaving for the one safe place, the more he identified it with her. Its lonely beauty, wild serenity and clear regard were hers.

Querida.

He turned back towards the telephones. If one were free, he would ring. If not, scrub.

Waiting for an *AllDay* switchboard operator to contact Normie McLaine, he told himself he was preventing a bigger mistake: going loony like Doc Monroe and ending up alone, burying a dog in a backyard.

The operator took so long to get through that after reintroducing himself to McLaine, Durman said: 'I'd hate to be reporting the start of World War III to you guys.'

'Four. World War Four,' McLaine said. 'The Napoleonic Wars were World War I. Read Fregosi's *Dreams of Empire*.' Durman had no chance to respond to this pedantry. McLaine said: 'Hang on.'

Durman could hear another voice yelling: 'Just cut the arse of it and bung it over. I'll do the bloody head.' When McLaine came back on the line, Durman had to remind him yet again who he was. 'You could've picked a better time, mate.' McLaine's growl was that of a dog disturbed on a bone. 'I'm trying to make sense of an A to Z of politics which seems to have no P.'

Anticipating a suggestion that he should ring back another time, Durman rushed into an explanation that he needed to see Bart Costello's daughter—an explanation made no easier by his embarrassment. He finished lamely: 'I didn't really get a chance to offer my condolences after the funeral.'

'Condolences?' McLaine's cynical tone made the word sound like a brand name for a condom.

'That's right.' Durman could not slow up. 'I was talking to you if you remember, went to get you both a drink and when I got back you were gone.'

'You took so long we thought you were skint.' Durman managed a laugh though he was imagining McLaine's droll's face with one end of the telephone sticking out of his mouth and the other giving him a new Adam's apple. 'So I owe you both one.'

McLaine was shouting at someone else: 'P—comes between O and Q. I want it yesterday.' To Durman, he said: 'Must go.'

'I need to see her,' Durman said. The plain truth. He did need to see her. Absolutely. And forever.

'Spike and Spigot,' McLaine said. 'Midday tomorrow.'

On his way to the Spike and Spigot, Durman passed the *AllDay* office.

Office and printing works. Ugly. Ugly enough to have been built by a cross-eyed kid given a fleet of concrete mixers to play with instead of a bucket and sand.

Turd-coloured concrete rising in a cluster of towers of varying heights from a podium.

An attempt had been made to gentle the childish brutalism.

The podium where it wasn't sheathed in green marble was sheathed in tinted plate glass.

Through the plate glass, Durman could see down into a basement level and across into the ground-floor level.

In the basement were the printing presses. Like mighty ships' engines with their ladders and catwalks, their shining steel and brass and their crew of dungareed machinemen. He pressed his hand against the plate glass as others were doing. It was vibrating from the run of an edition.

On the ground floor level was what Durman took to be the newsroom, a vista of high-tech word processors, their screens glowing eerily through the tinted plate glass, creating the impression the men and women sitting before them in chromium chairs were seeking to warm themselves at some weird, chill fire.

At the main entrance of the building were guards. Durman recognised their uniform: the dark brown and red V of Vigilanz Security.

## 20

The Spike and Spigot was on the slope of the hill crowned by the barnlike St Simon's. Durman wasn't surprised. Dad had always said Micks established watering points to stop them perishing of thirst climbing the hills where they built their churches.

Remembering Dad, Durman ordered a middy of Resch's before finding an empty stool and table. Resch's had been Dad's favourite beer until Resch left his fortune to the Micks.

At an adjacent table, a spry old girl with the air of a duchess down on her luck was wrestling with a copy of *AllDay*, her tongue out as she wrote in the newspaper and sought inspiration in her glass of sherry. 'Five across,' she said. 'Pseudo-fish did for King John.'

'How many letters?' Durman said.

The old girl gave him a haughty stare. 'This used to be the Ladies Lounge,' she said. She continued to wrestle with the newspaper, muttering her way through clues across and down, occasionally writing in a word. 'Bland Boy rocker,' she said. 'Anagram.'

'Bob Dylan,' Durman said.

'Never heard of him,' the old girl said.

'And if the pseudo-fish is seven letters, it's lamprey.'

'When this was the Ladies Lounge you didn't get pestered by know-it-alls.' The old girl went to the section of the pub reserved for Tote punters. Along with most of the others in the bar, she watched a colour television as a race was run, tore up her ticket and passed Durman on her way out. 'You're forgetting your newspaper,' he said.

'Isn't mine. Bloody rag. Form guide's worse than the puzzle and the shopping guide's worse than both.'

Durman retrieved the newspaper. He didn't get as far as Jackpot Crossword—NOW $35,000 BE IN IT TO WIN IT. He was halted by the picture of Patsee Urquhart on page 3.

Perky.

Smiling as she had in life.

But surely not in death.

Framed by the headlines:

> Retriever's ghoulish find
> COVER
> GIRL'S
> BODY IN
> LAKE
>
> Police scuba divers recovered the naked body of top cover girl Patsee Urquhart from one of the Centennial Park Lakes today.
>
> The recovery of the 26-year-old former Miss West Australia's body followed an incident in which a cocker spaniel in the park with its owner chased a duck swimming in the lake.

To the horror of the owner, the dog fastened on one of the body's wrists.

'All I saw was this hand rising from the water,' said the owner who preferred to remain anonymous. 'I screamed. It was as if the hand was waving for help.'

The owner then contacted the park ranger who in turn contacted the police.

A police spokesman said there would be a post mortem and that investigations were continuing. Teams of police were carrying out a search in the area around the lakes.

The body, identified by Patsee's trademark tinted hair, is believed to have been in the water for some time and had already been attacked by the eels which infest the park's lake system.

Patsee Urquhart first won fame as Miss West Australia. She went on to carve out an international career as a much sought after cover girl, known in London, Paris, Rome and New York as 'the kook from Oz' before baring all for Stud's Eye.

The kook from Oz.

Or cokehead?

Durman remembered meeting her at the Sydney Against Drugs bash. She'd been away with the Colombian pixies. And on the *Norn*. And not meeting her at Merv Vesmar's place. Was that why she hadn't shown? Was she already eel-bait? He was still staring at her picture when McLaine arrived, simultaneously apologising for being late and urging Durman to get him a drink. 'Guinness. And tell the barmaid I won't mind if she warms it between her tits for two minutes.'

The barmaid was wearing red dungarees. Durman ordered simply the Guinness and another Resch's.

McLaine raised the glass, took a sip and pulled a face. 'Still too cold. My fault. I should've told you three minutes. By crikey, I'll be glad to get south where you can at least have your Guinness at body temperature in winter.'

Durman, who'd expected Costello's daughter to be with McLaine, tried to restrain his eagerness. 'Ah, yeah, your antiques gallery. Is it still on?'

'On? It's imminent. And don't expect me to say I'm sorry—not with Merv Vesmar well on his way to becoming another Tyrannosaurus

Rex of media. The brain's there all right but all it can do is make the arsehole executives twitch.' McLaine's droll's face was gloomy but his eyes had a lurking glint. Slings and arrows, outrageous fortune, were his stock-in-trade. 'You were an executive,' Durman said. 'Your arsehole twitch?'

'Yeah.' McLaine's face became more mournful. 'And I was starting to like it. But no worries. Last shift tonight, free tomorrow and then you won't get me to look at anything newer than Victorian—and I don't mean the beer.' All the time McLaine had been talking, he'd been glancing at the copy of *AllDay*. 'What a waste,' he said. 'The beautiful kook from bloody Oz.'

Durman agreed and said he'd met her. McLaine said: 'Met her. I knew her when she was a pearl. Now she perishes on a midnight picnic. A picnic.' He saw that Durman was confused. 'Yeah, that's the latest.'

'She went solo on a midnight picnic?'

'Her? That pearl. Not even in this city. The cops reckon there was a guy with her. They get a little pissed, decide to go for a little swim, she gets into a little difficulty, the guy gets a little panicky. Eels ain't fun. And …' He finished his Guinness. Durman waited for him to offer to buy a round.

And waited.

But McLaine's meanness principle was stronger than his own. He picked up the Guinness glass. 'Make it four minutes,' McLaine said.

When Durman returned with the fresh round, McLaine spoke as if there had been no interruption. 'Cops got a tip-off from a caller who was in the park, saying he'd spotted a couple near the lake picnicking, frolicking naked.'

Frolicking, Durman thought. McLaine must've been thinking on a similar line. 'More like bollocking,' he said. 'The cops've appealed for the caller and/or the guy to come forward. Love cops—dote on them—when they're naive. There's as much chance of the guy or guys coming forward as there is of me raising the ghost of poor old Paddy White from his ashes in the park.

The pub was beginning to fill with counter-lunchers. Durman looked at his watch. 'She's joining us for lunch, is she?'

'Not her.' McLaine was finishing his Guinness as he headed for the door. 'She's not a Sally Ann into boozers.' He handed Durman his empty glass. 'But she is into generosity and all that.'

The tin-roofed, brick shed might have been a stable in a previous existence. Now, according to the white, spray-painted sign above its double doors, it was: HEADQUARTERS COSCOOP PROPRIETARY LIMITED—FASTEST GROWING MEDIA COMPANY IN BRICKPIT LANE.

Big-wheeled rubbish bins, lids hiding their contents, waited in the lane for a compactor truck. McLaine unlocked a wicket gate in the shed's double doors. He had to push. The shed was crammed with paper, bales of newspapers piled man-high, bundles of magazines, steel shelves packed with folders from which cuttings straggled and books, books, books, in shaky columns, on shelves, on chairs.

There were no windows. The only light came from an Anglepoise lamp focused on a table which was littered with more books and papers. At right angles to the table was a pinewood desk and next to it was a grey trolley on which was a typewriter.

She was seated at the trolley, typing, on her head a set of earphones plugged into a tape-recorder.

Above the table was suspended a shelf with four alarm clocks on it.

All stopped.

All showing different times.

McLaine moved sideways to come within her peripheral vision. Durman followed him and saw then that she was weeping as she typed. McLaine reached out and touched her on the shoulder.

One finger.

She looked round, her dark hair, backlit by the lamp, an aureole about her honey-coloured face. 'Normie.' Her starbust smile came and went. 'I did what Dad told me. I listened to the silence.'

For weeks Durman had been aware of the silence of Bart Costello speaking to him. Hearing her use the phrase confirmed his sense of her as the always-known stranger.

She took off the earphones and stood up, shaking her head to smooth the tangle of her hair. Her black polo-neck blouse emphasised the brownness of her skin. Her skirt was black-and-white houndstooth check, her stockings black and her shoes. She did not hold out her hand when McLaine reintroduced them but only said: 'I remember.' For which Durman was grateful. His heart pounding to the tips of his fingers.

McLaine was saying: 'The silence. He told me the same thing. I thought he was—you know?—raving.'

She disconnected the earphones from the tape-recorder and hit the reverse-wind button. The tape went gibbering back to the beginning before clicking off.

Everything she did had an easy grace. She went towards a fridge, dim in the far corner of the shed. When she opened it, its light illumined the corner and the single bed that stood there like a promise.

'Wine, red or white, or beer?' she said. 'Beer or wine, white or red.'

The gentle amusement in her voice told Durman that she was repeating a saying of her father's. She brought back what they requested: white wine for McLaine and beer—Cooper's—for Durman.

Nothing for her herself.

'Listen.' She pressed the tape-recorder play button. 'Listen to his silence.'

The hissing silence of blank tape lasted for at least seven minutes by Durman's estimate. Then came a staccato sound he could not place until she looked upwards at the roof.

Rain. Rain drumming on the tin roof.

Bart Costello's voice when it came sounded drunken, drunken in song.

A medley of fragmented Irish balladry in which the pipes, the pipes were calling and the pale moon was rising above the green mountains for the days of the Kerry dancing in the garden where the praties grow.

McLaine said: 'Crikey, I know this means something to you, darl …'

She held up her pale brown hand.

No ring.

'Jesus.' Bart Costello's drunken voice was gone. 'I pressed self-destruct. But I'm not destroyed. And you're the difference.'

A kind of prayer for she bowed her head. Bart Costello was a pro, dictating his story: 'Sydney from its foundation has been essentially a plutocracy, its veneer varying between the penal and the democratic. This plutocracy in serving the public interest—code for servicing the interest rates of its financiers—has always enjoyed the privilege of a currency alternative to money. Initially, this was rum—grog, vernacular for alcohol.

'Today the alternative currency is other drugs, especially heroin. And media baron Mervyn Vesmar is the most ingenious and wealthiest broker of this alternative currency—a great white pointer, constantly on the move in this city of sharks, undeterred by the net of anti-crime and corruption bureaucracies of which the Crime Commission Intelligence

Office is the latest…'

He was hearing the truth about Vesmar's organisation. Durman knew it. The truth he'd been clued on but failed to see. As he'd failed to see the real nature of the op. Doc Monroe had sussed it out.

Not Big Ig's rescue.

His delivery to execution.

And silence.

The silence also ensured by the deaths of Bart Costello himself, Father Voitre Solovjev and—had to be—Patsee Urquhart.

Yet before he'd been killed, Bart Costello had played a hunch: since independent circulation audits were not obligatory, the self-reported circulation of *Stud's Eye* could be inflated, to cover profit margins—which included secret drug-deal profits—the pattern for all Vesmar magazines.

Ingenious was right. Vesmar'd created a closed-circuit drug-smuggling and money-laundering organisation with its own security. The Unit *had been* reactivated. But privatised as Vigilanz Security.

Durman wasn't tasting his beer, he was tasting self-disgust. Anton had bullshitted him into believing he'd been hired by *the* government. It was *a* government, one of the world's secret power structures, the Tetra Triads, the Twin Ts, linking triads in mainland China, Taiwan, Singapore and Hong Kong. Vesmar was Twin Ts backed. The round-robin cheque'd been a Twin Ts cheque.

Hence Horrie Li with the impressive Honkers address.

*I had it for the address—you know?*

Big Ig hadn't been carrying *Stud's Eye* for a wank.

Or a call girl's address.

But for the address of the All Harmony Printing Company, PlasPacto Division, Urn Stones, Kowloon-side.

'End it,' Bart Costello's voice said.

From the dead.

McLaine was pro enough not to express surprise. And pro enough to ask the key question. 'Anyone else heard this stuff?'

'No one except you.' Her eyes held Durman's. 'And Uncle Jack.'

'Uncle Jack!' McLaine's emphasis was half envy. 'Just because Bart and him were in that wild mob together. Make no mistake, he's on the outer. This stuff's his ticket back.'

Sergeant Jack Sands. Still running quietly amok. Durman waited for her reaction. She said: 'That's got to be good.'

'Not as good as me getting it into print first,' McLaine said. 'I mean he's probably tipped it into some top cop's earhole already. And you know how long it takes a top cop to leak—about as long as a bub in a fresh nappy.'

'This Crime Commission Intelligence Office—what about it?'

Durman's question made McLaine frown. Not a guy who liked to miss a point. 'Could be. A secondment to the CCIO would make Sandsie as happy as a pig in shit.' McLaine was at the trolley. 'Good-o, you've done a black.' He was gathering carbon copies of the transcript. She found him an envelope. 'You're going to slip it to the *Herald*?' His droll's face fell in disgust. '*The Australian?*' More disgust. 'Where then?—the *Financial Review*?'

'Oi'm ethical, Oi am.' He was moving towards the door. 'Must get it into me own newspaper, right? And that's still *AllDay.*'

'In your dreams.'

'And yours. When you read your *AllDay* tomorrow, listen and you'll hear your father and me having the last laugh together.'

From the lane, they heard a single yell: 'On ya, Bart!'

Durman was conscious of her every move as she made a beguiling dance of the humdrum by returning to the tape-recorder. 'Normie didn't listen to all the silence.' She turned the tape to its other side. Again a hissing silence came into the room. And again Bart Costello's drunken voice, howling. He was in London, a wonderful sight. She said: 'We loved London.'

Durman said: 'You lived there?' She nodded and told him about it—the flat, the garden square behind it, the school she went to and the church—her voice more entrancing than her father's who was howling about people not growing potatoes nor barley nor wheat but gangs of them diggin' for gold in the street and the hills, the hills of Donegal so dear to him.

No drumming rain. Recorded at a different time? 'I've had a whisper Vesmar has hired a specialist. Name: Ross Durman. I've checked the cuttings. Nothing. He's due in Friday morning, ex-London. How he fits in, I don't know. Yet.'

She clicked off the tape-recorder. She did not need to ask how Durman fitted in. He told her. Astonished he was doing it.

Yet delighted.

Everything.

The death of his comrade-in-arms Helen. His expulsion from The Unit. His break-out ops. The encounter with her father. 'I hit him. Twice. Kidney punches.'

'You didn't kill him?'

What could he swear on? His love for her?

'Not guilty.'

'Someone did. Uncle Jack says …'

'They were together? He and your father? In the army?'

'Not exactly together. Dad was freelancing in south-east Asia back then and used to go out with the mob Uncle Jack was with. Parachuting into the jungle. Right into the trees. Big trees. The canopy. Then they lowered themselves on ropes.'

Durman had heard of the technique. And of the mob that devised it.

She was saying: 'Uncle Jack got snagged and one of the guys they were after was going to kill him.'

'Your dad intervened?'

'If you call falling on someone from a great height intervening, he did.' She laughed. 'Anyway, it did give Uncle Jack time to unsnag himself.'

Her laughter, her phrasing were an echo of her father's. Durman could imagine the gut-wrenching terror of the incident, the split-second courage, and knew the memory of them continued to drive Sergeant Sands.

She was not to be diverted from the point she had been making. 'Someone did kill Dad—the same person, Uncle Jack says, who killed Father Solovjev.'

Person. Durman moved towards her. Sergeant Sands must be losing it. Taking out Bart Costello and Father Solovjev would've been at least a two-handed op.

Anton.

Durman had seen it on his face. The lineaments of gratified desire. Not once. Twice. At the Australian Imperial Forces Club. And at Merv Vesmar's place. First, after the killing of Bart Costello. Second, after the killing of Patsee Urquhart—whose death Maree did not seem to have connected with what was on her father's tape.

And Anton was out in the city.

Anton and his necessary offsider, targets in their minds.

Maree.

The big green bins in the lane.

A layer of rubbish on top of her body.

The bin being hydraulically tipped into the compactor truck.

The truck dumping its load on one of the city's rubbish tips, followed by other trucks dumping their loads.

And a bulldozer covering the rubbish with topsoil.

He moved towards her.

'No,' she said. 'No.'

Fear in her voice. She had read his murderous thought. Yet misread his intent. 'I only want to protect you.' He looked around the shed. 'You can't stay here.'

'I'm not.' She made her way between bales of newspapers and columns of books to a door at the other end of the shed. She opened it and sunlight shafted in.

The door gave on to a backyard where a lemon tree and a Norfolk Island pine fought for space with a brick barbecue and a Hill's hoist bedecked with drying laundry. Beyond the pine rose the back of a terrace house—three storeys. 'I'm staying there with Normie,' she said. 'And Beth, his missus. They rented the shed to Dad.'

But Durman, still not sure she would be safe, wanting to convince her that he could protect her, broke the need-to-know rule by which he'd lived. And told her of the one, safe place.

Its name.

Its location.

'It's like you,' he said. 'You're my island.'

The bright Australian sun put a sheen as of velvet on her brown skin. 'I belong here,' she said.

'At least have lunch with me.'

'Too late.'

'Not now.'

'There's something you don't know.'

'We can celebrate Normie's scoop.'

From the terrace came a sound, startling in that urban setting, the ancient Aboriginal call of the bush: 'Coo-ee!' Which she echoed and re-echoed: 'Coo-ee! Coo-ee!'

Durman put his hands over his ears in mock distress.

She said: 'Beth's not as nimble as she was. Must've heard a rain forecast. I've got to get the washing in.'

'Lunchtime.'

Her nod was barely perceptible. Durman, like most men a believer in the power of posh over women, nominated the Regal Tower. 'You're sure you'll be all right?' he said.

Her starburst smile flashed as she made another dance from the humdrum at the Hill's hoist. 'Absolutely,' she said. 'I can become invisible when I want to.'

## 21

Along Bondi beach a red and white helicopter cut discs of sunlight as it swooped and banked on a shark-spotting flight.

Should be flying a grid-search pattern over the central business district, thought Durman, on what he'd made an obligatory run when he was staying at the bolthole, followed the sloping road to the steps which led to the cliff path.

On this low section, the limestone rock was undercut and hollowed by aeons of king tides and the path was slick from the seepage of underground springs. Out at sea, a couple of skindivers were spearfishing.

The path curved and Durman had two sets of steps to climb to reach the high section. Exactly the exercise he needed for the harvests ahead in the one safe place: digging spuds, hay-making, peat-cutting and bringing in the sheep from the hills.

He was not alone on the path. There was a two-way traffic of walkers, local and foreign. And other joggers: lissom young things, colour-coordinated from headbands to running shoes, matrons who looked as if they could make better speed with a supermarket trolley, and any number of guys, many in footy jerseys, some, as he was, carrying handweights, others formidable beer guts.

On the high section, the path curved and dipped and rose, narrow and unfenced along sheer cliffs against which the Pacific breakers growled. The view was clear south over the Waverly Cemetery headland where good surfers go when they die, south over Tamarama, Bronte, Coogee, Maroubra.

The names brought back the memory of Big Ig's chant in the Gulf of Siam. Durman touched the belt of the black bumbag he was wearing, the belt Big Ig'd used to tow him.

Southward beyond Maroubra—Aboriginal for where the shit hits the sea—the land resolved itself into a dazzle of light and a blue haze.

Last time, he thought. When he left, he would be heading north. And he still had a chance to persuade Maree to join him. Better than even chance. She, too, must know this was a city forever trapped in its criminal origins, its caste system, its privileges those of a gaol.

Merv Vesmar and his organisation were still untouched. Normie McLaine had bombed out. There had been nothing in the *AllDay* first edition.

Not a line.

And nothing in any of the other local newspapers to which McLaine, forgetting ethics, might've slipped the Bart Costello stuff.

Nothing on radio.

Nothing on television.

The city was still clammed up on its giggle as it had been clamming up since its beginnings. What was it Bart Costello had said on his tape? 'Making heroes of self-serving sheep-shaggers like Macarthur and monsters of honest men like Bligh.'

Total clam-up.

Unless Sergeant Jack Sands could come through. And pigs might fly to join the angelic host. If Bart Costello was right, cops were among the heroin inheritors of the Rum Corps who'd created the first alternative currency.

Durman paused, jogging on the spot, to study an Aboriginal rock carving.

A great shark with a smaller fish in its belly.

Sydney.

The Aborigines had seen it coming.

Durman heard it.

He'd resumed his run and was on a section of the path which closely paralleled the cliff edge. Behind him he sensed another jogger.

Heavy guy from the sound of his feet.

Aiming to pass.

Inside.

Durman broke stride.

The guy's shoulder charge did not quite make full contact. Over-confident dill. As he stumbled sideways, he began some deathless line. 'Anton …' Durman's foot went out and clicked the guy's heels together. The stumble became a fall.

A fall over the cliff.

A fall as silent as a dream.

Like Bart Costello? Durman was already turning on the question.

Offsider.

There had to be an offsider.

There was.

A young hoon, built like a brick shithouse, product of the natural selection of the city's league football.

Bred for bursts round, over or through opponents.

He ducked to go for Durman's balls and throat, aiming to spear tackle him over the cliff. Durman swung a handweight. Once was enough. The hoon's jaw cracked and he went down screaming. But he got to his feet, reaching round to his waistband. Durman hit him again with the handweight, dropped it and took the weapon the hoon'd been reaching for. Neat handful. Bad boy, carrying a weapon on what was obviously a bare-knuckle job. He was supposed to have gone off the cliff as if by accident.

The violence, as it does, had created its own suspension of time. Suddenly, a woman was screaming in fear. And a couple of dogs were yelping. Durman shoved the weapon into his bumbag and started to run. 'Got to call an ambulance.'

Another jogger held up a mobile phone. 'Already have, mate. And the cops.'

Weird.

There was more warning than condemnation in the jogger's voice. Durman knew he had to get off the path.

Pronto.

On the landward side, houses and backyards overlooked the sea. No way he could risk a shemozzle by cutting through someone else's property. As he ran, dodging joggers, he hurled his other handweight into the sea.

Anton'd always been mad as a meataxe. But controlled. What'd set him off? McLaine caught trying to get the Bart Costello stuff into *AllDay*? Had he revealed details of the meeting with Maree? The banshee screaming of an ambulance siren was approaching. On the landward side, wooden steps were built into a grassy embankment. Durman climbed them and found himself facing a playing field.

And a couple of cops.

Glocks still holstered.

His hand moved from the bumbag. One of the cops gave him a black-shades stare before going back to the main event: a kid with a brightly coloured kite. 'We've had a complaint, mate. Your kite's making too much noise.'

His offsider's two-way began to squawk. Durman sprinted for the road bordering the playing field, crossed it and found himself in a street at the end of which was the main road.

Buses. Cabs.

He'd already accepted that his bolthole was out. Anton's hoons had been wearing lightweight tracksuits. Odds were they'd pinpointed the bolthole and heel-shitted him from there.

Going through the revolving door of the Regal Tower into its enveloping sumptuousness gave Durman a sense of safety.

Illusory, he knew.

Exactly how illusory was made clear by the message handed to him by his favourite Swiss-movement flunkey.

Heavy envelope.

Heavy writing paper.

Heavy message: 'You're dead.'

The Swiss-movement flunkey was waiting and Durman could've sworn he heard the sound of the flunkey's brain moving on its bezels. 'Delivered five minutes ago, sir.'

His hesitation on sir was millimetric. 'You have a guest waiting.' His eyes had a blank unfocused look as he indicated with his head the direction Durman should take.

Maree was sitting in one of the foyer's peacock-backed cane chairs, facing the revolving door. He should've spotted her when he entered.

But she *could* make herself invisible.

Simple trick. She had exchanged an admired individuality for an ill-regarded stereotype. He apologised for not noticing her, realising as he did that he was failing a test. 'Let me get you a drink while I change for lunch,' he said.

'I'm not having lunch.'

But she *had* changed. Her dark hair was covered with a black crochet tam-o'-shanter. She wore a green jacket of some fake fur which looked as if she'd skinned it with a blunt knife from a wild studio couch. Under this, she had a dark grey, pink-sprigged dress. Her feet were bare in brown leather sandals from a time before bubblegum joggers.

He sat in a chair across from hers. 'You agreed. You agreed to have lunch.'

'I agreed lunchtime. I've got to go, Normie says and …'

'Normie? So what about his last laugh?'

Nothing could hide her starburst smile, its reflection in her dark eyes, her pride. 'Bart Costello and Normie McLaine's last laugh,' she said. 'Some people are taking it seriously—very seriously. Normie—and

Uncle Jack—say I should do a vanish.'

Somehow he'd missed the last laugh. But he was too vain, too eager to protect her from its consequences, to ask her about it. 'With me,' he said. 'Vanish with me. You know where.'

She trusted him as he had trusted her. 'No, my own country. Up near Manilla.'

'You're Filipina. I thought Spanish. South American.'

Her laughter had the spontaneity of a dawn bird's call. 'You're not the first. When Dad was working in London, I was taken for Spanish. Then we came back here, I was taken for a Pom. Funny that—sometimes accent matters as much as colour.'

'But your name—and you're going to Manila …'

It's not that Manila. It's Manilla, New South Wales. I'm a Koori.'

The word hadn't been current when Durman left Australia. She had to explain it. 'Koori—what you call Aborigine.'

He could not believe it. And he could not deny it—anymore than he could deny saying 'It doesn't matter' even as he realised that again he was failing a test. To say it didn't matter was to imply that it might. 'What I mean is … Come with me, I'll look after you.'

She rose. And he saw she'd reinforced her invisibility by her posture. No longer was she standing elegantly tall. She was bent to the stereotype. In the way she walked, too-—a kind of shuffle.

The revolving door took her and spun her like magic from his life.

But not his love. It rushed after her. And he followed it, wanting to protect her, wanting to warn her: don't smile, don't laugh, don't talk—your charm destroys the stereotype of your invisibility.

No one in a rush ever gets into an empty revolving door. But Durman made it in time to see her getting into a Subaru four-wheel drive. By the look of it—and him—Sergeant Jack Sands, fifteen years with the Highway Patrol, Drug Squad gun, brought down by a dog, had been flogging it as hard and as fast as he knew how on long, bush roads.

He spotted Durman and went into a strange pantomime. He covered his eyes.

Then his ears.

Then his mouth.

In his room Durman checked he weapon he'd taken from the hoon. Very neat. Short barrel. Walther automatic. TPH model—6.35 mm. One round in the chamber. Five in the magazine. He replaced it in his bumbag with his passports and money. He might yet need it more than both of them. Only then did he go through *AllDay* again.

Nothing.

Yet Maree'd said Bart Costello and Normie McLaine's last laugh was there.

Radio?

He turned it back and forth between noisy yet empty varieties of rock. He found Old Titanium Tonsils hanging onto the end of some Mantovani strings and pitching a sonorous folksy commentary. 'The sensational news in the first edition of today's *AllDay* makes it a collector's item. And I'm not just talking about when it says about Mr Mervyn Vesmar, but the way it says it…?

Nong.

Must've missed it.

Durman went through *AllDay* page by page. No picture of Big Ig. No mention of him.

OTT was saying: '… legally *AllDay* may be required to stick to the rules and put all correct solutions in the draw to decide the jackpot winner. But the offending puzzle was withdrawn in subsequent editions of the newspaper as—and I quote—"the work of a hoaxer inspired by a malcontent. Anyone repeating the material will be subject to the full sanctions of the law." Such sanctions, I'm advised prevent me broadcasting either the clues or their solutions.'

This commentary OTT followed with the oldie but goodie, 'Who's Sorry Now?'—as Durman thumbed through the pages of *AllDay.*

**ACROSS**

1. Place without fury of woman scorned.
3. Not brave stuff but there's a hero in it.
8. Go to it—or fish with it.
10. Marks the spot from which to go.
11. Chinese trading place.
12. Simian king of the Empire State.
13. It would be criminal not to know these initials.
16. You get one at 21.
17. Third person singular of most important verb.
18. Synonymous with plastic wrapping.
20. Lincoln's nickname.
23. Hurry for gold.
24. Goes with fro.
25. Receptacle for ashes but no bin.
26. With sticks these break bones.
28. Better than being down.
30. Better than being out.
31. Chinese measure of weight.

32. Kipling storied were just this.
33. Sounds like a moo of a foolish place.
35. Name to conjure with especially here.
38. Pop version's a toy, rest tend to be deadly.
39. Officially killed.
42. Abbreviated baronet.
44. Initially the late ironman.
45. Cleric with fatal letters following.
47. Paddy's kooky daughter. /
49. Time for possessive whisky drink (two words).
51. These secret societies have more interests than three.
55. Preposition of location.
56. Traditionally almost a national sport to do this (two words).
62. What addicts seek can be found unusually packed with reading matter.

**DOWN**

1. Goes with she.
2. Special news after a fashion.
3. Charles Kingsley's western.
4. Put on, then separate into categories (two words).
5. He did but see ER II passing by but had his initials intertwined with hers.
6. Eisenhower nickname.
7. The kernel of this brandy liqueur is peach or cherry.
8. Fine Vietnamese name.
9. To do this you may need cricketer's stomach.
11. Skippy's gait.
14. Plaster or theatre it's crucial.
15. Bullock Bill might've said this, hunting (three words).
16. Knock out.
18. Potent initials.
19. Antonym of fro.
21. Native birds established with thanks (three words).
22. Em's smaller half.
27. Victim of hairy meal.
28. Britain's official initials.
29. Nickname for Englishman.
30. Electrified particle's trip (two words).
34. Fond parents or whisky drinkers might say this.
36. Way out yes in Anglo-Spanish.
37. Officer's cross.
40. Upon my word, it's Greek for a piece of TV.
41. Priestly Welsh accountant.
42. Someone should've done this to Cleopatra's last pet.
43. Macbeth's lady damned it.
46. To use this in the plural is to be very irritated.
48. Finis by any other name still spells this.
52. Outer edge.
53. Weld section of circle.
54. Fi tends to be this.
57. You're off or you're this.
58. Initially your puzzler.
59. Warm footwear.
60. All right.
61. Work by author's own hand.

Working his way through the clues, Durman began to realise the puzzle was rough. When he'd completed it, he knew it was ready enough and underlined the words that counted.

*AllDay*'s high-priced ventriloquist solicitors and their more highly priced barrister dummies—interchangeable heads for prosecution or defence—might be able to put a legal lid on the puzzle. He ripped it from the newspaper. But the CCIO surely would not—could not—ignore its plain message?

No wonder Anton had gone meataxe. Merv Vesmar must've gone beserk and was pushing him.

Half right. Half wrong.

The steak sandwich he'd ordered from room service arrived. And the pot of tea. No booze. He was operational again. And his life was the objective. Meataxe Anton might be but he was also a hard nut, deploying teams as hard.

The hardest.

The ex-SAS guys he'd mentioned. Parachutists, he'd said, boathandlers. Shit, they were the crew of the pirate boat. And one of them was the sniper-executioner.

Durman poured himself another cup of tea. What would Anton make of the St Vinnies gear at the bolthole? Part of an alternative withdrawal plan?

With any luck.

Bad luck.

The Qantas voice had an English accent..'You're booked on QF1 to London a week from today, sir. When would you like to travel?'

'Now. Today.'

'I'm sorry, sir. That flight is already boarding.'

Durman had known it would be. 'Next available.'

'Monday.'

'Tomorrow. What about tomorrow? Or even Sunday. It's urgent.'

'I'm sorry, sir. Those flights are fully booked.'

'What are you, a bloody robot? You should know who I am. Bump someone.'

'Can't be done, sir. Do you want the transfer to Monday?"

'All right. All right—if that's the best you can bloody do.' Durman slammed the receiver down. No way Anton wouldn't be monitoring the airport. Remembering Anton's picklock expertise, Durman stuck a table across the door of the suite. The adrenaline surge that had carried him through fight and flight had ebbed.

He needed a kip. And Anton surely wouldn't try to serve Irish porridge here.

Anton did have other areas of expertise. When the telephone twittered, Durman was convinced it was Anton, calling to rubbish him, to get him off balance. It *was* Anton but at one or possibly two removes. 'I've been asked to bring a certain matter to your attention, sir.' It was his favourite Swiss-movement flunkey. Exquisitely polite and taking exquisite pleasure in his task. 'Your bill.'

Durman had evolved a technique for dealing with condescending hotel staff. He imagined them eating shit in their bedsit kennels. 'Listen,' he said, 'one phone call from me will sort this out.'

'My understanding is, sir, that it will take more than telephone calls to sort things out. Accordingly, I've been instructed to tell you that we need your suite immediately.'

Anton was pushing. Pushing hard to get him off-balance. Durman countered. 'Monday, I've advanced my departure date to Monday. Everything will be settled then.'

'Immediately, sir. I'm sure you would prefer that I not involve our security staff.'

Durman would prefer. 'I'll be right down,' he said. 'And I'll want to see the manager—the organ grinder, understand? I'm tired of dealing with the monkey's arsehole.'

He did go right down. Right down to the basement car park, carrying his holdall into which he'd crammed his gear and tipped the fresh bowl of complimentary fruit and a clutch of miniatures from the bar fridge. Anton had him on the hop. But he would still celebrate at Anton's expense.

The flunkey would give him no more than ten minutes before calling security.

Anton and his hoons would be expecting to pick him up as he left the hotel on foot.

## 22

Most of the cars ranked alongside the serpentine access ramp had ignition keys in for the benefit of the car-park attendants. Durman took a Rolls-Royce—Silver Shadow II—and a chance. As he drove towards the exit barrier, controlled from a glassed-in booth, he waved his room key and a $20 note. 'Be forgetting my head next,' he said to the attendant. 'No prob, mate,' the attendant said. 'I'll see reception gets your key.' He raised the barrier and Durman found himself exiting on to a road that ran by the side of the hotel. He checked in his rear-view mirror. No heel-shits on wheels. The traffic flow took him towards Circular Quay. There, in a side street near something called the Justice and Police Museum, he abandoned the Rolls—bonnet up.

Anton had pushed him into the streets because Anton and his hoons had been trained to operate in streets as much as in jungles. And Anton must believe that if he failed in the killing ground of the streets, he had a final—and best—opportunity at the airport.

Move.

Get off the streets.

Better.

Get Anton off his back.

The Venus de Milo was centred on a circular lawn round which a red-gravelled path ran under a grape-vined pergola.

Beautiful Venus.

Arms restored.

Good as new.

Except for the black moustache inked on her upper lip.

Behind Durman the roar of the traffic rapids of Parramatta Road was muted. He turned for a final heel-shit check. Nothing. With any luck, the Rolls had been found and Anton and his hoons had assumed he'd taken the ferry to Manly.

As it was, he could just make out the University of Sydney. Had some witty academic from his old uni inked the moustache on the Venus, guardian of the house behind it? Two-storeyed. Italianate cream stucco. Shady. Definitely shady. Unlikely any academic would have to come here. Those creeps had their annual crop of dewy students. Lie back and think of your high distinction, my dear, had been the joke in his time.

He stared at the closed-circuit security camera which covered the house's entrances and exits—so screened and controlled that no client need see another arriving or departing.

The Princess Celia Von Kronberg had her own monitor. She was waiting for him in the hallway, saying to the guy in the frilly shirt who minded the seraglio but didn't look like a eunuch: 'I'll call you if I need you, Michael.'

Michael didn't blink although she was in her basic working rig: black bra, panties, suspender belt, stockings and high heels. Maybe the guy *was* a eunuch.

She ushered Durman into a drawing room, a place of brocade curtains and couches and oil portraits. 'Welcome to the Pleasure Dome.' She gestured regally to a shining oak and gold tantalus on an equally impressive credenza. 'Help yourself to a drink.'

'That's not what I'm here for.' He was remembering her as less regal aboard the *Norn*—yet still potent.

Demanding.

Giving.

The memory may've shown in his eyes.

To prevent her getting the wrong idea, he drew the Walther.

Cool woman. 'I'm so sorry. But I'm not available to you at present, even at gunpoint.' Graciously, she indicated a large colour television on which a succession of prostitutes were showing what they had been born with and what they had developed. 'The pick of the house is yours. Now if you'll forgive me.' She left the room. He followed. 'That's not what I'm here for either.'

His arrival had interrupted her in the middle of putting on her full working rig in her dressing room where the monitor screen showed the front entrance. As she busied herself amid her racks of clothes and shoes, Durman stared at the portrait which decorated the room: Sir Walter Scott.

'I hated his work when I was at PLC,' she said. PLC. Presbyterian Ladies College. 'I became a fan only when I heard he'd said of his future daughter-in-law, "There's gold in her garters."'

Durman was prepared to bet there was gold in hers as well. Through the dressing room's other door was her bedroom, the silk sheets of the bed turned back from high-piled pillows.

Someone was in for a treat.

She was now in her full working rig: sparkly tiara on perfectly coiffeured head, eyes freighted with startled lashes, mouth lip-glossed, long blue silk gown, elbow-length blue silk gloves. Across her gown she wore a red and white sash with some kind of starry emblem attached to it. The gown sighed against the carpet as she led the way back to the drawing room.

'Bit early for a ball,' he said.

'For a formal ball, perhaps. But not to have a ball. My clients tend to have their own time frames and the one I'm expecting like so many Australian politicians gets off on royalty at any hour of the day or night.'

Actors are not necessarily prostitutes but prostitutes are necessarily actors. She was obviously getting into character for her client. Durman said: 'Anton's gone meataxe. The way we work, I can't contact him, he contacts me.'

'He hasn't?'

'Wrong kind. Meataxe contact. He's being stupid. Tell him from me. Tell him he's mad.'

She half-turned, managing the train of her gown as to the manner born. Against her mahogany tanned shoulders and decolletee glittered a parure that matched her tiara. '*You* want me to tell Mr Van Dieman *he's* mad.'

'Who better? In your game you don't survive without life insurance—and I'm not talking about the kind your friendly local commission artist sells.'

She had been walking back and forth. She halted. 'You mean you've recorded your information, put it in a safe place with a trusted person and instructions for the record to be sent to the appropriate authorities if any little thing like sudden death happens to you?'

'I thought you would know the drill.' He took out the lettercard he'd bought at the Bondi Post Office and written there. She held out her blue gloved hand for it. He said: 'If I gave it to you, you'd open it and read it—and suffer a little thing like sudden death.'

She gave the prospect consideration.

Smiling consideration.

'I must say I find it difficult to think of anything so lethal—especially after the revelations in *AllDay* itself.'

He had found it difficult to think of. But Anton would realise—would realise his innermost secret had been penetrated. 'Anton wasn't mentioned in *AllDay*. He's snow-white. And he stays that way—if he behaves, calls off his hoons. I'm not interested in what goes on here. I'm out of it Monday.'

'And if Mr Van Dieman doesn't comply, you mail the *lettre de cachet?*"

'I might hand-deliver it. Or have it couriered.'

'But it's pre-stamped.'

Quick, cool woman.

She was saying: 'In any case, I expect its destination will be The Rocks.'

Very quick. Durman'd established that the Criminal Commission Intelligence Office headquarters were in The Rocks. Appropriate, he'd thought, the location of Sydney's founding orgy. 'The Rocks,' he said. 'Or copied and hand-delivered to *AllDay's* rivals. TV. Radio.'

If Anton didn't agree and tried to block the insurance ploy, Durman wanted him to have to spread his hoons thin.

'You've thought of everything, she said.

He felt a butterfly flicker of panic. She'd phoned Anton, who'd told her to keep him talking. He glanced at a window. Not discreetly enough for this woman who made her living reading impulses, thoughts and secret desires.

From regal, she flared to full-on imperial.

Plus vestigial schoolgirl.

'I never dob anyone in.' She surveyed the drawing room. 'I prefer to maintain the Pleasure Dome as a sanctuary.'

She meant it. Father Voitre Solovjev should've been so lucky in his presbytery. Durman said: 'I'm grateful. Anton will be as well if you pass him my message.'

'You're sure you won't have a drink?'

'I'm on my limit.'

'Amazing.' Her scent had cinnamon in it. Smoky cinnamon. 'After what you've done, I find it truly bloody amazing that you have a limit.'

'What I've done?'

'Please, no false naivete. It sits on your mug like a clown on a coffin.' She was helping herself to a drink. Gin. 'Merv Vesmar was not my favourite person …'

'Nor mine.'

'But killing him was rather extreme.'

*Rather extreme.* Durman could not prevent a grin. The Princess Celia's mum would have been rapt. Her daughter did sound like one of the bunyip aristos Australia's first-in-best-dressed had tried to foist on the country. She said: 'Please. No denials. No alibis. Merv Vesmar was found shot yesterday at his country property which you know as well as I do—shot three times at close range.'

Copies of magazines and newspapers were laid on a side table for the benefit of clients who wanted to affect an interest in things other than the Pleasure Dome's stock-in-trade. Durman said: 'There's been nothing in the papers.'

'Two clowns on the coffin,' she said. 'You must know that when a Merv Vesmar dies, it's sometimes necessary to keep it hush-a-bye. If he'd had a heart attack at home, do you think, it would've been front page in *AllDay*?'

'Well, no. But maybe it would've been in the Jackpot Crossword.'

She was not amused. 'The Stock Exchange was still trading when Vesmar's body was discovered.'

'Yesterday, you say?' He was working out a time frame.

She thought he was still playing silly buggers and stamped her foot—fully in character now. 'Yes, I do say. And please, don't try telling me you can't remember yesterday was Thursday. The Stock Exchange is trading today, so the news of the death of the mighty Mervyn Vesmar will be revealed only after certain hedging precautions have been completed here and overseas to protect what were his interests.'

'Three times?'

'Shotgun, as you well know. Sawn off?'

Information was the tightrope on which she balanced her high life.

Information to hint she had—not to threaten to reveal. Like the Kook from Oz, Patsee Urquhart, had threatened?

But even hinting might be deadly for the Princess Celia were she to find out what Durman suspected. He said: 'Just talk to Anton. Tell him I've taken out insurance. The heaviest—involving what he's been planning for a long time.'

Her disdain may not've been truly imperial. It was real. 'No, Mr Van Dieman talks to me. Were I in the habit of talking to Mr Van Dieman, you would already be as he wishes you to be, dead meat.'

On the drawing room's black marble mantle was an ormolu clock featuring nymphs cavorting with satyrs. Or politicians. It began to chime. 'I'm afraid I do have an appointment.' Her startled eyes upped and downed him. 'You look as if you're country bound.' He'd bought himself a pair of R. M. Williams elastic-sidies, moleskins and a blue shirt. 'I'm off Monday.' Information was her tightrope. 'Thought I might go bush for the weekend. Any thoughts?'

'The Hunter Valley's always worth a visit. How are you proposing to travel—car?'

'Train.'

'Make it Mudgee then.' She held out her gloved hand.

Durman kissed it. She might not talk to Mr Van Dieman. Nonetheless, he would take bets that she would have one of her people ring Anton to get him to talk to her.

Exiting from the house, he was conscious of someone entering on the other side of the screen. The Princess Celia's politician client?

Die, you bastard. Die on the job.

And if the pollie did die, he would do so knowing the Princess Celia was a pro who knew when to open her legs and when to keep her mouth shut.

And vice versa.

It *was* the pollie. His white vehicle, the Commonwealth red C on its registration plate, was parked outside the next-door house. The chauffeur was in the front seat—reading *Stud's Eye*.

There ain't no justice. Durman headed back down the dead-end slope, off which the Pleasure Dome stood.

It had been a risk seeing the Princess Celia.

Downside: She had a description of what he was wearing, backed by security-camera tape.

Upside: She knew of his plan to go into the country. And he knew what was driving Anton. And how long and how hard it had been driving him. Anton had to keep himself in the clear. He might go for the insurance ploy.

Might.

The escalator to the Central Station access tunnel was stopped and littered with the remains of a Big Mac banquet. Durman took the stairs two at a time.

The tunnel—Devonshire Street—ran straight for at least 500 metres—a heel-shit's nightmare.

Durman lingered from time to time to inspect the wares of pedlars working the tunnel and to watch his back. No likely heel-shit lads. A couple of the pedlars were black Africans. Neat switch, their selling bangles and beads to the local natives. The murky grafitti that had decorated the tunnel was gone. It was now an underground gallery, bright slashes of tiles setting off vivid frescoes with music echoing off both.

The muso at the end of the tunnel was playing the sax. Tenor. A classy 'Sultans of Swing.' Durman wanted to be remembered if any of Anton's hoons came tracking him. He dropped a handful of coins into the muso's sax case. 'Play Loch Lomond.' A daft request.

As he emerged from the tunnel, the music followed him. bluesy yet somehow jaunty and sure. He was taking the high road. Bart Costello had taken the low road.

Half right. Half wrong.

In the great curved-roof concourse of Central Station, Durman checked train departure times.

Another change. No more the clicking, rotating name sticks. No more board. A bank of blue television screens. But the names were as he remembered them: Bathurst. Orange. Wollongong. Penrith. Emu Plains. Richmond. Windsor. And, yes, Mudgee.

He retrieved his holdall from the left-luggage office where he'd put it. The other travellers were also as he remembered them. Guys with sun-gullied faces in work-worn jeans, sweaty Akubras and stitched boots which made his own look flash. Women with enduring faces, baskets, blankets and bubs.

At the booking office, he asked for a ticket to Mudgee.

'Single or return?' The clerk looked Indonesian.

'Any price difference?' He wanted to be remembered. 'Or is it all the bloody same.'

'Not any price difference.'

'Return, mate. And how about I buy one for you, too.'

The clerk would remember him.

For sure.

Behind him in the booking office were a group of her people.

Maree's people.

Kooris.

Blokes in footy jerseys and shorts. Women in T-shirts and print skirts. Eyes deep-set, far-sighted from primeval hunting for fresh food, fixed now on tooth-rot tucker: lolly water and crisps. Kids skinny, mysteriously tow-headed.

He'd seen their faces before and not recognised them because of their invisibility factor.

They were the faces of the poor in a thousand photographs of the Great Depression.

Negatives.

Negatives in which the white positives now recognised their own past and their possible future.

And were fearful.

He had a mad impulse to say: Take it. Australia is all yours. Take it. You can't treat anyone white worse than you've been treated black.

Go to Manilla, tell Maree he'd never really wanted this country which was sick from second-guessing the world, this city whose nature a Koori rock carver had foretold: shark-like, insatiable, greed as perpetual motion.

As the train crossed the Harbour Bridge, Durman only glanced at Luna Park he'd noticed on his previous trip, concentrating instead on the harbour's exit between North and South Heads—and the wide free ocean beyond.

Mudgee had been a feint. He was on a North Shore line train. At each station, he left the train, getting back on in a different carriage at the last moment.

North Sydney. Waverton. Wollstonecraft. St Leonards. Artarmon. Chatswood. Roseville. Lindfield. Killara. Gordon. Pymble. Turramurra. Warawee. Wahroonga. Waitara—an ascension into Tudor nostalgia, magnolias, gardenias and old-money trees.

Hornsby was something else—a junction where suburban aspiration merged into the broader-acre mortgagedoms of Dural and the land lifted towards the Great Dividing Range over which lay the long, wide uncertainties of the inland.

## 23

The hand clutching the hammer banged against the rivet. The bell rang within. And the door to Doc Monroe's house opened slightly. Durman pushed it further open and got a whiff of the latrine smell. 'You there, mate?'

Doc Monroe was not there.

Not in the living room with his icons: the fulfilled Marilyn Monroe and his Legacy ward Big Ig, gazing at each other in the green-tinged light from the jungly garden beyond the French windows which were closed.

Not in the kitchen where a pair of yellow rubber gloves and blue plate of crackers and cheese made a still life.

Not in Big Ig's bedroom.

Nor in Doc Monroe's own. Only the .303 was in the rack. The Martini-Henry carbine was gone. Durman checked the .303. Magazine empty.

Not in the bathroom.

Which was what Durman needed. He unzipped his holdall. Time to begin playing his final hand.

Fifteen minutes later, shitted, showered and shaved, he was looking in the bathroom mirror at the clean-shaven face of a remembered stranger. He touched his broken nose. All he needed was a Groucho nose, moustache and glasses. He compared the mirror image with the photograph in the Irish passport.

Twins.

Out of the bathroom, he moved, fastening his bumbag, but now it was over a dark green and blue checked shirt and blue jeans and on his feet were the lace-up boots he'd been wearing when he arrived back in the city.

Where was Doc Monroe? Durman took the complimentary fruit from his holdall, found a terracotta bowl, finely glazed white splashed with blue within. He arranged the fruit in it. Mean. He knew he was. At least complimentary fruit was an acknowledgement of the tradition of the one safe place. This time he hadn't arrived empty-handed.

Cupping his less mean hand under a kitchen tap, he drank.

The water was like the city.

Bright but corrupt under a gag of chlorine.

Soon he would be drinking the water of the one safe place.

Spring water without taint.

Cheese and crackers he ate bite for bite with an apple. And found himself chewing paper: a tiny, sticky label. There were others on the fruit in the bowl—oval labels printed with the Regal Tower's logo. He spat the label into the kitchen sink and went into the living room. This was the place to lie up till jump-off.

In the garden wall was a blue door.

Ajar.

Maybe Doc Monroe was out walking beyond the wall. Durman pulled open the French windows.

The ecstatic buzz of blowflies was unmistakable.

And the stink of corpse flesh in the sun.

Doc Monroe was lying next to the grave he'd dug for Ace, the cockroach dog.

Lying with the Martini-Henry carbine in his hands, its muzzle in his mouth, its black-powder round exploded in his head.

Durman tugged at the blue door. A draught of air scented with eucalyptus and smoke sidled in like a blessing.

Suicide.

Suicide mimicking the killing of Big Ig?

But what about the twiddly bits?

Two unfired Martini-Henry rounds on the ground next to the corpse.

No one about to commit suicide by putting a gun in his mouth lays out spare ammo.

Nor does a frugal old guy about to commit suicide lay out a feast of crackers and cheese.

No way was it suicide.

Rubber-glove op.

Anton op.

The kill method, in line with Unit drill, was different from those used on the other targets in the sequence: Bart Costello,

Father Solovjev, Big Ig, Patsee Urquhart—just as the bareknuckle op on himself had been designed to be different.

No way was it suicide.

Murder.

And something worse.

So like a blow was his next thought that Durman doubled over.

Doc Monroe had been forced to do what he did.

Forced to hold the carbine.

Forced to put the muzzle in his mouth.

Forced to place his thumb on the trigger.

Durman knew the kind of drill. It was part of Unit training: Intensive Interrogation.

Aka torture.

A question put at each step of the drill.

In Doc Monroe's case the question: Where've you hidden your copy of Durman's letter?

For Doc Monroe—for anyone—an unanswerable question. There was no copy of the letter with a trusted person.

Doc Monroe had been tortured and murdered because of a bluff.

Durman turned from Doc Monroe's hard-staring eyes and moved closer to the open door and the bush air. But he couldn't leave. He couldn't rely on some bright cop sussing out the twiddly bits. Doc Monroe'd died a soldier's death in his own jungle. Suburban maybe. But as savage as the jungle for which he'd volunteered as a medic. Durman had to dismantle the evidence of suicide.

Rubber glove op.

He fetched the gloves from the kitchen and his holdall from the bathroom.

He had just managed to get the muzzle of the carbine from Doc Monroe's shattered mouth when the door-knocker banged. He completed his next moves: levering out the empty cartridge, levering a new cartridge in.

Explain that, Anton you bastard.

He heard the front door bang open.

Cops.

The Walther was in his hand.

'I don't think we should be doing this. If he's not here, he's not here.'

Man's voice.

'One quick pic—I've heard he keeps it like a shrine—and at least we can say we tried.'

Woman's voice.

Arguing in the doorway.

'No, let's go. This place stinks.'

'Oh, come on, it's cool.'

Journos.

Durman did not see them. Nor did they see him. He was out of there through the open door with his holdall. He did hear the woman discover the corpse.

Not so cool.

He was in one of those ravines of bushland, too steep and wild to be built on, that remind suburban Sydney of its pristine past.

Bees hummed. Butterflies flickered. Birds warbled. And as he made his way down the rough track, one fled for cover in a skitter of brilliant plumage and fantastic tail feathers.

Lyrebird.

First he'd ever seen in his life.

Maybe his last.

Anton the balls-up control specialist was sealing off to wait out the media mortaring and the CCIO probing, set off by Bart Costello and Normie McLaine's last laugh—going to ground, Anton, while he worked out his counter-attack and how to make good his plan.

The double-deal plan he'd been working on from the very beginning.

Which was why he—yes, Anton personally—had tortured Doc Monroe. Torture, death were what put the lineaments of gratified desire on Anton's face. Durman peeled off the kitchen gloves as if they were his disgust. The bastard should stick to S and M in the Pleasure Dome like any other law-abiding citizen.

The ravine was opening out. In this area, pedestrians were almost as rare as the lyrebird. When the journos—from *AllDay,* Anton would've arranged it—contacted the cops, prowl cars would outswarm the bees. Durman slung his holdall haversack-style as he'd done in Bangkok. Maybe here he would be taken for a bushwalker.

The ravine ended in a clearing and a hillock of gravel. A tubular gate was locked to keep out 4WD and trailbike jockeys. He climbed the gate and found himself on a bitumen road.

Time spent on reconnaissance is rarely wasted. The memory of Anton's pedantry mocked him. He wasn't sure where he was. But he had the sun to give him a bearing.

North to Manilla.

To her.

Querida.

The endearment he'd only dared utter to her in dreams.

Go to Manilla. Say it to her.

And take her to the one safe place.

Or lead Anton and his hoons to her?

She would be safer, invisible with her own people.

And with extra protection from Sergeant Jack Sands who owed it to her. A man who paid his debts: Sergeant Sands.

Durman doubled south along roads and through streets of houses so silent their inhabitants might all have died and been bricked up, the fate Doc Monroe had feared for himself.

Hornsby Station, Durman by-passed, heading down the line to Waitara, a quiet station, more easily checked for heel-shits.

At the limit of Durman's thinking—an unwelcome creditor—something was trying to claim his attention.

| 1 H | 2 E | L | L | ■ | 3 H | 4 E | 5 R | O | 6 I | 7 N | ■ | 8 N | E | 9 T |
|---|---|---|---|---|---|---|---|---|---|---|---|---|---|---|
| 10 E | X | ■ | ■ | 11 H | O | N | G | ■ | 12 K | O | N | G | ■ | E |
| ■ | 13 C | 14 C | 15 I | O | ■ | A | ■ | 16 K | E | Y | ■ | ■ | 17 I | S |
| 18 P | L | A | S | P | A | C | 19 T | O | ■ | 20 A | 21 B | 22 E | ■ | T |
| 23 R | U | S | H | ■ | ■ | 24 T | O | ■ | ■ | 25 U | R | N | ■ | I |
| ■ | 26 S | T | O | N | 27 E | S | ■ | 28 U | 29 P | ■ | O | ■ | 30 I | N |
| 31 L | I | ■ | T | ■ | 32 S | O | ■ | 33 K | O | W | L | 34 O | O | N |
| ■ | 35 V | 36 E | S | 37 M | A | R | ■ | ■ | M | ■ | 38 G | U | N | S |
| ■ | 39 E | X | E | C | U | T | 40 E | 41 D | ■ | 42 B | A | R | T | ■ |
| 43 S | ■ | 44 I | G | ■ | ■ | ■ | 45 P | R | I | E | S | T | O | 46 D |
| 47 P | A | T | S | 48 E | E | ■ | ■ | U | ■ | 49 A | S | O | U | R |
| O | ■ | S | ■ | N | ■ | 50 T | W | I | N | T | E | T | R | A |
| 51 T | 52 R | I | 53 A | D | 54 S | ■ | ■ | D | ■ | 55 A | T | ■ | ■ | T |
| ■ | I | ■ | R | ■ | 56 C | 57 O | 58 N | C | 59 U | S | T | 60 O | 61 M | S |
| 62 S | M | A | C | K | I | N | M | A | G | P | A | K | S | ■ |

He read off the words he'd underlined:

HELL HEROIN NET EX HONG KONG.

CCIO A KEY IS PLASPACTO ABE. RUSH TO URN STONES UP IN LI KOWLOON.

VESMAR M GUNS EXECUTED BART IG PRIESTOD PATSEE AS OUR TWIN TETRA TRIADS CON CUSTOMS.

SMACK IN MAGPAKS. EXCLUSIVE.

Rough all right. Very rough. But clear enough—though no mention of how the perfumed magazines prevented sniffer dogs from detecting the heroin.

Out of date already—Doc Monroe's name should be in it.

And it was something about Doc Monroe—something about his place that was worrying him.

The ticket he bought was to the outer-beach suburb, Cronulla. City hotels were out. Odds were his favourite Swiss-movement flunkey had tipped them off about his bill and his Rolls retreat. Which wouldn't help him evade Anton's hoons.

And if Anton wasn't buying the insurance ploy, his operation would be on the basis of the subject getting out of the city. He would've already checked the subject hadn't flown to another state capital—rearranged his ticket to exit from Melbourne or Perth, Brisbane or Adelaide. A check would be on at end-of-the-line stations and motels.

Like Cronulla.

Durman got off the train at Hell.

Town Hall Station, Sydney.

As a little kid, he'd always thought of it as Hell—its dark ceilings, its sombre stairways, its greasy escalators, connecting its various levels through which monster trains rumbled and screeched.

It had been brightened up. But the forlorn look of its travellers lingered like fear.

Move.

Hand. The hand clutching the hammer?

Half-in, half out of sleep and an unremembered dream, Durman's brain was racing but his conclusions were slow-motion.

Hoon on a sneak op, trying to get the Walther?

No way.

A hoon who'd got this close would already have offed him: smother, strangle, ear-pick, chop.

Durman shifted his head. The hand moved deeper under his pillow, gripped one of his boots and began to withdraw it.

Thief.

Brilliant.

Durman was lying on his right side, facing the thief and didn't want to risk a look.

Yet.

He mumbled. The hand halted before withdrawing the boot

completely. It then began a foray for the other boot. Durman would not have minded the boots. He had spare ones. But he had improvised a lanyard for the Walther by tying one end of the boot's lace to its trigger guard and the other end to his wrist.

He opened his eyes now grabbed a handful of the thief's hair with his left hand and banged his head downwards. It must've connected with the iron frame of the bed. The thief gasped in pain, his round face distorted in the glimmering darkness. Durman kept his grip on the hair. 'My other boot, mate.' The thief reached down and handed him back the other boot. Durman gave a final wrench to the thief's hair. 'Find a heavier sleeper.' The thief went the way he'd come, crawling on the wooden floor of the hostel dormitory.

Durman'd got there just before final check in.

Deliberately.

'Just made it,' the guy in the hostel's caged reception area'd said. Young guy. Spotty. He reminded Durman of the kid who'd passed him on the racing bike going up the Rose Bay esses. 'You've missed supper.' As if Durman were a younger kid, he'd handed him a Mars Bar and an apple. 'Mars Bar first.'

Hell.

It had been getting off at Hell that'd brought him to this brick box. He'd remembered clutching Mum's hand on the way through Hell, remembered something she'd said—the clincher in the argument she'd had with Dad after she gave his suit to St Vinnies: 'Well, at least they give battlers a feed and a clean bed for the night in that hostel of theirs.'

Durman settled his boots back under his pillow. Beneath the sheet and light summer blanket, his feet were resting on his holdall.

Around him two or three hundred guys shifted in their sleep. Like a herd of sleeping cattle, they seemed to take reassurance from their own night noises: snores, groans. The occasional cry. A whimper.

He too was reassured. He'd gone below the level at which Anton expected him to operate.

The sound of a bell woke Durman. And an announcement that breakfast was being served.

As he pulled on his boots, he scanned the other guys, looking for one with a bruised head. A futile exercise with these battlers. Many of them had bruises—from drunken falls or stoushes—and cuts and scars.

Breakfast in the big dining room was noisy. No chat. The sound of cutlery on plates of grub: cereal, sausage, eggs, bacon and mugs of tea.

Solid tucker.

Exactly what he needed to see him through this day.

Durman always counted his pennies. Bed and breakfast here had cost him less than having a shirt laundered at the Regal Tower.

The spotty kid was ending his shift, handing a clipboard to an older guy as Durman left the hostel. Above them hung a Mick crucifix.

Changing the guard.

The kid caught Durman's eye and called out: 'Goodbye, mate.'

## 24

Already the day had too much heat in it.

Sweating, he cut through Hyde Park past the Archibald Fountain where kids were splashing among its spouting bronze turtles as a click of camera samurai captured them on film.

At St James Station he made two telephone calls, the phone booth giving him a clear view back along the station access tunnel. In the first call he was ocker, demanding bloody assurances his Monday plane seat was definitely guaranteed. In the second call, he was Brendan Coyle modifying long-standing travel arrangements made in London.

Third call to be made.

But not yet.

Time: 09.35.

Hard day coming. If he didn't kill it shrewdly, it might kill him.

Yet he felt optimism. His edge over Anton. Surviving the critical night. The spotty kid's 'Goodbye.'

Goodbye. Hadn't heard it in years: God be with you.

His optimism rose. Anton might've exhausted his fugue of madness with Doc Monroe's death, might have seen the insurance letter for what it was: potentially lethal to him and his long-plotted dream.

He rose as he strolled the city's narrow-gutted streets, creating for any heel-shit the impression of a guy with two more days before he flew out.

Rose—until he glimpsed in a shop front the flicker of his own image repeated again and again and again.

His old bearded image.

Part of a ritual coda came to him: '… armed and dangerous. He should not be approached. Contact your nearest police.'

No qualms about approaching on the part of the shop's spruiker. 'We're knocking these sets out at cost.' He was gazing at Durman with generous rapacity.

'Just looking,'.

Just looking at his bearded image in a split-screen shot with an image of Doc Monroe.

Just looking at himself in his blue shirt, moleskins and R. M. Williams boots, walking past the good-as-new Venus de Milo—as originally featured on the Pleasure Dome security system.

Just realising, as the reporter kept the commentary down to hysteria, that he'd set a trap for himself.

And Anton had sprung it.

The Regal Tower logo stickers on the complimentary fruit.

The Martini-Henry carbine taken from Doc Monroe's mouth and loaded with a fresh round—the apparent suicide weapon turned into a murder weapon.

A murder weapon to which the logo stickers connected him.

The working reality behind the ritual coda, Durman understood: Anton had made a killing ground of the city.

The cops.

But part of this city's folklore was find the good cop in the rotten barrel.

And even if he found the good cop, he'd be held for questioning.

Deadline.

He had a deadline, beyond which shone the one safe place.

And he still had his edge on Anton.

Anton, the whizbang whiz.

Durman touched his bumbag where he'd put the insurance letter card.

His whizbang.

Delayed-action whizbang.

Move.

Do something.

Something Anton and his hoons—and the cops—would not expect.

Not so much them.

Anton, his shadow self.

Hide in the open. Make his last Saturday day in Sydney a Saturdee—kid's fun day, the kind he'd enjoyed before learning the true nature of the city.

Shooting in an express lift up Centre Point Tower, a giant rusty maypole, with a crisscross of steel guy ropes, topped by a huge golden knob, observation decks, eating places.

Taking snaps from up there: the Blue Mountains, the heat-hazed plains, the shimmering sea and the harbour's exit between North and South Heads.

Eating fish and chips with Shelley's lemonade followed by Street's ice-cream.

And once a sense of being watched.

A burnished head disappearing in the crowd: Syl?

Move.

Taxi first, then a bus—or Mercedes stretch limo—as the driver called it. Jokey guy. 'I'm George, your chauffeur.'

Out along Anzac Parade, no Champs Elysee, though designed to commemorate soldiers who'd saved Paris.

'Traffic conditions medium to chaotic for the time of year,' George said. 'I hope none of you ladies has left the iron on—and none of you gents has a weak bladder.'

Mum and Dad would've loved him. Bus driver as music hall turn.

Botany Cemetery's regimented forest of gravestones was continuing its slow march to the sea down the slope where Durman worked on his mother's grave.

He was finishing weeding it with a bricklayer's trowel, bought at the same hardware shop as before. Surprise. Surprise. The Chinese cab driver was behind the counter. 'My shop,' he said. 'Taxi part-time.'

Smart guy. He'd also provided a five kilo sack of mixed sand and cement and seeing Durman trying to pack it into his old holdall offered him a bigger sportsbag. 'Free umbrella,' he said clinching the deal.

Next to his mother's headstone, Durman placed a pot of yellow chrysanthemums. From the sportsbag, he took his 35 mm Pentax and knocked off a shot of the refurbished grave, the chrysanthemums shining like memories.

Tilted, his father's headstione, the military type he'd called a Gallipoli Biscuit though his war was a different one: Korea.

As if inclining towards Mum's. Bullshit. Their marriage, like their house, had been semi-detached. Dad had Jahbulon, the Sacred Word to Keep. And only now did Durman suspect there'd been as much sarcasm as pride in the way Mum used to cough like an unhappy bambi before saying, 'Grand Master'.

Anton, his hoons and the cops were looking for a fugitive armed and dangerous. And here he was safe with his dead.

Over the serried ranks of gravestone came the heartbeat of the sea. His heart beat with it, remembering how in the slop of the Gulf of Siam, Big Ig chanted the names of beaches: Cherry Venture … Tea Tree … Boiling Pot. And how in his own dream of the shark, the beach names were linked by the astonishing word.

He straightened the Gallipoli Biscuit and opened the sack of sand and cement.. He tipped most of it into a plastic basin and carried it to the nearest tap where he added water, partially mixing it into the sand and cement with the trowel.

On the way back, he scrunched through a spill of sand from a grave that had been reopened higher on the slope across the path from Dad's.

The storm that the heat of the day'd been incubating broke first in a hot gust of wind and the flat patter of raindrops.

He shook the basin of sand, cement and water. Wouldn't it? He opened the umbrella—orange and white—and propped it on top of the Gallipoli Biscuit.

The storm was quickening into a monster, heavy, black clouds rolling up to cover the sun and wind-driven rain slashing down.

Stockwhip cracks of lightning lit the gloom and thunder rumbled like a heavy artillery barrage. A lifting barrage, moving closer as if to protect troops advancing on their objective.

Crouched under the umbrella, Durman went on mixing his plaster. Too sploshy. He added what was left in the sack, mixing it in with the trowel and getting the mix on his hands.

Great fun.

He looked across the path and up the slope. A guy, made bulky by a green-hooded poncho, was coming down the slope towards the reopened grave.

Gravedigger coming to inspect his work.

Spade in left hand. Umbrella in right.

Stubby effort.

Unlike his unopened.

Cover. Durman moved behind the Gallipoli Biscuit, dropping the basin and trowel and scrabbling in his bumbag for the Walther as the guy brought the stubby umbrella to bear. It gave an apologetic belch.

But the impact and whine of its round striking the top of the Gallipoli Biscuit and ricocheting were vicious.

Walther up to return fire, Durman pressed the trigger.

Nothing.

Jam.

Grit from his hands.

The guy was coming on.

Anton?

Certain he had a defenceless target in his sights.

Dead certain.

Outmanoeuvred, Durman. thought. Pushed into a killing-ground, grave waiting. Pushed to the limit. He grasped the Gallipoli Biscuit on either side and rose with a roar, lifting it from its seating as the wind got under the orange and white umbrella and sent it flying.

Other shots struck the Gallipoli Biscuit before Durman was on his antagonist, ramming him so that he went down. Again and again, he brought the crushing weight of the Gallipoli Biscuit down until he heard ribs crack and his antagonist lay inert.

For a lightning-lashed moment, he left the Gallipoli Biscuit untouched before lifting it off.

Not Anton.

The rangemaster Roy Rankin, his stubby umbrella cover concealing the fat barrel of a silenced Welrod.

Durman'd counted the rounds fired. Four. He pulled the Welrod from Rankin's hand.

'Come on, Anton, I've taken out your offsider,' Durman yelled. 'Now it's your turn.' Lightning ripped the sky and thunder rolled, making his yell puny.

Ridiculous.

Under Rankin's poncho, he expected to find the Vigilanz uniform. But Rankin was in plain clothes. clipped on his belt a two-way radio, wrecked in the struggle.

Rankin did things by the book. He would not've gone in without reporting his position and his intention.

Move.

Durman stripped the poncho from the body and put it on. It might confuse Rankin's mates. The monster storm had grown fiercer, wilder, the sky darker as the rain sluiced blood from the Gallipoli Biscuit.

He had come here to strengthen it, not leave it lying tumbled. He moved to slap a layer of cement from the basin onto the crumbled seating. And another before lifting the Gallipoli Biscuit back into position and re-settling it.

Lightning fed on itself, flash on flash, thunder rolled continuously and was cut by a rhythmic clatter.

Chopper.

Merv Vesmar's Black Hawk.

From its underbelly a cone of white light was sweeping the terrain. Durman rolled Rankin's body into the open grave and followed it in, face down.

The Black Hawk was overhead. Durman pressed closer into the inert flesh of Roy Rankin which gave off the citrusy, spicy leathery scent of his aftershave while under it lingered the charnel stink of corpse. Durman pressed even closer, cringing from the feared impact of heavy-calibre machine-gun rounds.

Crazed.

Convinced that Anton had somehow known he was coming to the cemetery and had prepared the open grave for him.

The Black Hawk swung away. Durman continued to press himself down, the rain pattering on the poncho. The edge. He still had his edge. He pulled himself from the grave. The Black Hawk was hovering at about 30 feet, 500 metres away, its cone of light focused on the orange and white umbrella, caught between an angel's wings.

Two ropes dangled from the Black Hawk. Down them a couple of hoons were rappelling.

Move.

He squirmed round, grabbed his sportsbag—and found himself staring into the pain-maddened eyes of Rankin who'd clawed himself upright in the grave.

Did he have a yell left?

No way.

But maybe a whisper about the target's changed appearance. The Welrod belched apologetically. Rankin's face simultaneously jerked back, disintegrated and disappeared.

Hollow-point load.

Along the cross path he slithered until he reached a down path where he switched to a crouching run. If the hoons came on Rankin's body in the grave, it would give him extra time.

Not much.

Hoons not into prayers. The Black Hawk was quartering the far left of the cemetery where he had glimpsed a market gardener's shack on the way in. He passed a broken column and a Celtic cross. Ahead of him, through the wind-driven curtain of rain, a dark figure flitted on a cross path.

Backstop.

He should've realised: Rankin had circled up from the beach to take him by surprise but left an offsider to block the line of retreat. Durman went right at a hard run, passing urns, obelisks and sarcophaguses, statues with upspread wings, statues with outstretched arms. He swung left, moved forward on another down path, left again and he was behind the backstop, crouched in ambush behind a gravestone.

Durman touched the nape of the backstop's neck with the Welrod. The backstop bent away from the gun, hands scrabbling and turned, holding a huge bunch of roses which flared blood red in a flash of lightning.

His comrade-in-arms, Helen, blood from her severed aorta, flowing in the valley between her breasts.

Blonde this woman. Tall. Short hair pasted to her head like gold leaf. Cool. 'You're not going to arrest me, are you?' Quick. 'I mean, what's a few flowers?'

The huge bunch of roses still had a name card attached.

'Drop them.'

'I know cops're meant to be rude.' But she did drop the roses. She was wearing a long, dun-coloured DrizaBone.

'Open it.' Underneath, she wore a black tank-top, black shorts and black bovver boots. Tits like grenades. She was standing on a grave slab which sagged into a shadowed cache near the headstone. Durman ran his hand over her.

No weapon on her. No two-way.

She said: 'Honest cop—pay for your feels, do you? Or expect them free like French fries.'

'Vehicle,' he said.

She gathered up the roses. Twice on the down path, she stopped to grab more flowers from graves.

The cemetery petered out. No perimeter wall. No fence. Only a dirt track. As if the gravestone forest was surrendering to the sea. To the right were a cluster of white storage tanks and the yellow cranes and stacked containers of a shipping terminal. The chopper was still over on the left, hovering at ground level. Searching the shack? Durman motioned her right. 'Dead end,' she said and led him down a slip road to the beach, going right at the double, the rise of the first sand dunes covering them from the chopper.

About 500 metres on, a stormwater creek had carved a narrow boiling channel in the sand. Durman slung his sportsbag haversack-style and shoved the Welrod into his bumbag. She jumped first, holding the flowers. He was in mid-air when the flowers hit him, blinding him, sending him into the torrent which swept him floundering in the poncho, weighed down by the sportsbag towards the roaring surf. He went under and felt a surge of Gulf of Siam panic.

And Big Ig was dead.

The sandbar saved him—the sandbar formed at the mouth of the creek by the action of the sea against the torrent. His feet touched bottom and he struggled upright.

She must've stopped to watch when he first went in. She was only about fifteen metres away, running towards the sand dunes, the flaps of her coat lifting in the wind like wings.

Angel of death?

Angel of life?

He dropped the sportsbag above the highwater mark and went after her, squelching through the heavy sand, drawing the Welrod.

Hoping.

He would not've caught her. But the round from the Welrod was close enough to freeze her in fear of another—freeze her face up in the sand, her legs spread.

Cool. Quick. Irrepressible.

'Pig. Had your free feel, didn't you? Might as well have the rest, eh?'

He could've. As he could've killed her—except he needed her. Could've hit her—except he needed her unmarked. She hadn't had the chance to count the rounds. The menace of the Welrod got her to her feet and back to the sportsbag which she picked up.

Ahead through the driving rain—200, 300 metres—was a lighted building. As they approached it, she said: 'Yarra Bay Sailing Club. What about a drink?'

Peck-peck questions. Like a bird guarding a secret nest. She skirted the club car park. The vehicle was on an access road to a picnic area.

White Holden utility.

Rain snare-drummed on the roof of its cab as she put the sportsbag under cover in the back. The surf boomed. The wind howled.

Rock around the barometer.

The Black Hawk added the clatter of its rotors. Had it picked up the ground-search team? Durman slid into the cab beside her and she started the engine.

Cool. Quick. Irrepressible. Take charge.

'Your place or mine?'

'Name.'

'You're not really a cop, are you?'

'Name.'

'Salli, with an "i", you know?'

'Patsee with two "e"s. Salli with an "i"—doesn't anyone spell their name properly here?'

She gave a snort of laughter. 'Smyth's my surname. Smyth with a "y". Salli Smyth.'

'Van Dieman.' He was testing her. 'Anton Van Dieman.'

She passed the test. 'That's Dutch, isn't it?'

'Left here.' He wanted to get off the main road into the side streets. Just another utility meandering home through a suburb. He kept giving her directions until they emerged on Anzac Parade. 'Your place in the city?' he said.

'Crim, aren't you? Made that gun yourself, didn't you?' It was his turn to laugh. The makers of the Welrod, designed originally for World War II special ops, might also have been amused. 'Out of the Bay, aren't you. Overstayed your work release, didn't you?'

'Something like that.'

Traffic was heavy. Heavier the better. The storm had eased. As they drove past Long Bay Gaol, she said: 'You weren't on work release, were you? You broke out, didn't you?—using your home-made gun.'

The gatehouse at an angle to the perimeter fence he'd noticed when driving with Sergeant Sands was still there. He pointed to it. 'Ladder up to the roof. Same ladder from the roof and across to the perimeter fence.'

'And then you jumped and ran for it, didn't you?'

The traffic was thickening, slowing to a crawl. Beyond Maroubra Junction was the reason: a big van lit up like a blue Christmas tree with a flashing sign—POLICE. A cop with a flashing light baton was waving selected motorists towards the van.

Breathalyser van.

Durman tucked the Welrod under the poncho. As the utility came up with the cop, Salli Smyth leaned across him and said: 'I want him done now. We're on our way to Mum's and I think he's had too much already.' The cop looked at her and at Durman. 'I'd like to help you.' Between the cop and the van, a prowl car was parked, its crew using this choke point to check for the armed and dangerous fugitive. 'Oh, come on,' she said. 'It doesn't take a minute, does it?' The cop waved her on. 'Just get your Mum to talk to him,' he said. 'That's what my wife does with me.'

'That's not what I would do with you.'

Another test passed.

Time: 18.45.

## 25

Taylor Square had never been square in any sense. Diamond-shaped. Rough diamond. Durman remembered a scruffy green centre. Nicknamed 'Gilligan's Island' where wild winos played drunken chicken with the traffic. Was that before or after a clump of palm trees like ambitious dish mops? Both palm trees and the winos were gone. The square had been renovated again. Old harlot Sydney slapping on another layer of make-up.

Her place was in a lane nearby—a sandstone cottage squeezed between taller terraces. Outside, it was nondescript to deter thieves. Inside, the rough-hewn sandstone, lit with Tiffany lamps, made the living room a luxurious cave: polished wood floors, red Persian rugs, bird paintings, two grape coloured couches and a teak coffee table on which was a silver jug full of flowers.

'Yours?' Durman said. 'Or theirs?'

'So I supplement my income, doesn't everyone?—global economy means local economies.' She'd insisted on shopping. One bottle of red. One of white. In a blue plastic bag. She poured the red. He waited till she'd drunk before taking a sip—which was more than enough. 'It's a blend,' she said. 'And I think the pinot's bullying the merlot while the cabernet's creeping up on them both to mug them.'

Wine and cheese. Not Doc Monroe's frugal mousetrap and crackers. Pepper cheese. Brie. Fruit cheese. Jarlsberg and something she called Blue Castello as if she'd made it herself. Wine and cheese. Crusty bread and black olives.

Time: 19.15.

Eating: good way to kill time.

'Great cheese,' he said. 'And all from flower-rearranging.'

Her eyes were green. Her teeth white and sharp on the food. And on her words. 'Drongo. I said supplement.' Durman did not reply, waiting for her to elaborate. She did. A mistake? Sign of a cover story? 'There are a lot of lonely people out there, I help to bring them together.'

'Computer dating service?'

'Crap. Dinner parties. Start with a Chinese banquet for twenty or thirty and with any luck, you get it down to two-for-tea for life—or til the tea gets cold.'

'The same thing happened in the Bay. No banquets. Gallons of tea.'

'What did you do?'

'I got caught.'

'How long did you get?'

'Too long—which was why I left.'

'You'll go back for even longer if they pick you up.'

'No chance. I'm out of here.' He made a flying motion with his hand.

'Airports aren't that easy these days.'

He touched the Welrod in his waistband. 'My final pass out. No more Long Bay Hilton. I'll take my chances in the other place—and I don't mean heaven.'

She rose. Fit. Sure of herself, carrying the bottle of red, her glass and the bottle of white in the blue plastic bag.

The bedroom had enough brass for a band—the bed itself all winking knobs, a brass stand loaded with hats and belts, a big brass ring, suspended from the ceiling on brass chains, on which was draped a mosquito net.

Off the bedroom was the bathroom. This was one woman who bore watching. She had the same idea about him. Her eyes did not close as they showered together, the cold water melding them as it washed away the summer sweat and the stink of their fear. She had taken the bottle of red into the shower cabinet and drank from it before giving the wine to him in kisses until they moved together beyond the level of kisses, gasping as if drowning. 'How's the blend now?'

The blend was not perfect. It lacked trust as the Welrod balanced on a towel rail within his reach made clear.

Sex as armed truce.

Sex: better way to kill time.

Time: 20.10.

When he came from the bathroom, he was checking the action of the Welrod. And from the bed, she checked them both. 'Interesting comparison.'

Her blonde hair was soft now. Baby soft. Her eyes were not.

She gave him more winey kisses. The white wine from the bottle in the blue plastic bag.

Tired sex, he thought. Someone ought to write a song. Maybe someone had. A blues. He turned to her in a wave of sleep and they made love again.

Like dolphins.

Away in the wave of sleep, he was conscious of her raising his head to caress it, holding it against her breasts, whispering tenderly…

Of her getting astride him.

And dreamt again he was with all the fish of his boyhood swimming around him, opening their mouths to identify themselves: Leatherjacket. Bream. Catfish. Trevally. Mackerel. Yellow Tail…

And—sudden as sin—the great white shark was upon him. It swallowed his head so that he could not breathe.

Yet he could see.

A marvellous mermaid with sea-blue tinged breasts astride him.

A murderous mermaid—Salli with an i. Her knees were on his upper arms, pinning them. Her left hand—tight, strong—was clutching his throat and the ends of the blue plastic bag which covered his head. Her right hand held the Welrod.

Unit drill. Vary the kill method.

Bart Costello thrown from a cliff.

Father Voitre Solovjev golden bullet.

Big Ig sniper round.

Patsee Urquhart drowned.

Doc Monroe fake suicide.

Now Durman was to die in his own gas.

Be removed from here.

Dumped.

Motel or park?

Naked.

Plastic bag over his head.

Hands on his cock.

A wanker who'd died trying for a cheap thrill.

He bucked against her weight and the gathering blankness. Salli with an i tightened her grip on his throat.

He bucked again and twisted sideways. She rammed the Welrod hard against his forehead.

Going…

Had he counted correctly?

Going…

His life under the hammer.

He bucked, twisted and bucked again. She pressed the Welrod harder against his forehead. 'Be still, creep, can't you?' she whispered hatred as fiercely as she'd tenderly whispered love. 'Or I'll have to make a bloody mess of you.'

He could not be still. He bucked again and again in the approaching orgasm of dying—and rolled with her towards the edge of the bed, dragging the mosquito net.

And she had to make a bloody mess of him.

Had to try.

The click of the Welrod's hammer on the empty breech as much as their fall to the floor made her release her grip on his throat. He pulled the blue plastic bag from his head and sucked in gulps of the city's hot breath as if it were mountain air in the one, safe place. 'Six rounds, you bitch. You knew it was a Welrod, not a home-made job. Rankin's Welrod. You should've checked the mag.'

He should've checked her. She got in one vicious blow with the Welrod, its heavy barrel raking across his broken nose. Yet he had judged her correctly. She was fit. Not aerobics fit.

Hand-to-hand.

Foot-to-balls.

And all moves in between.

'You killed Roy.' She was on his back, arm round his throat, hand pushing to break his neck. 'Roy. You killed Roy.'

On the floor, Durman yanked the brass stand down. The stand hit her, enabling him to get on top. Rankin's comrade-in-arms. As Helen had been his. He could not kill her. He did truss her. Wrists and ankles with belts from the brass stand. And he gave her four hats: head, tits, quim.

His change of clothes—doubly protected by the holdall and the sportsbag—was drier than he expected. He hung them in the bathroom with the ceiling fan on and went to the kitchen to make coffee.

She did not want any. He needed it. 'You had a knock-out drop in your mouth, right? You dissolved it in the wine and gave it to me.' She was silent, already considering her next move. He said: 'You'll get a bonus for trying.'

Mourning is repetition. 'Roy,' she said. 'You killed Roy Rankin.' Not a question. An elegy for Roy Rankin. The sniper who took down Big Ig? And her comrade-in-arms. For sure. Where was Cain's woman when he killed Abel? Holding Abel down? 'He was good,' Durman said. 'Like you. He got close to body-bagging me. But how do you know I body-bagged him? I might've left him back in the cemetery tied up—like you.'

'Written all over your face, wasn't it?'

The lineaments of gratified desire.

Something else he shared with his shadow half, Anton Van Dieman.

Durman's watch alarm whined.

Time: 21.15.

He showered again and shaved. Blue shirt, silk Paisley tie, moleskins, R. M. Williams elastic sides and a blazer. The contents of his bumbag, he split: British passport, ticket and money in his inside blazer pocket, Irish passport, other ticket, letter card in a slim briefcase taken from the sportsbag.

When he came from the bathroom, she had moved towards the telephone. He plugged it in.

From his inside pocket, he took his British passport and plane ticket and checked them.

She said: 'Decided to try and get an earlier flight out, have you?'

'With planes, who knows? But with operators like you around—and you can tell Anton I said so—the safest place is inside the airport security area.' He put the Welrod in the briefcase. 'I'll dump this before I go through security, of course—no need for anyone to know it was empty.'

He lifted a hat to kiss her.

She spat in his face.

Salli with an i, Smyth with a y would be free within an hour, he bet himself. And would be leading the charge at the airport on Monday—yeah, with her weapon retrieved from its headstone cache. Tricky moment that. Had he made her retrieve the weapon then and there—or tried to himself—she might have countered. And brought the chopper on to him.

Taylor Square was one of the city's unsleeping eyes and its news vendor got editions of the local newspapers earlier than usual.

*AllDay's* Sunday front page was black-bordered and carried a picture of Mervyn Vesmar.

Visionary. Powerful. Steadfast.

Headline:

> TRIAD DEATH PLOT VICTIM
> By-line: Eric Ramsey, Editor-in-Chief.

Heavy title.

Heavy bullshit.

> The proprietor of *AllDay*, Mervyn Vesmar, was the victim of a Triad plot to silence him because of his unrelenting campaign against the evils of drug-trafficking.
>
> Mr Vesmar was shot three times at his country property on Wednesday. News of his death was withheld to create a better chance of immediately tracing his killer, believed to have been an overseas specialist on contract.
>
> The extraordinary nature of the projectiles used in the shooting showed that he had made enemies of Asia's most evil drug cartel, China's secret Triads, compared to whom Japan's Yakuza are tattooed babes in arms and Italy's mafia variants, ice-cream sellers gone wrong …

Durman was smiling. He already knew the extraordinary nature of the projectiles. Still smiling, he turned to: RISE OF THE MEDIA MASTER: Full story, tributes Pages 7, 8, 9, 10.

And there he was.

Shifty. Weak. Cowardly.

A fuzzy photograph, taken from the Pleasure Dome tape.

But he was no longer bearded.

And he was no longer smiling.

The beard had been air-brushed out.

> MANHUNT: POLICE STEP UP SEARCH
> Police last night were intensifying a nationwide search for Ross Durman, known to have been a recent guest at Mervyn

> Vesmar's property.
>
> Durman, believed to be armed, is wanted for questioning as to his whereabouts on Wednesday. Police had already been seeking him for questioning in relation to the death of Doc Monroe, found shot at his home on Thursday.
>
> 'We cannot rule out the possibility of a link between the deaths of Doc Monroe and Mervyn Vesmar,' a police spokesperson said. 'We are sure that Ross Durman can help us with our inquiries.'
>
> Police were following up a report that a man answering the fugitive's description got off a plane at Alice Springs, then hired a car to travel north on the Stuart Highway to Darwin.

The gathering darkness had not lessened the heat of the city. But coldness had grown in Durman from his solar plexus, chilling him.

Anton, balls-up control expert, was way out in front of him. Anton had him fitted up for the death of Doc Monroe *and* the death of Merv Vesmar.

Not only that, Anton had made Vesmar's Triad backers the villains, knowing secret organisations will wear any label as long as their efficiency is not eroded. And the accusation that the Triads had arranged the killing of someone as powerful as Mervyn Vesmar could only enhance their power.

Time: 21.45.

And he was standing there like a piss icicle.

Move.

The Law Courts were less than 50 metres away. A squat complex of buildings which seemed to cower before the challenge of the city's endemic corruption. Sandstone. Durman made one of his bets that way back some of the sandstone had been stolen to build Salli with an i's cottage.

Outside the Law Courts' railings were two red post-boxes. Durman already had his lettercard in his hand.

Anton might be able to con this city which was into being conned the way some of its people were into S and M. But the Triads would not be impressed to learn Anton Van Dieman was Bart Costello's source in a move to destabilise and succeed Mervyn Vesmar as blue-eyed gweilo and holder of a rich drug fiefdom in fee not-so-simple.

Had to be.

Anton was the only one who knew about the hiring of a specialist called Durman.

The only one not mentioned by Bart Costello. Journos protect their sources even when they're crims.

The lettercard was addressed to the Director General, Crime Commission Intelligence Office, Post Office Locked Bag 1.

Locked bag. Someone was trying. No need to risk a direct approach to the Crime Commission's headquarters in The Rocks.

The lettercard fell into the post-box as silently as a leaf.

Delayed-action whizbang.

Behind the post boxes were three public telephone booths. Durman made a call from one.

Again he was Brendan Coyle.

Very Irish. And very much in a hurry.

Time: 21.57.

But not in a panic.

And no piss icicle.

He still had the edge.

In Birchgrove, Durman told the cabbie to drop him outside a white weatherboard bungalow in Louisa Road from which came wafts of rock music and barbecue meat.

Party-time.

The cabbie'd diagnosed him as having the symptoms of a cold and kept asking him if he was sure he had the cure the provided. Durman assured him he had. The cabbie insisted on repeating the cure: 'First, the vodka. Stolichnaya is good. But Kirsch better. From Adelaide. Then the black bread with mustard. English mustard. This starts double fire in stomach. No more cold.'

Durman tipped him. 'Get yourself a medical degree.'

The cabbie reached inside his jacket. Durman, keyed-up, barely prevented himself from smacking the cabbie who was saying: 'I have a medical degree. Only these AMA bastards will not let me practice. I was on KGB blacklist. Now theirs.'

Louisa Road had gone even more posho. And arty. Posho artists? In Sydney?

The wharf was as he remembered it. Long Nose Point Wharf, jutting out into the reaches of the harbour.

Time: 22.25.

From the direction of Balls Head came the roar of a boat. Durman moved away from the wharf lights with their dance of moths and dropped the Welrod into the harbour.

The boat throttled back and sidled alongside the wharf.

Twin-hull. Yellow. Water Taxi.

Its cox'n was a chunky guy with a grey scrub of hair, red polo shirt, white shorts and bare feet who handled the boat as if it'd been built around him at birth.

'Boss said an Irishman. I thought you might be late.'

'Sure, I would've been if the directors of the last company had gone on any longer.'

'Business, eh?'

'Indeed.' Durman flourished his briefcase before packing it in his sportsbag. 'Assessing companies for European investors. There's some disquiet at recent happenings.'

'She'll be right.'

Optimism as lunacy.

The cox'n had the boat at speed—20-25 knots. As they passed under the Harbour Bridge a train roared over them.

To port was the fried-chicken stern-wheeler, seen during his first trip on the *Norn* with Anton.

Up you, Anton.The towers of the harbourside inched their lights towards the distant stars.

A barquentine passed under sail—ghostlike as if bringing settlers in for the first time.

Dead ahead, the looming stern of a container ship.

To starboard, the Opera House. From sea-level, its shells with their lighted, glassed-in fronts had a different aspect. Not conspirators' cowls as they were from the Regal Tower.

Mouths.

The gaping mouths of giant, attacking sharks.

An Aboriginal artist had foreseen it. Had a later artist confirmed it?

The container ship was making about six knots. From its portside, a floodlit Jacob's ladder was slung. The cox'n brought the water taxi in handily so that it came stern-first to the Jacob's ladder and was not caught by the suck of the ship's hull. 'Jackpot,' the cox'n said, assaying his tip.

His sportsbag slung on his shoulders, Durman reached for the Jacob's ladder and began to climb. Behind him the water taxi sheered off, its engine note rising as it turned for its base.

As he climbed he was wondering about the other passengers who were taking the slow way home. He rehearsed a cover joke for them.

How many Australian businessmen does it take to change a light bulb?

I don't know.

Depends on how many can be spared from cooking the books.

He reached the top of the ladder, smiling.

He'd done it.

Killed the day that could've killed him.

## 26

In London, Durman slept at Grantham House, seventeen storeys of instant corporate prestige, hemmed in by 20, 30 and 35 storeys of greater prestige. From his office a section of the dome of St Paul's could be glimpsed like a thin slice of Christmas duff. He was happy with this accommodation, his natural meanness aggravated when he wasn't on expenses. And he was saving on an hotel, making himself scratch feeds and crashing on the camp bed he kept in the closet of his office along with blankets, tucker and winter-summer gear.

Above all, he was in the bubble, Unit slang for minimum contact status when on the run. His minimum contact was with the unavoidable secretary-receptionist Suzie Downie, whose work area was three times the size of his office and four times as luxurious: a power boudoir where trailing ivy—and Suzie—sought to come to grips with the Apple, Xerox Fax and Commander telephone system through which she created a flaky entrepreneurial facade for her fly-by-nighters.

Among mail, waiting to be sent to his GPO Poste Restante, Glasgow, was a letter from Anton on *AllDay's* letterhead.

> TO WHOM IT MAY CONCERN
> The bearer of this letter, Ross Durman, has undertaken a confidential and hazardous operation for this organisation in a delicate international situation, the core objective of which he achieved to our satisfaction despite manifold difficulties.
>
> In addition, the bearer tested the integrity of this

> organisation in an ultimate way, demonstrating its impregnability to every kind of attack, including rumour and poison-pen missives.
>
> We unreservedly recommend the bearer for operations which similarly challenge his skill, judgement and ability.

Surreal.

Not arty surreal.

The surreal generated when a secret world masqueraded in the open.

Anton's letter of reference was not meant to be used. It was designed to rubbish him about the part he'd played in bringing Big Ig into a sniper-executioner's sights. Was it also rubbishing him about the delayed-action whizbang? Durman did not want to believe—any more than he wanted to believe the title under Anton's signature.

The huge granite axehead of Australia House lay between the traffic streams of the Aldwych and the Strand, waiting for a mighty tycoon to fit a big enough haft to it to bring it crashing down on the forlorn remains of Fleet Street.

In the marbled reading room, Australian newspapers were on file for nostalgics, optimists and sceptics. Allowing for the time-lapse of his boat-trip Durman scanned the newspapers for reports on the effect of his whizbang.

Nothing.

He couldn't believe it. Still nothing—although in the *Financial Review*, he came across a paragraph headed CAN DO. This said that Jerry Telfer and Ray Turnbull had joined forces to provide the broad-spectrum coverage of the healthcare industry.

The story that counted was in *AllDay's* business pages.

> NEW CHIEF TAKES CHARGE
> AND TELLS IT LIKE IT IS
>
> The board of the AllDay Organisation yesterday announced the appointment of Anton Van Dieman as its new chief executive officer.
>
> Mr Van Dieman was formerly a specialist consultant in Canberra. His duties there gave him a wide-ranging

experienceof media and an intimate knowledge of media professionals at every level.

He worked closely with the founder/proprietor of the AllDay Organisation, Mervyn Vesmar, the hunt for whose killer has switched overseas.

Australian police have asked Scotland Yard and Interpol for help in tracing Ross Durman, believed to be travelling on an Australian passport in the name of Leslie Burnett.

In a statement, Mr Van Dieman said: 'As Chief Executive of the AllDay Organisation, I want to deal first—and I think finally—with any lingering effect of allegations that the late Mervyn Vesmar was somehow linked with trafficking in the drugs he hated as much as he hated the traffickers, the so called Twin Ts—the Tetra Triads.

'These allegations have already been exposed as both spurious and malicious by the fact—the uncontroverted fact—that Mervyn Vesmar was the victim of a hired Twin Ts assassin.

'Further evidence is available and should be made public.

'Within the Crime Commission Intelligence Office, a confidential paper is being circulated about a dawn raid carried out by Hong Kong police on the All Harmony Printing Company, specifically its PlasPacto Division, where magazines of the AllDay Organisation are shrink-wrapped to Australia.

'According to this confidential paper, no evidence was found to connect PlasPacto or the AllDay Organisation.'

'Excuse me.' It was a bloke and his missus—definitely his missus—wanting to know whether the price of their house in London would be enough to buy one in Sydney.

Durman, intent on staying in the bubble, simply showed them *The Sydney Morning Herald* property section and returned to *AllDay.*

Taxpayers could have been spared unnecessary expense had the CCIO listened to *AllDay.* This newspaper's position has always been that the allegations on which the CCIO saw fit to act were the work of a hoaxer inspired by a malcontent.

'The malcontent, one Bart Costello, was notorious as a drunkard whose AllDay file was marked NOT TO BE EMPLOYED—a reputation he consummated by taking his own life.

In mitigation it can be offered that he was the hapless target of disinformation. This is the position maintained by self-confessed hoaxer Norman McLaine, a former employee of the AllDay Organisation.

'He it must be said is now enjoying his retirement. AllDay has decided not to use his lapse to challenge his right to the company contribution to his superannuation benefits.'

Anton, balls-up control expert, was in top form. Durman strode from Australia House into the 40-watt London sunshine.

Normie McLaine'd gone to water. Gallipoli was written on the heart of one cohort of Australians. Mont St Quentin on the heart of another. Tobruk, Kokoda on the heart of yet another. Kapyong. Long Tan. On the heart of Normie McLaine's cohort was written superannuation.

Locked Bag 1.

Someone had tried. And Durman had tried. But he should've remembered the old Anton's speciality: locks. He would've placed a kettle with a key to monitor incoming CCIO mail.

Fax?

Not unless it was personal to the Director General.

And not even then.

In Sydney, who guards the guardians had long ago become who humbugs the guardians, and if the guardians winked as they were humbugged—well, that was part of the giggle.

Durman waved down a cab. There was another guy he could contact.

The lifts in Grantham House creaked as if the stress of their users had infected them. Emerging on the fourth, Durman met Suzie Downie rushing to be late for an early lunch. She was wearing one of the hand-crochet outfits he thought of as her Cottage Loaf Club uniform. White with pink ribbons threaded through the collar and cuffs.

Scatty. Dumpy. Imperious. He had a flash of her dealing with Princess Celia Von Kronberg. Queen Victoria receiving the Countess of Crud. And he was the Count. 'Washing. Biscuit crumbs. Sleeping in your office. Some of my other clients feel it's not quite—you know? One even suggested buying a cardboard box and paying your bus fare to Waterloo. And that desk of yours higgledy-piggledy.'

She handed him a business card. 'Oh, you have visitors. I didn't want them cluttering up reception.' Her tone put the visitors in the same category as biscuit crumbs. 'Asking about your Mr Durman. Very insistent. I . . .'

Express-train talker, Suzie Downie. One of the few things that could halt her had done so: lift doors.

The business card was printed in red.

Lucky red.

Horrie Li red.

He stood ahead. Durman motioned him back into his chair. The other visitor preferred to remain standing. Sikh. Little Boy Blue. All six foot plus and 200 pounds of him. Blue turban. Blue suit. Jacket open. Durman would take bets he was carrying more than the dagger enjoined by his religion. Surreal Horrie Li acted as if Little Boy Blue wasn't there.

So did Little Boy Blue.

And he wasn't.

Unless Durman made a wrong move.

He'd been allowed to get behind his desk.

Higgledy-piggledy.

He began to sort out the jumble of papers and video-cassette containers. 'My secretary's been nagging me.' He reached over and handed Horrie Li one of the *Olympic Glory* tapes. 'Great stuff.' Then he found what he needed. He held it up. And faster than Little Boy Blue could clear his silenced pistol from under his jacket, Durman pulled the pin. 'This isn't here.'

Yet Horrie Li knew what it was. 'M26 A2, grenade, hand, fragmentation.' He spoke as if reciting from an ordnance catalogue. Durman had no need to tell him what would happen if he gave the word and Little Boy Blue fired for effect. The lever he was holding down would be released and the grenade would explode in 4.5 seconds, sending lethal metal shards throughout the office. 'Admirable.' Horrie Li was tapping his hand gently against the *Olympic Glory* tape container. 'Now we have a civilised formula for a balanced discussion.'

Horrie Li's presence had a fated inevitability about it—as there was a fated inevitability about Durman's giving Horrie Li the gist of the fax he'd intended to send him.

‘Fascinating.’ No more the red Santa, Horrie Li was steel grey from hair to shoes. ‘Absolutely fascinating your imagining we could not deduce what you have deduced.’

‘He gets away with it, then?’

‘I did not say that.’ Horrie Li’s manner was as silky and tough as his suit. ‘But Van Dieman, as you should be aware, has valuable skills not found in the computer files of executive head-hunters. Until we find a successor, he retains his position.’

‘Then you eliminate him.’

‘No, you—I hope—eliminate him.’

Ace of spades.

The smoothness with which Horrie Li produced it silenced Durman. Horrie Li said: ‘Think of the shock he will experience after we tether him for you in any killing ground you care to nominate.’

Temptation time.

Bart Costello.

‘You will be eliminating him in the full enjoyment of his ascendancy.’

Father Voitre Solovjev.

‘The fee—500,000.’

Big Ig.

‘Swiss francs.’

Doc Monroe.

‘Krugerrands.’

Patsee Urquhart.

‘No charge for personal pleasure.’

‘I draw a line.’

Horrie Li’s fingers stopped tapping on the video container. ‘Not at informing obviously. At killing? But you are being hunted as the murderer of Mervyn Vesmar.’ Durman let it pass. He’d wondered whether he would’ve shot Vesmar if armed with a Kalashnikov AK47, firing 7.62 mm rounds instead of a toy version firing paint balls. And had decided he would have. Horrie Li was saying: ‘I do not think you killed him.’

‘He deserved to die.’

‘Three shots. Close range. Mervyn Vesmar must surely have known his killer to let him get close.’

‘A specialist can get very close in the bush.’

‘And you are such a specialist. I defer to your expertise. Perhaps you can enlighten me as to the peculiar nature of the loads used in the killing—the extraordinary projectiles.’

'You should've been a cop.'

'I was. Hong Kong police. Now tell me about the extraordinary projectiles.'

'You're no longer a cop. I don't have to tell you anything.'

Little Boy Blue who wasn't there yawned.

Count-down yawn.

Durman held up the grenade that wasn't there to remind Little Boy Blue to stay cool.

Horrie Li started tapping the video container again. 'You cannot tell me about the projectiles because you do not know what they were.'

Horrie Li *had* been a cop. He knew the Aussie cops had withheld a description of the projectiles to use it to trap any suspect who might describe them.

Or rubbish any nong who might confess to the killing.

Durman said: 'I draw the line at drug-traffickers.' Horrie Li smiled. Even his lips had a greyish tinge. 'But the drug-trafficker in this instance is Van Dieman. It is because of him you have been blamed for the death of Mervyn Vesmar—not to mention Doc Monroe—killings for which Van Dieman himself was responsible.

'Anton killed Vesmar?'

'He had motive. He had opportunity. He used projectiles designed to implicate the society to which I have the honour to belong.' Horrie Li spoke of belonging to the Twin Ts as proudly as he'd spoken of being with the Hong Kong police.

'You don't need me. Bodybag Anton yourself. Maybe he'll bodybag you in the process. Then another pair of you can have a go until the whole mob of drug-traffickers like you is gone.'

'Ah, yes—the internecine response. That is why you were prepared to inform. Understandable. Less understandable is your general attitude. Drug-traffickers like me. Kharma. Or as Americans say—what goes around, comes around. Opium was dumped on my compatriots in the past. Inestimable fortunes were made here.' His gesture encompassed London. 'The number of victims was also inestimable. Now when we undertake a reciprocal deal with heroin, a superior derivative …' His grey smile came and went. 'We are vilified like common bankers who turn their clients on to easy credit, raise the usury rates and watch them twist in the winds of drought.'

'It's the combination. Drug traffickers *and* secret societies. I draw the line at that.'

Horrie Li brushed something from his suit. 'My grandfather was a law-abiding citizen. In 1869, when secret societies—yes, including the triads—were outlawed in Malaya, he decided, not without risk to fortune and life, to relinquish his membership. He was about to give effect to this decision when he became aware that one powerful gweilo secret society had been exempted from the law, The Free Masons.' Durman couldn't help laughing. Horrie Li's solemnity. The memory of Dad toddling off to Lodge.

The incongruity.

Hilarious.

Horrie Li did not share his amusement. 'Secrecy is power,' he said. 'Power is secrecy.'

'And time is money. And a rolling stone gathers no moss unless he's a drug propagandist with a guitar. And half a loaf is better than no bread.'

Horrie Li stood up. 'Lunch, of course. We can discuss the fine detail—killing ground, et cetera. But first a glass of sherry wine in El Vino. I love its vestigeal ambience of Grub Street, the faint echoes of the liberties of Alsatia, the itchy symbiosis between hack lawyers and hack journalists.'

'I'm busy.' Durman shook his grenade fist. 'Very busy.'

The office was decorated with posters of sporting heroes. Horrie Li glanced at these and fixed his attention on Durman's underpants and socks drying on the radiator. 'Yes, you do seem to keep busy. A pity. I must console myself with the thought that I have taken what may be a last chance to see you …' His timing was nice. 'In any case, if you change your mind, I'm at the Hilton until 3 p.m.'

Little Boy Blue who wasn't there opened the door for Horrie Li who carried a black attaché case.

Like Dad's.

The peaceful, suburban, secret devotee of Jahbulon.

Justification for the not so peaceful Horrie Li and the secret Twin Ts.

Little Boy Blue who wasn't there turned in the doorway. His pistol which wasn't there either was cocked and aimed: Heckler and Koch VP70, calibre 7.65 mm or 9 mm? No question it was aimed to kill, head shot.

Seconds stretched and broke like hours on the calculus of shot velocity, the slammed door and the grenade blast. Horrie Li did not give the word. And Little Boy Blue who wasn't there left behind a grin with as much mirth in it as Singh the lion whose name he bore.

Durman looked at his grenade.

Bloody thing was going to rust—the amount of sweat on it. He reinserted the locking pin and placed the grenade on his desk.

Time: 13.35.

'I do wish you'd let me tidy your desk.' Suzie Downie was back from lunch and picking up her remarks exactly where the lift doors had halted them. She sniffed.

Disgusted.

Mystified.

She hadn't smelled fear before and was moving to fulfil her wish until she saw the grenade. 'Oh, my God.'

'Don't worry,' he said. 'It's only a replica—video promotion gimmick.'

She was pink and white like her outfit—possibly pinker after a glass of wine with her lunch. 'Nasty-looking thing, isn't it?' she said. 'Cross between an avocado and a pineapple.'

Sabre-tooth tiger.

Women, he believed, had gentled the sabre-tooth down to the domestic moggie by calling it 'kittie-kittie.'

To forestall her at his desk, he piled up the *Olympic Glory* tapes and realised Horrie Li had kept the one given him. Choice. *Aussies and Kiwis*—including the greatest Herb Elliott and Jack Lovelock.

Suzie Downie was folding his washing.

He scribbled her a memo: 'Ross Durman has been fired and his whereabouts are unknown. Under no circumstances is he to be given a positive reference. In the unlikely event of his seeking the derisory commission owed to him, tell him we will see him in court.'

She was trying to pair off his socks. 'You should buy all one colour.'

'I need this typed up.'

She absorbed the memo at a glance. 'I hate to say it. But I'm glad. I never did take to him.'

'You didn't even meet him.'

'He was sloppy. Those *Olympic Glory* videos he sent from Australia—just addressed to you. Sloppy print. No covering letter. No signature.'

Durman waved the memo. 'For the file.'

'Copy to Mr Li?'

Shrewd. She'd assumed the sacking was the result of a complaint by Horrie Li. She gave the desk a longing look. But 'file' was for her a stronger trigger word than 'tidy'.

Time: 22.40.

Australian time.

Surreal.

Ross Durman was gone as other employees had gone to maintain that core identity. To himself, he was always his alias Ross Durman. To others he was any number of persons.

His shadow half Anton Van Dieman would be strutting his stuff as chief executive of *AllDay* and perving on the porkable journos. Intimate knowledge of media professionals was right. Anton'd porked as he disinformed and disinformed as he porked in the hotter beds of Canberra, back when The Unit was active.

Temptation time again.

Stronger.

Horrie Li was still waiting.

He'd said they would tether Anton on any nominated killing grounds.

Durman had a flash of which one: The hi-tech newsroom of *AllDay* with the journos crouched before their cold-fire computer terminals.

Cut the bastard down there.

And watch the bloody headlines spring.

Hatred surged.

Hatred under pressure too long.

Never vented.

After Helen's death, a secret inquiry'd discussed whether he should—could—be given another chance. Anton'd said: 'Not again.'

The kind of remark that always leaked from secret meetings.

A betrayer's remark.

A hyena's remark, made knowing the prey was already down.

Durman picked up the telephone to call Horrie Li. But the old Anton was going to get his for a body-bagging he didn't do. Durman tapped in the *AllDay* number.

Progress.

His call from London bounced off the satellite to *AllDay* quicker than his Bondi call had gone over the local wires.

Mr Van Dieman was in a meeting.

'Tell him his mate Leslie Burnett is on the line.'

The meeting must've been *coitus interuptus*. Anton was breathless. Durman wasted no time: 'Get out of there. Your Twin T friends are planning to tether you on a killing ground for body-bagging Merv Vesmar.'

Anton laughed. 'You're dead, mate, as you should've been. Gave you three to scare the shit out of you. Fourth had your name on it. But I decided to do you slowly. Why are you calling me with wild bullshit?' His laughter echoed out of space as if it'd been there from time's beginning and would continue til time's end.

Durman didn't know why. Then.

He *did* know the peculiar nature of the extraordinary projectiles used on Mervyn Vesmar.

And he did know Vesmar's killer.

Only one person could've gone man-hunting with a shotgun. Yeah, a Purdey—best London gun.

Only one could've taken the shot loads from three cartridges and replaced them with solid charges.

The extraordinary projectiles.

Three favourite Sydney police commissioners.

Hear no evil.

Speak no evil.

See no evil.

Three tiny bronze monkeys.

The three tiny bronze monkeys he had purchased and given to Sergeant Jack Sands to mark their meeting in the Chinese Gardens.

Sergeant Sands hadn't been running quietly amok about a mega-drug deal, trying to get back on-side. He'd been seeking payback for the murder of his mate Bart Costello who'd helped him through a scrape.

In a war that wasn't a war only a confrontation.

In which he'd served with a legendary wild mob.

Squadron 1, the Borneo Scouts.

Durman touched the grenade. Horrie Li'd rubbished it as part of the civilised formula for a balanced discussion. Horrie Li had done so because he did not intend Durman's elimination until he was certain the Van Dieman contract was not being taken up.

Time: 14.06.

Bundle and go.

In Horrie Li, he'd sensed something he only now realised had been in Mervyn Vesmar and was in Anton. They were not people of a given country. They were denizens of a worldwide power nexus in process of becoming, financed through revenues screwed together by desperates preying on each other to obtain the drug of their choice.

Suddenly, the instant corporate prestige of Grantham House was flimsier than ever and the vast warren sprawl of London with its millions of inhabitants had shrunk to a condemned cell.

Move.

The Thames Embankment was busy with walkers who looked to be turning Dr Johnson's cheery remark about the man tired of London being tired of life into a grim prophetic utterance. They seemed exhausted, caught between the quiet river's undercurrent of greater days and the traffic snarl's presage of ultimate entropy. Durman, in the bubble, avoided eye-contact and the beggars with equal intentness.

A couple of times, he doubled back to throw any heel-shits and crossed the road at a run to get up to the Embankment entrance to the Savoy. The same ageless guy was still dispensing the same white hand towels in the hotel dunny. Durman left by the Strand entrance, avoiding the temptation of the American Bar.

Harder than he intended it to be. After his celebration drinking as Brendan Coyle on the voyage back, he'd gone into what he liked to think of as remission.

Somewhere in the limbo between hangover and never again.

Now, never had ended and he craved a drink.

From the river, he told himself. Have one from the river. The joke did not quench his craving. He stayed away from the river—and out of the booby-trap pubs—working his way round through Trafalgar Square into Piccadilly.

His tourist Pentax was up for shots of little cock Nelson on his phallic column and Eros and his metal mound.

Statues should be switched.

The sun was shining into Green Park.

Impossible to believe that it was the sun of the same planet as the sun that shone on Australia.

Possible to believe that the earth'd originally been two hemispherical planets which aeons ago collided and fused, each retaining its own sun.

He knocked off a couple of shots of the park with Buckingham Palace beyond.

Poor bastards.

On he went—a snap-happy tourist again—past Hyde Park and into Knightsbridge. Arab women, faces veiled in black to conceal their attractions. Sloane Rangers, chins veiled in Hermes scarfs to conceal from the world that they carried the dreaded recessive-chin gene of England.

He was taking the long way round to avoid the perimeter security on the Houses of Parliament, Whitehall and the Palace. All he needed on this bound was a cop, polite as a penguin, instinctive as a wolfhound, asking to see the inside of his sportsbag.

And there was another reason. He found it beyond Knightsbridge on Brompton Road next to the Victoria and Albert Museum. At first, he assumed it was part of the museum.

No museum.

The church she'd told him she'd gone to.

Querida.

Maree.

Vast joint, the church. Ornate. Gilded. But with the same smell of incense as the brick barn in Surry Hills.

And silence.

Different from the silence of Bart Costello.

A waiting silence.

Nearby, across Brompton Road in a side street was her old school. Plain red brick. But same name as the church: Oratory.

The flat was where she'd said in Collingham Road, opposite a grey-stone church.

The garden square was behind the flat. He peered through a gate, seeking some after image of her. His scrutiny attracted the suspicion of a trio of mothers—two brunettes, one blonde—with their kids in the garden. Yeah, he sent them the thought, I'm sick—love sick. What a world where that makes me threatening.

Near the church a van was parked.

White. Bouquet of flowers on the side.

Florist's van.

Coincidence?

Life was full of them.

Some fatal.

He broke into a run, listening for the van's engine to start. Or a door to slam, indicating a heel-shit.

Nothing.

Not crossing Fulham Road. Nor Kings Road.

Along Chelsea Embankment, the river was gilded by the setting sun.

One coat.

Its mucky grey showed through in harridan streaks.

The Pentax he used to knock off more shots: Chelsea Bridge and

Battersea Park across the river.

There were few walkers here. Yet he sensed he was being watched. He turned. Across the road—high, small balcony, mansion block of flats—a guy had him in his sights.

Durman went sideways on to the ground.

Hard landing.

And the guy was laughing.

Big bastard.

White towelling bathrobe.

His gun, a shoulder-mount camera.

But he stopped laughing and left the balcony when Durman focussed the Pentax on him.

A luckier Romeo between bonks by the look of him.

Durman grinned and got to his feet. Romeo had gone back to Juliet. Good bonking luck, Romeo. Watch the bastard, Juliet.

The gilded river rolled on. Its bed must be strewn with weapons going back all the way to the Celts and the Romans, the Saxons and the Normans, the odd German bomb intermixed with swords, dirks and spears.

In his sportsbag, Durman had a bottle of Oban malt—half-full not half-empty. He was an optimist. From the bag, he took the M26 grenade and lobbed it into the river to join the other deadly weapons. If he hadn't decided the Oban deserved sweeter water than Thames, he would've sent it to join the grenade so strong was his conviction that a swig now might be as lethal to his chances of getting back to the one safe place as the grenade might've been to Suzie Downie.

No way she would have resisted the urge to tidy his higgledy-piggledy desk. No way could he have risked her fiddling with a replica grenade that would've blown her higgledy-piggledy.

Bloody higgledy.

Bloody piggledy.

## 27

To reach Glasgow, a city he'd once laughed to hear described as Mediterranean by a woman he knew in Melbourne, Durman had a routine: Earls Court to Heathrow. Shuttle from there. Cab to George Square.

He was lucky with his cabbie. Aiming to strengthen the bubble, he said: '*Sprechen zie Deutsch?*'

'Aye.' The cabbie was pricing Durman's sheepskin coat. 'Aye, Ah dae but Ah prefer Yiddish.' He glared. '*Ich bin ein giftiger swerg, verstanden zie?*'

He did. I am a poison dwarf. The cabbie was recalling the nickname given to Scottish soldiers in the occupation forces. He maintained a tirade of broad dialect and mein fuhrers all the way to George Square.

When Durman paid him the exact amount on the meter, he said: 'Danke mein fuhrer. Gas chambers straight ahead.'

What was straight ahead was the City Chambers—Glasgow's town hall, a building so fantastic that Durman half-expected to see the local councillors dancing from it and leading the citizens in a wild reel on the square. He was delighted—the cabbie had him fixed in his mind as a rotten, tight-fisted German.

Only one letter at the GPO Poste Restante. Urgent from The Hon. Secretary of the All Ireland Whole Earth Liberation Society: a request for a further meeting at the same place to discuss the previously discussed matter of a mutually beneficial nature—and a reminder of a service rendered.

The same place was Letterkenny, County Donegal. The Brendan Coyle passport was the service.

Durman replied on post office bought stationery: 'Nothing would give me greater pleasure than another meeting in the same place. Unfortunately, I am suffering a severe case of the trots—an ailment I'm sure you understand—and may have to lie up for as much as two months but will advise.'

He signed it Brendan Coyle. The letter, addressed to the Hon. Secretary, care of a post office box in Armagh, went inside a larger envelope addressed to Suzie for forwarding.

The extent of newspaper coverage tends to vary in inverse proportion to the distance of the newspaper from the subject matter. In the *Glasgow Herald*, Durman found himself in a single paragraph under the heading MAN SOUGHT.

He headed for St Enoch's Station. Make that one month's lie-up. At St Enoch's, he began his guaranteed heel-shit shaking drill on the Clockwork Orange, the city's subway system, its parallel tunnels linked by shared station platforms and its trains running clockwise and anti-clockwise round the city.

After a couple of hours of switching trains and directions across the platforms of various stations—Buchannan Street, Cowcaddens, Charing Cross, Kinning Park, Hillhead, Partick Cross—he was certain he was not being heel-shitted.

His exit station, he varied. This time it was Govan Cross. The best. There was a cab rank across from the station. And it was tribal ground.

His grandfather'd worked as a boilermaker in the Govan shipyards before emigrating to Port Adelaide. Durman had a vague memory of an old man with a brogue you could've cut with an oxy-acetylene torch, talking about the incredible—really incredible—racket made in the Govan shipyards.

Now Govan was as quiet as it had been before it took on the Industrial Revolutionn and defeated it. No hulls. Only red sandstone tenements that, cut by demolition, had the look of beached liners.

What the woman in Melbourne'd meant by Mediterranean, he could see. Rain was needling down as though cold drop-forged from the solid grey sky. Yet the people had a certain swagger.

Been there.

Done that.

Bombproof.

Like his grandfather.

Atavism can be stronger than any rule. Durman, waiting for a cab in the lea of a blue police box, took the half-full bottle of Oban from his bag and had a swig for his grandfather.

'See's a drappa that, man.'

Surreal.

Not a beggar. A guy who looked as if he'd had a few bottles. And shared every one. Old British Army jump smock. Axe-handle shoulders. Bald head cocked. As benign as an eagle. Durman passed him the whisky bottle. The guy took a pull of it and wiped the neck with his hand before passing it back. 'Thanks, pal.' He meant pal.

'Aussie?' he said.

What with the whisky and not knowing his origin had been inscribed on his face by the sun, Durman was surprised out of the bubble. 'That's right.'

'Aye, Ah thought so. Wis wae the Aussies in Korea. Royal Australian Regiment. No' bad people, Aussies. Mark you, they'll hiv tae be twice as good as they think they are tae be half as good as they'll need tae be when their luck runs out.'

And went on his way, limping.

A chieftain of narrow streets.
But not mean.
Brought home by some overwhelming power.
Which Durman could feel.

Hail or rain, sleet or shine—and all four could happen in an hour—Durman walked the macadam road and the causeway that connected the airfield island to the main island and his one safe place, the slow booming of its waves rolling from the west to break on its peerless white sands while the sound travelled on over the coastal plain, over lochs and peat bogs to curl and lift and murmur against its mountains where grazing sheep patched the green like snow and the topmost summit—faith had carved a mountain here—bore a statue of a woman holding a child for this small world to see.

Hail or rain, sleet or shine, remembering how burn-bagging files, he'd come across a report about security for the island's rocket range and the fact that the outer perimeter was patrolled by ex-servicemen armed with pick handles. Some bureaucrat humourist had noted in the margin: 'Re Woomera. Should we try nulla-nullas ?'

And through that lame joke, he'd found his one safe place. Hail or rain, sleet or shine. This was shine, the booming of the waves and their murmur linking the cries of seagull to raven, oyster-catcher to curlew and the air lively and warm as if the rousing bees had already distilled all their honey from the heather.

Or her.

Maree Costello.

He had not even kissed her. But so what? Sex was only a tributary.

Not the mainstream of love.

Not the ocean.

Querida.

M'eudail—in the language of the one safe place.

She was it. It was her.

The macadam road rolled on south. He turned east on to a dirt track. Off the dirt track, next to a ruined house—old when a prince with a price on his head and no takers was hunted here—lay a well, its stonework mossy, its water clear. He took a swig of the Oban and cupped a handful of the water to his mouth.

Sweeter than Thames or any other water of his travels.

The sweetest.

From the well side, he could see, jutting into a loch, the rounded peninsula on which his house stood: white plastered, dormer-windowed, blue-grey slates, its outbuildings drystone and thatched—ancient black houses as enduring as those who'd built them.

At the loch's edge, reeds tuned themselves to the wind. Water lilies shone white and gold. And a too-eager trout silvered the air and rippled the surface.

His one safe place.

His forever more.

He knew now why he'd called Anton to warn him he was to be tethered on a killing ground.

Anton had no safe place.

As Durman walked on, a lark rose singing a descant to a figure in the landscape whetting a scythe. The figure raised a hand and all the while the lark was singing and rising and singing until it disappeared in the blue of the sky but still its song came down.

So powerfully did the song conjure Maree Costello that, coming to his door and reaching for the key above the lintel, he was convinced she was within, waiting for him.

M'eudail.

Darling.

And so fierce was his conviction that he pushed the key past the slight obstruction which might otherwise have alerted him.

Only when he felt the tremor of an electric shock run to his heart did he realise he'd closed the circuit on a whizbang.

Too late?

Yet everything slowed as he dived sideways, trying to get out of the blast line.

Time to wonder about the whizbang.

Anton's Irish porridge?

Time to realise Horrie Li—'last chance to see you'—must've known about the whizbang but wouldn't've revealed it was in place even if he'd taken the contract to body-bag Anton. Horrie Li had been intent on closing another kind of circuit on both Van Dieman and him.

Time to puzzle how he'd been tracked to the one safe place.

Not by heel-shitting.

The Clockwork Orange was heel-shit proof.

The guy at Govan Cross who'd broken the bubble?

Never.

Maree?

Tortured to make her speak.

'No!'

Half-right. Half-wrong. His fate.

The roar of pain had carried him back to the Gulf of Siam slop and Big Ig towing him while chanting the surf breaks: 'Butterbox... Winki Pop... Bondi... Tamarama...'

Durman knew he needed a word to pass from the surf breaks to the beach of silence.

The sacred word.

Too late?

Never too late.

He'd said it in a dream.

This was no dream.

Say but the word!

He said it.

Not Jahbulon.

MORE FINE FICTION IN THE PRESS ON SERIES

1. Peter Corris, *Wishart's Quest*, ISBN 978 1 921509 54 4
2. Michael Wilding, *The Prisoner of Mt Warning*, ISBN 978 1 921509 56 8
3. Phillip Edmonds, *Leaving Home with Henry*, ISBN 978 1 921509 55 1
4. Inez Baranay, *With The Tiger*, ISBN 978 1 921509 57 5
5. Ross Fitzgerald & Trevor L Jordan, *Fools' Paradise*, ISBN 978 1 921509 58 2
6. Victoria Thompson, *City of Longing*, ISBN 978 1 921875 36 6
7. Peter Corris, *The Colonial Queen*, ISBN 978 1 921875 31 1
8. Michael Wilding, *The Magic of It*, ISBN 978 1 921875 37 3
9. Morris Lurie, *Hergesheimer Hangs In*, ISBN 978 1 921875 34 2
10. Garry Disher, *Play Abandoned*, ISBN 978 1 921875 33 5
11. Inez Baranay, *Always Hungry*, ISBN 978 1 921875 30 4
12. Ian Callinan, *Dislocation*, ISBN 978 1 921875 38 0
13. Félix Calvino, *A Hatful of Cherries*, ISBN 978 1 740971 67 6
14. James Murray, *Shark City*, ISBN 978 1 921875 35 9
15. Peter Corris, *Standing in the Shadow*, ISBN 978 1 921875 32 8
16. Michael Wilding, *Asian Dawn*, ISBN 978 1 921875 39 7
17. Colin Talbot, *Ah, Sweet Mystery*, ISBN 978 1 921875 93 9
18. Morris Lurie, *Hergesheimer in the Present Tense*, ISBN 978 1 921875 95 3
19. Michael Wilding, *Little Demon*, ISBN 978 1 921875 94 6
20. Félix Calvino, *Alfonso*, isbn 978-1-925003-20-8